THE POWER OF GOD

Edited by Linda Ellis Eastman

Professional Woman Publishing
Prospect, Kentucky

THE POWER OF GOD
Copyright © 2012 by Linda Ellis Eastman
All rights reserved.

Published by:
Professional Woman Publishing
Post Office Box 333
Prospect, KY 40059
(502) 228-0906
www.pwnbooks.com

Please contact the publisher for quantity discounts.

ISBN 13: 978-0-9858142-6-7

Library of Congress Cataloging-In-Publication Data

Cover Design and Typography by:
Sential Design, LLC — www.sentialdesign.com
Photo credits: Evgeniya Moroz/Dreamstime

Printed in the United States of America

TABLE OF CONTENTS

TABLE OF CONTENTS
—CONTINUED—

TABLE OF CONTENTS
—CONTINUED—

ABOUT THE AUTHOR

LINDA ELLIS EASTMAN

Linda Ellis Eastman is President and CEO of The Professional Woman Network (PWN), an International Training and Consulting Organization on Women's Issues. She has designed seminars which have been presented in China, the former Soviet Union, South Africa, the Phillipines, and attended by individuals in the United States from such firms as McDonalds, USA Today, Siemens-Westinghouse, the Pentagon, the Department of Defense, and the United States Department of Education.

An expert on women's issues, Ms. Eastman has certified and trained over two thousand women to start consulting/seminar businesses originating from such countries as Pakistan, the Ukraine, Antigua, Canada, Mexico, Zimbabwe, Nigeria, Bermuda, Jamaica, Costa Rica, England, South Africa, Malaysia, and Kenya. Founded in 1982 by Linda Ellis Eastman, The Professional Woman Network is committed to educating women on a global basis regarding, self-esteem, confidence building, stress management, and emotional, mental, spiritual and physical wellness.

Ms. Eastman has been featured in USA Today and listed in Who's Who of American Women, as well as Who's Who of International Leaders. In addition to women's issues, Ms. Eastman speaks internationally regarding the importance of human respect as it relates to race, color, culture, age, and gender. She will be facilitating an international conference where speakers and participants from many nations will be able to discuss issues that are unique to women on a global basis.

Linda Ellis Eastman is also founder of The Professional Woman Speakers Bureau and The Professional Woman Coaching Institute. Ms. Eastman has dedicated her businesses to increasing the self-esteem and personal dignity of women and youth around the world.

Contact:
The Professional Woman Network
P.O. Box 333
Prospect, KY 40059
(502) 566-9900
lindaeastman@prodigy.net
www.pwnbooks.com
www.protrain.net

THE POWER OF GOD

ABOUT THE AUTHOR

CHERIE DAVIS

Cherie Davis specializes in training, mentoring and advising people in the role of leadership. Her passion for leading and developing others has been demonstrated through a 30-year career in hospitality management. Concurrently, she served as an officer in the United States Army Reserve, both on active and reserve duty, in the United States and in Germany. In service to her country, Ms. Davis went from the rank of an enlisted soldier to a Captain in the Military Intelligence Corps.

At 36 years of age, Ms. Davis gave up her lifestyle in the United States to work and travel while circumnavigating the globe. Her activities included working with women and families of third world countries, teaching about preserving the underwater environment as a Master SCUBA Diver Trainer, and working to return orangutans to the wild in an orangutan rehabilitation center in Asia. Her solo backpacking journey began in Chile, ended in Italy, took her to thirty countries, and ended following her 40th birthday.

Most recently, while holding the position of general manager of an upscale, green-certified hotel, Ms. Davis founded her own company, Lifestyle Presentations. As the CEO of Lifestyle Presentations, she is recognized as a motivational and inspirational speaker regarding leadership, hotel management, sales training, green business initiatives, and the benefits of a green environment. She is recognized as a community leader and serves on a number of non-profit boards. Cherie Davis is a Rotarian and a Christian.

Contact:
Cherie Davis
Lifestyle Presentations
PO Box 7653
Long Beach, California 90807
cldnla@aol.com
562-989-1010

ONE

BIRTH OF A MISSIONARY

By Cherie Davis

*A **missionary** is a member of a faith based organization that is sent into an area to do evangelism or ministries of service, such as education, literacy, social justice, health care and economic development.*

Perhaps you are like me: you are familiar with missionaries or have heard of people who go on mission trips. Like me, you may have been interested in going to a foreign country to help people in need. What kept me from pursuing this interest was always, "How would I get the money? Could I get time off work? What could I really do or offer to be of benefit to others?" In the past I did believe in miracles in the lives of other people, but I could be skeptical when it came to my life. Then life changed.

God's First Work: As we say, "A funny thing happened on the way to The Forum." On a bright sunny day in Los Alamitos California in June 2011, there was a raffle to win a free mission trip at my church. I purchased four tickets just as a donation – I NEVER win raffles. While filling out the little orange tickets, I said to God, under my breath, "It would be just like *You* to have me win this missions trip," as God had always tugged on my heart to do a missions trip. You know what happened next: I did win it. Actually, God assigned it to me. The First Miracle. *Ephesians 1:11*

God's Second Work: Technically I didn't need to raise the $2,900 that I needed for the trip, but God had laid it on my heart that if I were to be a missionary I would need to do everything the other missionaries had to do. The church provided a letter to the team and I sent one to every friend, business associate, and family member. This letter was designed not only to get donations so I could pay for the trip and raise money for the orphanage, but also to reach out to give others the "opportunity" to be part of God's work. The fund raisers that our group would do would also help with funds. To my surprise, in less than three months the money came in. God had moved people to invest in his kingdom. The Second Miracle. *2 Corinthians 9:8*

God's Third Work: Having been chosen by God, Pastor said I could choose from the 19 locations, worldwide, where our church was conducting mission trips. I had always wanted to go to a *certain* very poor third world country and this *certain* very poor third world country was on the list! I prayed for guidance; God put it on my heart that I could not ask for that *certain* place that I really wanted. It was His trip, and I was to ask Pastor where they needed me. My response: "Really God?" There were countries on that list where I really didn't want to go. For weeks I struggled and negotiated with God. I remember gripping the steering wheel while driving to the church to choose which mission trip I would take, when I finally accepted that I wouldn't ask to go to that *certain* very poor country. When Pastor asked me my preference, I meekly replied by asking him "Where do you *need* me?" "Israel," was his reply. Inasmuch as the Israel trip would take place within the next 30 days, I was unable to go. "Where is your second greatest need?" I asked. Pastor asked if I could go to this *certain* very poor third world country – my original first-choice country. Immediately, in my heart, I heard the words, delight yourself in the Lord and he will give you the desires of your heart. The Third Miracle. *Psalm 37:4*

God's Fourth Work: My business is partnered with a school and I mentioned to the principal that I was going on this mission trip, in the hopes of getting some lightly used lost and found items to take to the orphans. Unbeknownst to me, the school of 700 elementary students and faculty created a large bulletin board with a map of this *certain* very poor third world country and pictures of the orphans that we would be helping. A few nights before the team left on the trip, the students, their families, and school faculty came to my place of business and brought 26 full oversized plastic bags of clothes, shoes, backpacks, and toys, plus five cases of school supplies. This mission trip resulted in reaching nearly a thousand families here at home. After arriving at the orphanage and presenting the donations to the orphanage, I showed pictures of the school, the bulletin board, and the children who had donated all these items to the orphans. The pastor's wife was especially grateful for the clothes. She explained that every year they try to give the children some new clothing for Christmas, yet this year 25 of the children were so seriously ill that they had to spend clothing money on doctors and medicine and therefore were unable to provide clothes for the children this year. God answered their prayer and more surprising was that God used me! The Fourth Miracle. *2 Corinthians 9:9*

God's Fifth Work: I was told that each member of the mission team would have to lead devotions and teach some bible classes. I have many life experiences and am considered an accomplished professional; however this news brought sheer terror to my heart. I had been saved at an early age but had spent a great deal of my life as a prodigal daughter. I didn't know the bible very well, so I Googled bible studies and researched devotions. Surely I could figure this out, but I didn't. Even on the plane I still had nothing; I prayed and prayed and asked God what could I teach the children that could be meaningful? Then the Spirit spoke into my heart, *Jesus calms the storm.* The orphans had storms so I would use their storms – hunger, sickness, loneliness, fear, abandonment – in the teaching. I knew the story from Sundays at church and Christian radio, but how would I actually connect with these children? As I started to introduce myself, the Spirit put it in my heart that it wasn't important who I am, what was important was who they are. God has given me the gift of languages, so in their language the Lord helped me ask each of the children their names, and tell them how nice it was to meet them. God gave me all the words I needed, not only for that lesson, but for leading devotions as well. Satan had tried to minimize what had happened, by whispering in my head, "these were only children, they're easy to speak to", but I knew what had happened was inspired by God. God had said He would give us the words to speak and he did. I was so energized and amazed that, through God, I was able to connect with these children. The Fifth Miracle. *Luke 12:12*

God's Sixth Work: It was a hot day in Asia, so after teaching my bible class, I was sitting under a tree and marveling at how much God was doing! I have seen and done much in life, but all this left me a little speechless. It just so happened there was another church group at the orphanage at same time and we had become friends. As I sat under the tree in awe at how God was using me to speak to these children – use me of all people! – the pastor of the other group sat down next to me. He had just finished a bible lesson to these same children. He asked me about the lesson I had taught. Now I was very excited to tell anyone about what God had done – I rattled off the whole thing. Then this pastor said to me, "God has used you to speak to my heart. I am struggling with some things right now and your words were what I was supposed to hear!" Now normally – I'm not so sure about all that – but somehow this time I knew that God, in His over-and-above way, was speaking to that pastor and to me by saying – it wasn't just children – that God could use me anywhere and with anyone! The Sixth Miracle. *1 Peter 4:11*

God's Seventh Work: On Christmas Day, another team member and I switched cameras as my battery had gone dead. I took out that team member's camera memory card and put in it the side pocket of my backpack. I remember this distinctly! Then when I went to return it to the team member – it was gone. We looked everywhere. The loss of the camera card and all their mission and Christmas photos – was devastating to me. I take responsibility very seriously and I had hurt these people by losing their pictures. I asked for forgiveness and the injured party quickly not only granted me over-and-above forgiveness but also led me in a prayer. He was genuinely more concerned about me being able to forgive myself – which he could see was a very hard thing for me to do – than he was his own loss. This amazed me. I had never seen that type of forgiveness! The Holy Spirit spoke to my heart and helped me understand what forgiveness really was and felt like, that day. It changed the way I forgive today. But wait, there's more! Later the team members found the memory card and said maybe they hadn't given it to me after all, ***but I know they did!*** Clear as if God was in the room I heard in my heart, w*hat was intended to harm me, God used for good. Genesis 50:20.* Satan had tried to ruin this experience, but God had used it to teach me about forgiveness! The Seventh Miracle. *Matthew 18:21-22*

God's Eighth Work: A teenage member of our missions group became very sick. By the time the girl reported her illness, she was already in the second day of vomiting and diarrhea, and could not keep down food or drink. As a result of my travels and training, I understand the importance of traveling with a comprehensive first aid kit. The medical kit had what she needed, and together with hydration salts and lots of prayer she got back on her feet. One more day may have resulted in a trip to the hospital. I know that through the laying on of hands and praying for the young girl, God could heal her. But that night I finally understood the parable of the Talents. Now I knew that all my travels, hardships, training, and languages were all meant for something. I never knew what God's path was for me and certainly didn't think I had what it took to do His work. This day, God had shown me the talent that he placed in my care, to use for His good. The Eighth Miracle. *Matthew 25:14-30*

God's Ninth Work: As we had our farewell assembly, the children went on stage and told us how wonderful we were. A sudden urge came over me to speak to these children. I went up on the stage and the following parable came to me: When Jesus was in the temple with his disciples, he saw the rich putting their gifts in to the temple treasury. He also saw a poor widow put in two very small copper coins. Jesus told the disciples that the others had given out of their wealth, yet the poor widow had given more because she gave all she had. As in this story, we had given much to these children. They gave us their love, attention and care; in their poverty they had given us much more; they gave us all they had. *Luke 21.* I went on to explain that the seventeen of us were only the messengers and deliverers! We brought gifts from people half-a-world away – our friends, families, local businesses and a school of children and their families that gave freely and prayed for their well- being. I walked away in absolute wonder for I knew that these had not been my words, they were God's words. The Ninth Miracle. *John 3:34*

God's Tenth Work: There were 170 children at the orphanage and we discovered during our final moments there, that *some* of the children would receive cards from the missionaries with whom they had interacted. God put it on my heart that every child should receive something, so we were making cards for the others but there was not much time. Hopeful that we had enough, we passed out the handmade cards as we were departing. I was giving cards to a group of children but suddenly ran out. There were another 30 children who had not received anything. I couldn't bear to see their sad faces and my heart began to break. Suddenly the children who had already received cards saw the situation and came to me to return their cards so that I could give the remaining children a card. In their poverty they understood the principle of giving. I was moved to tears by their loving gesture. Actually it was God showing me how these children genuinely loved others as they loved themselves. The Tenth Miracle. *Philippians 2:4*

God's Eleventh Work: I was recently in Japan for business and was invited to dinner with a prominent and high-ranking gentleman who is the chairman of our very large company. He is also a highly respected reverend in the Shinto faith. The chairman began to explain the Shinto faith to me during dinner. Though a little uneasy as this is a work relationship, I explained my beliefs as a Christian. This discussion lasted for hours. In the taxi back to my hotel, I was sure that you could see that I was glowing from the events of the evening. How does a small town girl from Ohio have access to such a powerful man, let alone witness to him about my faith? God is an amazing God. The Eleventh Miracle. *Luke 21:13-15*

God's Twelfth Work: I was tempted to title this section "Last Miracle," but I realized that there are no *last* miracles! Since my experience as a missionary, I have fallen back in love with my faith. I am more diligent about obeying the word of God and have been able to speak boldly about Jesus. It is clear to me that my life is in the middle of radical change for the Lord as a result of that mission trip. The Twelfth Miracle. *Romans 12:2*

A missionary was born out of the will of God and the guidance of the Holy Spirit on that sunny June day in 2011. I did not have extraordinary circumstances, unwavering faith, or a great deal of wealth. God met me where I was and took me to a place I couldn't even imagine.

* **Post Script:** Last week I decided to continue work in this *certain* very poor third world country. I am convinced we will continue to see miracles in giving as we work to raise the finances and supplies needed for another successful mission trip.

Consider this...

God used a woman who didn't have the money or time to do missionary work. Are you willing to let God provide for your needs? *Philippians 4:19*

Do you have desires of the heart that may be miraculously filled by God? *Psalm 37:4*

The Spirit gave a woman, with limited Biblical knowledge, the words to speak, teach, comfort and lead others. Would you like to be used by God? *2 Timothy 3:17*

After a lifetime of searching, a small town girl learned about the purpose and talents that God had given her. Do you wonder where your purpose or talents lie? *Romans 9:21*

Given the chance, would you like to be called to do work for God's kingdom? *John 15:5*

What if "yes" is all you need to experience miracles in your life? *Deuteronomy 15:10*

Are you waiting for the right circumstances? What if I told you that they are here, now? *Isaiah 6:8*

God uses others and intercedes supernaturally to our benefit when we step out in faith. Do you feel that it is all up to you? *Philippians 4:19-20*

Do you fear reaching out in such an endeavor? *Deuteronomy 31:8*

How do I get started?
Pray about doing missionary work, both here and abroad.

Read the Book of Acts in the Bible and study the early missionaries of the Bible.

Go to your current or local church and inquire into mission opportunities.

Here is a list of Christian Mission organizations that may have opportunities for you.

International School of Ministry: www.isom.org

Church Mobilization: www.churchmobilization.org

Service International: www.serviceinternational.org

Mission Frontiers Magazine: www.missionfrontiers.org

GOD Aid/ Giving Children Hope: www.gchope.org

Hopeforce Disaster Relief: www.hopeforce.org

U.S. Center for World Mission: http://uscwm.com

A Global Aids Perspective Enterprise: http://www.agapeincintl.org

The Voice of the Martyrs: www.persecution.com

Travel the Road: http://traveltheroad.com

Heavenly Treasures: http://heavenlytreasures.org

The Joshua Project - Unreached Peoples of the World: www.joshuaproject.net

Mission Frontiers Magazine: www.missionfrontiers.org

Great Commission 2020: www.greatcommission2020.com

World Vision: www.worldvision.org

May the peace of our Lord, Jesus Christ,
and the Holy Spirit dwell within you.

Notes:

_____

_____

_____

_____

_____

_____

_____

_____

_____

_____

_____

_____

_____

_____

_____

_____

_____

_____

_____

_____

ABOUT THE AUTHOR

DANA CONNOR

Dana Connor is an Author, Speaker and Certified Professional Life & Transition Coach. Her memoir, *Celebrate Your Scars: A Survivor's Story of Childhood Abuse* was released in December, 2011. She is the President and CEO of It's About You! Her company offers personal coaching, retreats and workshops on topics such as "Celebrate Your Scars," "The Superwoman Syndrome," "Building Positive Self-Esteem," "Let it Go: Releasing Anger & Resentment Positively," and "Finding Your Normal after Abuse."

Dana has also created the Memory Coaching System, a system created for people diagnosed with dementia, Alzheimer's Disease, or other memory issues helping them to stay at home safer and longer.

Ms. Connor holds a Bachelor's degree in Business Administration and Marketing and a Master's degree in Conflict Management from Sullivan University in Louisville, KY. She is a Certified Youth Minister and holds Certifications in Women's Empowerment Coaching, Professional Coaching, and Diversity & Women's Issues Training. She is a member of the Professional Woman's Author Institute as well as the Professional Woman's Speakers Bureau.

Contact:
Dana Connor, CEO
It's About You!
P.O. Box 221615
Louisville, KY 40252
Dana@ItsAboutYouCoaching.com
Website: ItsAboutYouCoaching.com
Twitter: @Its_About_U

TWO

WE ARE NEVER ALONE

By Dana Connor

Has there been a rough time in your life when you remember wondering how you would make it through? Hopefully, you can look back now and realize you were not alone. You may be skeptical to say God was with you, but just maybe you will believe God worked through someone or something else. I fully believe God helps us find and leads us to people in our lives who will be there for us – especially during the more challenging times. Even when we may not have someone physically present with us, He is letting us know that we are not alone in other ways, just as I felt when I was a child.

My childhood was not the easiest as I remember it. My first memories consist of watching my mom and siblings being beaten by my dad. I vividly remember as a child having a sense of protection or security surrounding me when I was alone and listening to my family endure such pain. Ever since then, I have been sensitive to try and feel what or who is surrounding me. I haven't done any major studying of angels, but you cannot convince me that my beloved family members (maybe some I didn't even know) are not watching over me and my loved ones. I can feel their presence, even when things are going well, and especially during the more difficult times.

Grandpa, my favorite person growing up, passed away when I was 14 years old. You better believe I have felt him with me ever since. He and my grandma were my safety nets, and though it has been 26 years since I lost my grandpa and four years since Grandma left us, I still feel them near me today. I believe God is with us always and sometimes He shows Himself through people, music, nature, and other circumstances. Therefore, I realize that God may have had a hand in placing some people who came into my life at specific times, especially when I needed extra guidance or support.

My thoughts naturally seem to divide into three primary areas as I write this chapter. One is the image of footprints, just like the poem "Footprints in the Sand." The second is the thought of angels - like our guardian angels, and the third is the people, music, and nature that just come into our lives. I love the poem "Footprints in the Sand" and have included it below for you. I did not list an author because so many people have claimed to write it that it is hardly cited anymore.

FOOTPRINTS IN THE SAND
One night I dreamed I was walking along the beach with the Lord.
Many scenes from my life flashed across the sky.
In each scene I noticed footprints in the sand.
Sometimes there were two sets of footprints.
Other times there was one set of footprints.
This bothered me because I noticed that during the low periods of my life
When I was suffering from anguish, sorrow, or defeat,

I could see only one set of footprints.
So I said to the Lord, "You promised me, Lord,
That if I followed you, you would walk with me always.
But I noticed that during the most trying periods of my life
There has only been one set of prints in the sand.
Why, when I have needed you most, you have not been there for me?"
The Lord replied,
"The times when you have seen only one set of footprints
Is when I carried you."

(Too many authors have claimed this to give credit to any specific one)

I love this imagery. First of all, walking alongside with Jesus – how cool is that? Then to realize that when there was only one set of footprints during your hardest times it was because Jesus was carrying you - Wow! If we could only always feel Him carrying us at those times, life would seem so much easier! Whoever was the original author of this poem was trying to assure us that we are never alone, and even when we may feel we are alone, especially during those treacherous times; that is when we need to remember that we are being lifted up.

I also find it interesting that this poem takes place while walking on the beach. We have the sand so we can see the footprints, but let us not forget we also have the ocean next to us, and the ocean is significant. The ocean can easily represent the ups and downs of our lives. The calming sound of the waves lapping over each other flowing in and out with the tide is a very peaceful image. Also, we have the water itself that can represent healing. These two characteristics represent the good times in our lives. Yet, water is very powerful and can be destructive. This can represent the harder times we have experienced in our lives.

No matter what was going on in our lives, whether the ocean waves were peacefully flowing or crashing loudly, our Lord was right there with us through it all. In order to better personalize "Footprints..." write down the specific image, message, or line from the poem that means the most to you.

_____

_____

_____

_____

_____

2- Angels

I am a strong believer that we all have guardian angels of some sort looking after us. Not that they can protect us from everything, but I'm sure they do their part that we don't even realize. As I mentioned earlier, I felt a presence with me as a very young child and that presence made me feel safe during some very frightening times. I do believe my grandpa could have been and still is one of my guardian angels since he died when I was a teenager. Maybe because I have lost a good deal of loved ones in my life is why I feel that they are my angels. I simply call them my angels now, but I can't help feeling that they are looking after me. How could my own parents, grandparents, and close friends who have gone before me not do so if they have the power? It makes sense to me, so I hope it makes sense to you. If nothing else, it sure is a comforting thought to know that you are being watched over. The more you believe it and are open to it, the more you can feel it. Can you think of a time when you perhaps felt a divine presence with you?

_____

_____

_____

How many times have you experienced a "close call" and you said, "Someone was looking after me." Have you ever really stopped and reflected on that statement and who it may have been watching over you? If you believe you have the spirits of those who have gone before you looking after you, write their names here:

_____

_____

_____

3- People, Music, & Nature

Have you heard the saying, "People come into your life either for a reason, a season, or a lifetime?" It comes from a poem by Michelle Ventor. I had never really thought about this saying much until a few years ago when someone shared it with me as a reference to me entering her life. As I pondered, I thought of several people who came into my life for specific reasons, and some who stayed longer – for seasons or more. Then I thought of those that I have been blessed with to share a lifetime, either most of mine or a great deal of their lifetimes. I thank God every day for being blessed with these wonderful people!

Reason, Season, or Lifetime

People come into your life for a reason, a season or a lifetime.
When you figure out which one it is,
you will know what to do for each person.
When someone is in your life for a REASON,
it is usually to meet a need you have expressed.
They have come to assist you through a difficulty;
to provide you with guidance and support;
to aid you physically, emotionally or spiritually.
They may seem like a godsend, and they are.
They are there for the reason you need them to be.
Then, without any wrongdoing on your part or at an inconvenient time,
this person will say or do something to bring the relationship to an end.
Sometimes they die. Sometimes they walk away.
Sometimes they act up and force you to take a stand.
What we must realize is that our need has been met, our desire fulfilled;
their work is done.
The prayer you sent up has been answered and now it is time to move on.
Some people come into your life for a SEASON,
because your turn has come to share, grow or learn.
They bring you an experience of peace or make you laugh.
They may teach you something you have never done.
They usually give you an unbelievable amount of joy.
Believe it. It is real. But only for a season.
LIFETIME relationships teach you lifetime lessons;
things you must build upon in order to have a solid emotional foundation.
Your job is to accept the lesson, love the person,
and put what you have learned to use in all other relationships and areas
of your life.
It is said that love is blind but friendship is clairvoyant.
— Michelle Ventor

I love when someone has come into my life and after a while I look back and realize they were sent to me most likely by God. My high school counselor once told me I had a gift for finding the people I need in my life, especially when I go through tough times. I can now see that it wasn't me finding them – it was them finding me as a gift from God. This causes me to reflect once again on the poem, "Footprints in the Sand" as a symbol of us not being alone and having those who come into our lives walking our journey with us. They, whether it be God himself or someone who is being Christ-like to us, are walking each step with us. I can name several people throughout my life since I was quite young that I felt were here to walk a part of my journey with me. Likewise, as I matured further, I began to understand that there are people in my life who I am meant to walk and accompany on their journeys. They may be only sent for a reason or a season, but the imprints they leave on our hearts last our lifetimes.

Use the chart below to list the people who may have come and gone from your life, but you can list them as a reason, a season, or those with us for our lifetime. Can you specifically name what the reason or season was?

	Check if Reason, Season, or Lifetime			
NAME OF PERSON	REASON	SEASON	LIFETIME	NAME REASON/ SEASON

-Music-

I strongly believe God communicates with us through music. Music can be healing and soothing and sends us messages if we are open to receiving them. I was fortunate enough to experience many retreats in my youth. Songs were always being utilized as a part of the theme or message people were trying to share. Those songs are still a part of me and remind me of that message or memory, and it feels refreshing to hear that message again. I don't think it is always a coincidence when I hear these songs again, especially when that message coming through the song is what I needed to hear.

There was a time that I was angry about some things happening to a couple of people I love. It was one of the few times I just wanted to stay angry at God instead of finding comfort in my faith. I was walking alone and all of a sudden one of my favorite retreat songs started playing. I was really surprised to hear it on the radio station to which I was listening. It was rare for this station to play this song, but there it was, Barry Manilow singing "I Can't Smile Without You, I can't laugh and I can't sing, I'm finding it hard to do anything..." I felt like I was singing to myself the message, *Hello, I can't continue to be angry with God.* He was reminding me through this song that all things are easier with Him. By the end of the song, I was singing along, smiling and feeling much better. I was beginning to let Him in again, and I was smiling and singing about it! Write down a song title or two that is special to you and seems to speak to you, sending you positive messages:

_____

_____

_____

_____

_____

-Nature-

   I firmly believe God reaches us through nature. For some people, nature is their spiritual sanctuary rather than a church. If you quiet yourself and listen to the sounds around you and let yourself see all of God's glory and creation around you – how can you not feel closer to God? I can walk out my front door and go for a walk and just feel better because I am a part of His creation. Many times I will choose not to put the ear phones on and just listen to nature – to hear the messages God may be sending me. The birds singing, the wind blowing, flowers and trees blooming or swaying – it all brings a calming peace within me.

   Is there a specific or special place where you like to be with nature and can feel God present with you? If not, is there a place you can think of that you would like to spend more time that may allow you to enjoy nature and possibly experience God within you?

_____

_____

_____

_____

   Does one or more of these three areas of emphasis help you feel you are never alone and help you feel closer to God? If yes, then focus on the one where you feel Him with you the most, where you can receive

His messages. He won't be calling us on our cell phones or sending us a text message, but that doesn't mean He isn't sending the message we need to hear through someone or something else. We don't have to be religious to feel God's presence or to experience His presence through others. That is the beauty of God and the power of God. I encourage you to be open to experiencing God passing his unconditional love for you on through a song, an experience in nature, a friend or even a stranger, and perhaps even through a guardian angel watching over you.

ABOUT THE AUTHOR

ELEANOR BECKER

Eleanor Becker is a mother, wife, pastor, leader, teacher and lover of God and life. She serves as Associate Pastor in one of the largest churches in America where she oversees weekly gatherings and large ministry events for thousands of women. As an ordained minister she has accumulated wisdom and practical insight into life issues through many years of ministry at the local and international level. Through teaching, training, and one-on-one sessions, she empowers women to embrace and walk in their God-given calling. She is passionate about seeing women take their role in society and wield their influence for good.

Marriage and ministry have been Eleanor's life choice for over 29 years. She is the mother of three and the grandmother of one. She has learned to fight for her family through her husband's tragic burn accident and a negative prognosis over her eldest son. She has walked through the pain of separation from family, country, and all that is familiar to follow her calling from her home in South Africa to the shores of the United States. The victories and lessons learned along the way are part of her strength and her story.

As a pastor, her passion is to see women fulfill their God-given destiny by taking their place in society without shame or condemnation. She has worked to train and equip female leaders both locally and internationally. Together with her husband she has planted local churches both in the USA and the Philippines. Her work stems out of her passion to see women rise up, see their beauty and become more than they ever dreamed possible. Put simply, Eleanor believes in women, their influence, and the good they can bring to their lives, their family, their community and the world.

Contact:
Eleanor Becker
PO Box 1427
Loma Linda, CA 92354
(909) 553-2974
eleanorvz@gmail.com

THREE

THE POWER OF GOD IN YOU

By Rev. Eleanor Becker

How close is too close? Getting into an elevator inevitably brings up the inkling to establish your personal space when suddenly surrounded with strangers in a tight space. People respond differently to this scenario by either making odd comments to wipe out the awkwardness or trying hard to pretend they are not really rubbing elbows with total strangers and focus on anything but the people. The space is too close for comfort and would be avoided if possible, by most people.

It's much the same with people you do know. If you are honest with yourself you will admit that your first response to a dinner invitation often is not thinking how great it would be to get close. Rather, you wonder who else would be there, how long would you have to stay, what if you don't like it, how can you find an excuse to not commit right away but take time to think it over and make sure nothing better comes up. You don't mean to be rude, but love your own space and comfort.

Closeness may bring a loss of sorts in that when you are close to people, your own way is not always going to happen. You desperately want the benefits of close relationships but when it comes down to the wire, too many people opt out of relationships in which they lose comfort and control. Avoiding closeness has become a way of life for many people and a huge part of modern culture, but presents major challenges in your relationship with God.

God is a close God! He is not a High Power we acquire and set aside until we are in need and ready to use it. He is a relational God and totally interested in having a relationship with you that is very personal and at times uncomfortably close. God is not out to spoil your fun or make your life miserable by being close to you, but rather to bring real meaning, life and power to you that you won't find any other way.

You may believe in the power of God, know about the power of God and even want it, but as long as it is a fact and entity you believe in and even admire from a distance, it can't benefit you. While religion may help you be a better person by teaching you to be good and change your behavior, God's plan is much more than that. God wants to be close to you, closer than even next to you. The Bible teaches that God is IN the believer and the believer is IN Him. Christianity is about a life changing experience and power filled living when you invite God into your life by accepting Jesus Christ as your Savior.

People often blame God for not being there for them when they need Him. They think God owes them favor because they believe in God and try to live good lives and even go to church. They live in frustration, knowing God is all powerful yet never experiencing that power in their lives. You can talk a lot about the power of God, but it will always seem out of reach to you personally and meant for other people, while God really intends to be the power IN you. There is a difference between knowing and believing in the power of God, and having the power of God manifest itself in and through your life.

Take a look at these scripture verses in the Bible that speak very loudly to this truth:

(Underlined for emphasis)

Galatians 2:20 New King James Version

I have been crucified with Christ; it is no longer I who live, but <u>Christ lives in me</u>; and the life which I now live in the flesh I live by faith in the Son of God, who loved me and gave Himself for me.

Romans 8:10-11 New King James Version

And if <u>Christ is in you</u>, the body is dead because of sin, but the Spirit is life because of righteousness. But if the Spirit of Him who raised Jesus from the dead <u>dwells in you</u>, He who raised Christ from the dead will also give life to your mortal bodies through His Spirit who <u>dwells in you</u>.

Romans 8:9-11 The Message Translation

But if God himself has taken up residence in your life, you can hardly be thinking more of yourself than of him. Anyone, of course, who has not welcomed this invisible but clearly present God, the Spirit of Christ, won't know what we're talking about. But for you who welcome him, in whom he dwells—even though you still experience all the limitations of sin—you yourself experience life on God's terms. It stands to reason, doesn't it, that if

the alive-and-present God who raised Jesus from the dead moves into your
life, he'll do the same thing in you that he did in Jesus, bringing you alive
to himself? When God lives and breathes in you (and he does, as surely
as he did in Jesus), you are delivered from that dead life. With his <u>Spirit</u>
<u>living in you</u>, your body will be as alive as Christ's!

Colossians 1:27 New King James Version

To them God willed to make known what are the riches of the glory of this
mystery among the Gentiles: which is <u>Christ in you</u>, the hope of glory.

The word "in" in "Christ in you" is the same word used in the
original language of the Bible, for a baby "in" the womb, being "in"
a city or being "in" darkness, clearly meaning Christ being more than
"with" or "near" you, but inside the believer.

This truth distinguishes Christianity from all other religions in
the world. In other world religions, followers or disciples have to work
their way to the god they worship or explore the god they believe to
be somewhere inside their own being. It requires works, efforts and
initiation on the part of the "lost" person who "seeks" the god through
sacrifice and own actions, never really getting any security if they are
truly successful or not. With the God of Israel, Abraham, Isaac and
Jacob – the God of the Bible – it is different in that He initiated a
relationship with people by sending His Son from heaven to earth as
the sacrifice and restorer of close relationship with Him. Before you
could choose God, He chose you:

Romans 5:6-8 New King James Version

For when we were still without strength, in due time Christ died for the ungodly. For scarcely for a righteous man will one die; yet perhaps for a good man someone would even dare to die. But God demonstrates His own love toward us, in that while we were still sinners, Christ died for us.

The scripture right before the above quoted verses also states the dynamics of what happens when a life is totally devoted to Jesus Christ and it's more than you trying hard to be a loving and good person. It shows that God, through Jesus Christ His Son and the Holy Spirit of God, take residence inside of you and become the power you need to live life God's way.

Romans 5:5

...the love of God has been poured out in our hearts by the Holy Spirit who was given to us.

It is totally possible to live as a Christian and not live in the power of God, but live a life of defeat and wondering why God is not helping you when you think He should. It is like inheriting a million dollars and never making a withdrawal and actually use it! In the Bible, Paul calls it "carnal Christians" referring to those who have accepted Jesus as their Savior but live lives in their own power according to their own will and way of thinking. You can be on your way to heaven and still live a defeated life while you are on earth.

This does not mean that you can do something to avoid all the trials and tough times in life. When God lives in and through you, He is the one who empowers you to go through the valley of the shadow of death (Psalm 23) and not give up till you reach the other side of the valley. Life is not fair but God is just. Bad things happen to good people and that is why you need God's power in you to fight the battles and overcome each trial. The Bible says that death is the final enemy you will overcome when you follow Christ through death into eternal life. Life still happens, but the difference is living as a believer in Jesus Christ in your own power, versus in the power of God that works in and through you as you submit to Him.

The power of God comes with the presence of God. Where God is present, there His power is and where He power is, there His provision and miracles are. With His presence and power also come spiritual insight and wisdom to know how and when to fight against the plans of the enemy in your life. In this way you will thwart many of the plans of darkness to steal, kill and destroy (John 10:10) in your life when the Holy Spirit who freely lives inside of you empowers you fight the good fight of faith. The Word of God is your sword (Ephesians 6:17) that you have to use by speaking out God's promises for your life in a loud voice. Many battles will be won this way before it even start, others you will have to endure and walk though till you come out the other side with thankfulness and praise on your lips.

How does this happen? How do you get the power of God to manifest and operate in and through your life so that you don't have to be tormented by the issues and circumstances of life? The key is found in the following verses:

Ephesians 3:16, 17

...that He would grant you, according to the riches of His glory, to be strengthened with might through His Spirit in the inner man, that <u>Christ may dwell in your hearts</u> through faith

Revelation 3:15, 16

"I know your works, that you are neither cold nor hot. I could wish you were cold or hot. So then, because you are lukewarm, and neither cold nor hot, I will vomit you out of My mouth.

It is by faith in Jesus Christ and in His Word and believing that He is who He says He is that Christ dwells in your heart, according to the Ephesians scripture mentioned above. The Revelation scripture helps us to understand that God sees our hearts, He is not unfamiliar with what we truly believe and how devoted we truly are to Him and hates half-heartedness. He uses graphic language in this verse, which indicates God's absolute resentment of lip service and make-belief relationships with Him. He is not fooled but a jealous God – He wants to give you the desires of your heart, but you need to give Him all of your life in total devotion to His Word.

God demonstrated His desire to be close to you by giving His own Son to die for you on the cross at Calvary. Someone dying for you – now that's close! Someone rightfully said that you make a living by what you get, but make life by what you give. Jesus brought life by what He gave to all mankind who would accept Him, and He invites you to become part of that life. He gave His life and died for you, now He is asking you to die to your own will and way and give your life to

Him so that He can calm the storms in your life and give you powerful living on earth, and peace and assurance that you will live for eternity.

Do you really believe? God's power is not available to you if you don't believe that Jesus was raised from the dead and is alive as we speak. God promises in scripture quoted earlier in this chapter that the same Spirit that raised Jesus from the dead, will dwell in you – if you believe and receive. Do you believe that God is big and powerful and can bring thunder storms, cause the ocean to not flood the earth and keep the moon in it's place, but have a tough time believing He wants to work His power through you? You are not "becoming" God or a god, that's not what is said, but God will empower you to live victoriously, to the degree you let Him live in and through you.

How do I let God's power into my life? You do that through total devotion to Him and faith in Him and His Word, but also through total submission to Him. You have to die to self and trust God. Don't learn the hard way that your own strength at times will not be enough and end up with a broken life and dreams. Get to know God's Word, learn from Him, get familiar with the way things work in the Kingdom of God and let go of your own way of doing life and start doing life God's way. Submission and sacrifice is a small price to pay to get rid of you human thinking and bad results in areas of your life, and gain God's perspective and live above the circumstances. How do you live above the circumstances? The answer: By not becoming the problem or the storm, but rising up and looking down on the storm by the grace of God in you.

People often have a tendency to become part of the storm when the storms of life hit. When people don't treat you right, your kids go south or the bottom drops out, you do not have to be identified with that storm and become part of it. You are not the storm! Separate yourself from the storm by trusting God and let Him fight for you. When you get to a place where you can separate yourself from the situation and make a decision to follow God's way and respond without reacting, you are on your way to victory.

The way to activate the power of God in you is to remain totally submitted to God in all circumstances. Not a passive submission of sitting on the sidelines of life doing nothing and waiting for God to do something, but actually actively display your faith in God by remaining in faith about the situation. If you remain in faith your actions will show it and your words will confirm it; as you trust God for your answer, you believe and say what God's Word says about the situation.

Here are some indicators that you are in faith and letting the power of God manifest through you:

- You don't become part of the storm in your life, but look down on the circumstances that are against you. You may feel the pain and not understand why things are happening, but you remain in faith that God is working in the situation and will turn things around for your good. (**Romans 8:28**)

- You never let go of the promises of God to you that you find in Scripture. For example: He will direct your path (**Proverbs 3:6**). You believe in your heart that, as you live in faith and submitted to God's word, He is working in ways you don't see at the time, to bring you to the place of promise in your life.

- You are able to act in contrast with your situation. When someone hates you or gossips about you, you can show them love; when everyone is out of patience, you still have hope and faith; when things are chaotic around your house or job, you are calm and in faith for God to work it out to your best interest. This is called the Fruit of the Spirit – the fruit of having the Spirit of God and His power on the inside of you. **(Galatians 5)**

The fruit of the Spirit is what will show outwardly that you have the power of God in your life the same way fruit on a tree shows what kind of tree it is. It is not what you receive and not know you have it, but it is what shows on the outside when you experience the opposite. The fruit of the Spirit is love, joy, peace, patience, kindness, goodness, faithfulness, gentleness and self-control.

The way you know whether you have it is when…

- you can <u>love</u> when you are not loved

- you have <u>joy</u> when others freak out

- you have <u>peace</u> while a storm is raging in your life

- you <u>patiently</u> wait when something you want is not happening

- you are <u>kind</u> to those who are rude to you

- you do <u>good</u> when no one is good to you

- your remain <u>faithful</u> when you are being disappointed

- your <u>gentleness</u> is known while others act harshly

- you have all the reason to attack, but you don't and <u>control yourself</u>.

It is so amazing to think that the God of the Universe wants to live in you and that He already bought your soul with His blood that was shed on the cross where He died. It is miraculous and supernatural, yet not rocket science and hard to figure out. God is love and created man for relationship that was severed in the Garden of Eden when Adam and Eve sinned against God. God is still love so He sent His Son Jesus to come to earth to build a bridge for man to have a close relationship with God once again. Jesus completed His assignment when he died on the cross, raised from the dead, ascended to heaven and send His Holy Spirit to dwell in you as believer.

John 15:4-5, 7-8

Abide in Me, and I in you. As the branch cannot bear fruit of itself, unless it abides in the vine, neither can you, unless you abide in Me.
"I am the vine, you are the branches. He who abides in Me, and I in him, bears much fruit; for without Me you can do nothing.
If you abide in Me, and My words abide in you, you wil] ask what you desire, and it shall be done for you.
By this My Father is glorified, that you bear much fruit; so you will be My disciples.

The power of God is available to you. The same Spirit that rose Jesus from the dead will dwell in you if you are ready to become less so that God can become more and endue you with power from on high. Don't just admire and talk about the power of God, but know that it's God's will that you will function in full capacity of who God created you to be, fueled by power from heaven so you can live in victory on earth!

ABOUT THE AUTHOR

E. JOYCE ROLAND, RN. PhD, MSN,CNE

Dr. E. Joyce Roland is a doctorally prepared registered nurse with expertise in women's health from a wholistic perspective (mental, physical and spiritual). She is currently an clinical associate professor of nursing at North Carolina Central University, Durham, North Carolina. She is also president and founder of Roland Essential Services, a personal service entity that focuses on Wellness and Health Maintenance, Career Coaching, Leadership Development, Stress and Conflict Management, as well as the mental, physical and spiritual health of women. She is a teacher, writer, and researcher in mental and physical wellness for women, and especially for African American women. She has co-authored several books in the PWN series, the most recent of which were *The Young Woman's Guide to Personal Success(2007), Survival Skills for African American Women(2007), The BabyBoomers' Handbook (2008),and Wellness for the African American Woman:Mind, Body &Spirit(2009)*.

Dr. Roland has a BS in Nursing from Winston-Salem State University, a masters degree in Nursing from Seton Hall University, South Orange, NJ, and a doctorate in Community Psychology from North Carolina State University, Raleigh, NC. Since 1978 she has worked as a nurse educator and research psychologist. In 1999 she completed post-doctoral studies in Alcohol and Substance Abuse Epidemiology (as it relates to women) at the Alcohol Research Group, University of California, Berkeley (1997-99), and most recently completed research on posttraumatic stress disorder among women veterans (2004-06). She enjoys working with women, adolescents (male and female), teaching them self-care and self-improvement strategies and providing mid-career advice to women. She also teaches courses on health and aging.

Her most recent community work has been with a Durham based Rites of Passage program for African American girls and with the Urban Ministries of Durham – a community agency for the homeless - teaching life skills development for women and preparation for re-entry into society. She also serves as a support group leader for women in the maintenance of breast health. She enjoys travel and has visited Mexico, Haiti, Barbados, and other Caribbean Islands. In 2004, she traveled to England with a U.S. contingency, visiting Coventry Cathedral to discuss and learn more about strategies for promoting peace and reconciliation in the world.

Dr. Roland is a member of the Professional Women's Network, a life member of Delta Sigma Theta Sorority, and a member of N.C. League for Nurses, the American Nurses Association, as well as the Central Carolina Black Nurses Association. She is an active member of St. Paul AME Church in Chapel Hill, NC, serving on the Christian Education Board and the Health committee. She also sings in the choir. She enjoys reading, writing, crocheting and quilting.

She is married to her husband, Lewis, and has three fabulous adult daughters: Leslie, Kaifa, and Lisa, a son-in-law (Richard), and two beautiful granddaughters, Cameren and Asha, and one grandson, Richard III.

Contact:
E. Joyce Roland, PhD, MSN, CNE
125 Hidden Springs Drive
Durham, North Carolina 27703
Phone: (919) 598-1917
E-Mail: jroland67@gmail.com
www.protrain.net

FOUR

I BELIEVE IN MIRACLES

By Dr. E. Joyce Roland, PhD, MSN

When discussing the power and the impact of God in our lives, the question often arises about one's belief in *"miracles"*. Many of us may express doubt about the power of the God we say we believe in, and sometimes question the occurrence of *"miracles."* Given our busy daily involvement in extraordinary events witnessed on T.V. and in our lives, one might be hard pressed to pay attention to or acknowledge events that might indeed be miracles. In this fast paced world where nothing seems new under the sun, we may be less inclined to believe in "miracles" as such, and even less likely to characterize the numerous phenomenal "events" in our lives as *"miracles"*. Thus the question we ask: "Do you believe in miracles"? Do you believe miracles still occur, and if so another question is may be "with and for whom?

Let's take time to define the term *"miracle"*. What is a *"miracle"*? Are we all in accord with what the term means? According to Webster's online dictionary, a *miracle* is "an extraordinary effect or event in the physical world that surpasses all known human or natural powers, and is ascribed to a supernatural cause." A *miracle* might also be described as an "event or effect manifesting or considered as a work of God"; Now that we know what this phenomena entails, let's talk about our beliefs about it.

I think if we were really honest with ourselves, we would acknowledge and recognize miracles happening in and around us every day. Let's consider for example, the changing of the seasons, beautiful flowers blooming without our assistance, caterpillars turning into butterflies, and healthy newborn babies born every hour of every day. In my estimation every one of these events or acts of nature we take for granted could be considered a miracle. However, it seems we do tend to take these God-directed orchestrations for granted. Let's talk about "miracles".

Miracles are described widely in biblical times. You remember, don't you? The feeding of the five thousand people with five fish and 2 loaves of bread; Jesus raising Lazarus from the dead, three days after his death, and Christ's numerous instances of healing the sick and afflicted during his lifetime; we remember well the story of manna from heaven to feed the multitude of Israelites trying to escape King Pharaoh's wrath. That story also was surrounded by another miracle; the parting of the Red Sea by Moses. This miraculous act enabled the Jews to cross over to the other side as the waters swallowed up Pharaoh's army.

Those who believe in a risen Christ attest to the miracle: Christ arising on the third day after a public crucifixion and burial at sundown on what we now celebrate as 'Good Friday'. The Bible and modern day Christians believe that he arose on the third day and spoke to his mother Mary, as well as a number of his disciples as he walked away from the tomb. Those who consider themselves "born-again believers" would probably be first to admit their unwavering belief in Christ's resurrection and ascension as a miraculous event. These kinds of events may certainly be seen as miracles.

Miracles are cited throughout the old and new testaments and usually attest to some unusual and unexplainable event. We have heard these stories since childhood if we attended church and Sunday or Sabbath School. Somehow, some of us don't think of them too much in the 21st century. When we do think of them, we seldom think of them occurring in the here and now. Why? Perhaps we think all the miracles have been performed, and only could have been performed in Jesus' time and by Jesus' followers. Since he is no longer with us in the flesh, perhaps we think the miracles have stopped. Let's consider if this is indeed true. Think carefully. Have there been miracles in your life that you can recollect? Write a memory of one:

_____

_____

_____

_____

Have there been "miracles" in the centuries since Christ's birth, death and ascension? I think every day Christians would agree that miracles do still occur. One miracle we all can certainly attest to is the daily awakening we experience after a restful night's sleep. We generally approach sleep as a way of resting our bodies and readying ourselves for the next day. But we should recognize that when we awaken the next morning through no effort of our own, we have experienced nothing short of a miracle. Think about that! Awakening each day to a new day can be seen as a miracle. Certainly we should express prayers of gratitude both on lying down and on arising. We do not have control over whether we wake up or not. Would you not call that a "miracle"?

Let's start with our awareness of miracles cited in the scriptures. What miracle resonates more with your belief in the power of God? What undergirds your belief that perhaps miracles do still occur? What are some of you most favorite remembrances of miracles told to you by your mother, grandmother, or experienced by you or a family member? Take a moment and use the space below to jot down one or more notions of miracles that you truly build your spiritual existence around.

_____

_____

_____

What did you come up with? What did you come up with besides the Virgin birth? Do you believe today that miracles such as those described in biblical times no longer happen on a day- to day basis? One of my favorite biblically based miracles happens to be the miracle of Jesus' Immaculate Conception and birth: Mary being chosen by God, to be with child, with Joseph agreeing to serve as her husband, as directed by the Holy Spirit. Being of a scientific mindset (a nurse you know), I tend to base most beliefs on some scientific principle, and although at times I find the "Virgin Birth" a bit difficult to wrap my mind around, my mind can accept it if I think of it as a miracle. How likely is this event to have happened? If I believe in the Bible and the imminent revelations and teaching in the Bible, I can hardly refute the "Virgin birth".

_____

_____

_____

The other miracle that stays with me is the circumstance under which Jesus turned water into wine and created enough food for thousands from two small fishes and five loads of bread to feed a multitude of people. We can't just believe the miracles we like. A miracle is a miracle. If we acknowledge belief in these Biblical miracles, then we should accept and believe in the "Power of God" to provide opportunities for us to experience miracles in the 21st century. If you (we) do believe these miracles happened, what is to prevent them from happening again in our lifetime? Take a moment and write out questions that perplex you as you contemplate miracles.

_____

_____

_____

_____

Let's continue to take our thoughts to a higher level. Should we expect "miracles" or do they occur as happenstance? Should we get down on our knees and pray for miracles or will they just happen because God loves us? Are these spiritual occurrences or irrational beliefs, and what do they have to with the 'power of God'? Can we claim what we think of as miracles as genuine representations of the spiritual realm? I like to believe and, in fact, I strongly believe that miracles continue to happen in our lives. I think if we believe in miracles and live out our faith in God, and believe in miracles we will recognize these continuous blessings when they do occur. The question again may be how is a "miracle" to be perceived or recognized in today's society when it seems that so much is governed by technology.

I, for one, am writing this chapter because I have over the years experienced and witnessed events that I would call miracles. The year 2011 brings to my mind at least two miracles that occurred within my family. I can go back even as early as 2004 when I walked around about a day and a half with a swollen left leg which was later diagnosed as a DVT or deep vein thrombosis. Again, as a nurse, I have known many individuals who experienced a clot, and for reasons that we don't understand, the clot moves quickly throughout the body, and frequently causes death before the individual even knows what happened On this particular day I had the presence of mind to call for a quick doctor's appointment, and I was sent to the emergency room right away for a sonogram. Thank God for modern medicine (a miracle of technology right there). There, behind my left knee, was a clot that obviously interrupted the flow of blood from my lower left leg to my lungs and heart. I think this was one of my first wake-up call regarding modern miracles, although now I know others have occurred.

Miraculously, I believe God did intervene in the discovery of this problem, and in the subsequent healing process. Although I had no reason to believe I had a clot, someone suggested that I might want to have it checked out. I had already lost a sister at the age of 35 to a cerebral aneurysm. So there should have been some spark to alert me to the possibility of circulatory problems in my own body. At the time, however, there was no thought by me that my body might have developed this clot, which could have instantly killed me, had it broken off and migrated to my lungs or heart. I had had no recent surgery or any injury that might have alerted me to the possibility of an event such as this. I did recall later that I had fallen in July of 2004 (almost 6 months earlier) while traveling in London, and had sustained an injury to the shaft of my left leg which I now remember took a while to stop bleeding. The injury had been cleansed and a Band-Aid placed on the spot. I thought nothing of it at the time because the bleeding soon stopped, and I was able to continue my activities of daily living. I happened to be in London on a spiritual trek, and I remember spending several more days walking around without a problem, and came back to the U.S. and immediately resumed my usual daily activities.

What had happened as I recalled later, was that I sat on an airplane for at least six hours without much moving around, and this allowed the blood cells to accumulate around that area that had been bleeding. Six months later in late December, the clot broke free somehow and began to cause my leg to swell. After the sonogram, I was immediately placed on bed rest for about 10 days having to give myself daily Heparin injections to prevent more clots, and on bed rest to keep the movement of my lower leg to a minimum. By the grace of God, the clot did not progress. I stayed on blood thinners for about 3 - 6 months until all evidence of a recurrence of the clot was gone. I was never even hospitalized. Ironically, during that same week another friend of mine was hospitalized with clots in both her lungs. She had undergone knee replacement surgery, and subsequently suffered a blood clot. Miraculously, she survived her clot also, and is still with us today. Tell me what you will or may, both of these incidents represent a miraculous experience to me. I could have ignored the pain or put off going to the doctor, but God directed my path and led me to solutions that I am sure saved my life.

It might be stated here that miracles don't always appear as overtly as happened in the "clot" story. In 2011, our household again experienced two miracles related to health issues. One day my husband on a routine doctor's visit learned that his PSA test (test for Prostate cancer) was elevated. Again following good medical advice, he went to his private doctor who referred him to Urologists who soon confirmed via biopsy that the elevated PSA test did indeed indicate a growth in his prostate gland.(It is said by many doctors that a man might not die from prostate cancer, but there is a good chance they might die with it, meaning that the chances of a male over 70 dying *from* prostate cancer were slim compared to the possibility that he might indeed be diagnosed with prostate cancer, and die *with* the cancer, not because of it, because prostate cancer occurs quite frequently in older men. Again because of my exposure to the medical field and having seen some of those prostatic cancer cases, I became somewhat apprehensive. I remember almost losing my composure, imagining the kinds of consequences, this might mean to my husband and our family. But something kicked in, (faith and determination and belief in a higher power), and I knew I had to be strong for my husband, myself and my children. If I had become upset and fallen apart, he would have thought all possibilities of a positive outcome were nil. We stayed with the process of "watchful waiting" for about a year.

After some time, my husband soon confided in me that the biopsies to detect growth of the tumor were quite painful, and he did not know if he could continue to endure them. He decided he would rather go ahead and have the surgery and remove the cancerous growth. So we moved to step two in decision-making, and decided to investigate the kinds of surgeries that were available for the type of cancer that he had. The time it took to come to that decision gave us time to think about and adjust to what being diagnosed with cancer meant. Again, we were sent to a specialist who listed the options, alternatives, and the kinds of surgeries and outcomes that were possible. We prayed about it, and read about different procedures, as well as talking to others who had undergone prostate surgery, and finally opted for a procedure that would require very little threat to his life, but offered a good chance of removing the cancerous growth for good. Very little blood would be lost and a huge incision would not be necessary. With the specialist's help, my husband decided on "Robotic" surgery, and we asked for prayers from our church family, immediate family and friends. To make a long story short, my husband entered the hospital on a Monday, had the procedure on Tuesday, lost hardly any blood, tolerated the surgery well, and was discharged from the hospital the next day. I took him home on Wednesday around noon time after only a day and a half in the hospital. The surgery had lasted all of two and a half hours and even with his age and a long history of type 2 diabetes, he was out of the hospital, and up walking around in less than two days. Another miracle in my book! The miracle of modern medicine, but also the miracle of faith, belief in God, and the confidence in a very skilled surgeon, brought us back to the reality of God being at work in our lives. We could have become disconsolate, depressed, and unforgiving, and full of self-pity. Instead, we called on the power of God to intervene, and assist us in making the procedure as benign as possible, as well as assisting him in a speedy recovery. The tumor was found to be malignant, but had remained encapsulated (no metastasis) and therefore, led to no complications. I could hardly believe it. After about three weeks, he was up and about gradually returning to normal physical activities. From that experience I also became more attuned to the role faith plays in believing that this type of outcome is possible. Can you recall similar experiences in your life that could be considered miracles? They happen all the time. We just don't recognize them as such.

_____

_____

_____

_____

Let's pause again and have you consider the miracles that might be happening more often than you realize in your life. Have some of these come to mind? What about your faith? We all talk about "faith" the size of a mustard seed, but often have no idea to what we are referring. Faith is a benign, abstract notion that very few of us appreciate or acknowledge. Oh, we walk around saying "I have faith that this will happen" or "with God's help this will happen". But how would you really describe your faith? (See end of chapter for scriptures on same).

_____

_____

_____

_____

I wanted to write this chapter because I have come to believe in miracles from real life experiences. To be truthful, I think one has to experience certain phenomena in order to recognize miracles when they do occur. Our belief system plays a great role in our ability to attribute unexplained events to power beyond our control. As I think about my own journey through the six decades that God has allowed me to be on this plane, I can recall very vividly some events that can only be attributed to the "miracle working" power of God.

The third event I mentioned above had to do with my daughter who walked around for years with a tumor in her body of which we knew nothing. On a late night in March of 2011 we received a call from an emergency room in Colorado because she had experienced what was thought to be a heart attack at 41 years of age. Again, God intervened by surrounding her with smart capable doctors who did not stop until they determined what had caused this potentially life-threatening situation. A small tumor was finally discovered in her urinary tract that caused her to feel faint and black out every time her body carried out its natural functions; again, it is my belief that to discover this tumor and remove it from such a delicate area was indeed a miracle. She is alive today, and doing well with no complications or recurrences since the surgery. I could probably go on and on in sharing events that I now can look upon as managed by God's hands.

Lastly, I'd like to add that as a labor and delivery nurse who has participated in and witnessed a number of babies brought into this world, I've always considered the entire process of birth from conception to delivery to be nothing short of a miracle. A tiny rapidly deployed sperm enters a seemingly foreign environment, but somehow makes its way through an unknown path to a tiny ovum (egg) lying dormant in the mother's secret, fertile hiding place (the fallopian tube). The sperm and ovum meet there, and if all conditions are right and in order, a conception and fertilization takes place. Although this happens like clockwork, all conditions and environments have to be ideal for the best outcome – a newly developed perfectly formed human being. The woman's body must then prepare itself to accept or reject this foreign object. Be that as it may, if all goes well, nearly 280 days or 40 weeks are required before this phenomenal occurrence presents as a finished product. The most miraculous part of this whole process is that the mother's body changes to accommodate all the nuances of a normal gestation, and then prepares itself to expel this new life into a totally unfamiliar environment to which the neonate and the mother must adjust. This new human is thrust into a totally foreign environment into which it now must adapt. No more envelopment in warm protective fluids in the mother's womb where it has received all its nourishment necessary for growth and development for nine months. In thinking about this phenomenal process which repeats itself over and over again, time and time again in the creation of new life, I become even more attuned to the miraculous nature of human birth. No evolution here! A baby every time in the same way unless the mother requires a C-Section) to bring the new being into the world. In my world view, this too, is the essence and evidence of a supernatural occurrence (a miracle). The mother (and father) are then charged with making sure this new creature maintains, adapts and develops in its new environment, and to its greatest potential. A Miracle? Indeed it is, and this process is not complete until about 18 years have passed. Living and being alive, and reaching one's pre-ordained potential is nothing less than a miracle!

Thus the birth of humans and all species in nature can be considered miracles as the "Power of God" continues the cycle of creation - creating a new species in the likeness of itself over and over again. Take a moment and write your own reaction to these miraculous events. How can we doubt the "Power of God"? God is the Alpha and Omega – the beginning and the end. Do you still doubt the occurrence of miracles? Can we not call "birth" one miracle that has continued throughout the centuries? Having given you something to set you thinking, now you can move on to describe miraculous happenings in your life. Take a moment to recall and re-live miracles in your own miraculous life.

What else can be said about the magic of miracles? How about the survivability of the human species? Some say there is always a constant balancing of nature. Only the strong survive! Not really sure of that, but we can all recall many instances over the years when events have happened that have seemingly miraculous endings. The hurricane that circumvents a city or a house and all inhabitants are spared, or the flood that destroys houses, and people are found clinging to trees and debris, and rooftops in an effort to survive. In all of these instances, miracles occur and I see it as tangible evidence of the power of God at work in midst. As children of God, we need to remain cognizant of the many tiny miracles that occur around us and that we take for granted. Count your blessings, and know that continued faith and trust in a higher power will sustain us through many seemingly trying times, but with unwavering faith and trust in the power of God, we will continue to witness more miracles in our lives. To God be the Glory! Great things He has done! Great things He will do!

Biblical References to Miracles and Faith:

2 Kings: 4: 8, 38, 42; 2 Kings 5:1 – 19;

2 Kings 19: 14 -19; (Significance of prayer)

Nehemiah 13: 4-31 (Faithfulness);

1ˢᵗ Samuel 3:1 – 21 (Listening to God);

Psalms 61:1-8. (Hope in God)

Scriptures taken from the African-American Devotional Bible: New International Version. The Congress of National Black Churches, Inc. Zondervan Publishing House.

Notes:

_____

_____

_____

_____

_____

_____

_____

_____

_____

_____

_____

_____

_____

_____

_____

_____

_____

_____

_____

_____

_____

ABOUT THE AUTHOR

BONITA F. BASARA

Bonita (Bonnie) Basara is a mentor, trainer and coach. She has held a variety of positions in the customer related fields over the past twenty-five years.

Ms. Basara received a Bachelor of Arts Degree in Management and Marketing from Saint Martin's University at the age of 52. After a brief break of a few years she obtained her Master of Science Degree in Human Resources, and simultaneously a Certificate in Organizational Leadership from Chapman University at 56 years of age.

Bonnie is a member of Altrusa International of Olympia which serves the community needs and challenges; by working locally as caring, concerned individuals making handmade chemo caps for cancer patients; collecting children's books for the local food bank; stuffing diaper bags with books and materials to encourage reading to newborn babies for the local hospital; providing deserving high school students over $9,000 in awards and scholarships per year; and working together as a powerful association of clubs and districts. In addition, she is a member of American Association of University Women (AAUW) and the National Association of Female Executives (NAFE), and The Professional Woman Network (PWN).

Her passion is assisting others to recognize their true potential and truly believe that education is never too late. Her plans for the future are to expand and develop her own coaching business "Excel in Life." She is focusing on women's issues such as: Diversity, Self-Esteem, Women's Wellness, Customer Service and Financial Independence. Bonita is available as a keynote speaker for personal and professional coaching sessions.

Contact:
Bonnie Basara
Telephone : (360)556.0474
Email: bonitabasara@yahoo.com
www.excelinlife.net

FIVE

GOD WASN'T READY FOR ME

By Bonnie Basara

This is my story of how I came to the conclusion that
God wasn't ready for me.

As I was growing up I never felt I was that deeply spiritual as other people I would meet. Don't get me wrong I believe in God and Jesus Christ, but I felt I just didn't have that deep commitment of spiritual faith.

My earliest memory of being exposed to religion was when I was about four or five years old and going to the Church of the Advent an Episcopal Church in Cape May, New Jersey with my mother, father, and brothers and sister. I would get bored listening to the sermon so

most of the time I'd fall a sleep. As I got a little older I would stand
with my sister in the church choir and afterwards go to Sunday school.
So this was my beginning exposure to learning about God and Jesus.
When I was about seven my father moved our family to Camden, New
Jersey and we started to attend St. Paul Episcopal Church in Camden.
My father would drive us to church and come back to get us when
church was over. He never really explained to us why he didn't attend
church with us anymore. My sister and I joined the girl's choir and
my brothers served as acolytes during Mass. Once mass was over with
we would then attend Sunday school. Through my growing up years
I would attend the different activities the church would have such as:
Thanksgiving Bazaars and dinner, Christmas Pageants, Palm and Easter
Sunday sunrise services, and the all important church picnic.

When I was thirteen I made my Confirmation and First Holy
Communion, and became a full fledge Episcopalian. Again, I believe
in God and Jesus Christ, but I felt I just didn't have that deep
commitment of spiritual faith.

The neighborhood I lived in was much diversified in ethnicity and
religious faiths. As I got older I found out my parents were originally
Roman Catholic and my three older brothers and sister were baptized
Roman Catholic. My parents had a difference of opinion with the
priest and so my father told my mother we should pick another faith
and church to attend. By the time I was born my parents converted
over to being Episcopalians. My parents felt both religions believed
in the same things fundamentally just the Episcopal faith didn't have
the Pope as their leader. As I grew older I became more of a liberal
thinker about religions and not as hung up on doctrines as much as
faith development. Again, I believe in God and Jesus Christ, but I felt I
just didn't have that deep commitment of spiritual faith.

When I met my husband Brian and found out he was Roman Catholic and we started to talk about getting married and possibly having children I knew he wouldn't convert to being an Episcopalian so I decided to maintain peace in our marriage I would convert to Roman Catholicism, after all my two older brothers converted to being Roman Catholic also. Again, I believe in God and Jesus Christ, but I felt I just didn't have that deep commitment of spiritual faith.

Brian joined the Air Force six months after we met. A year later he went to Vietnam. We got married a year after he came back from Vietnam in his family church. Brian, my husband was assigned to Dover AFB in Dover, Delaware after we were married and we settled in a little town called Smyrna about fifteen miles north of Dover. At Easter we went to the local Catholic Church there for services, and I was very disappointed with the homily topic. The priest read a letter from the Pope expressing his views on birth control. I felt he should have been talking about why we are celebrating Christ rising from the dead instead of focusing on this letter which in my opinion should have been put in the church bulletins. The next Sunday I went to the local Episcopal Church and felt more at home. The priest from their came to our home to visit, luckily Brian wasn't there, and we talked and I explained about me converting and I was very confused in my level of commitment to Brian in practicing being a Catholic. He said to me that he believed that God had a plan for me and that I should make an effort to accept his guidance in my conversion and to give it a chance. Needless to say I didn't go back to either church or any others for several years after. Again, I believe in God and Jesus Christ, but I felt I just didn't have that deep commitment of spiritual faith.

Three years after we were married Brian received orders and we were transferred to Langley AFB, in Hampton, Virginia. Within five years of marriage we had two sons Brian Jr. and John, twenty-two months apart and they were baptized in the church where we were married. We didn't attend church at all after they were born it just didn't seem important to us at the time. Again, I believe in God and Jesus Christ, but I felt I just didn't have that deep commitment of spiritual faith.

We lived in Virginia for five years when Brian received orders to go to Bitburg, Germany. He went over first to find us an apartment to live while he was worked at the air field. In the meantime my sons and I stayed with my parents till we received order from the military that we go accompany him. By this time the boys were five and three. Brian found us a nice apartment about fifteen miles north of Bitburg and our landlord lived below us and they had a girl eight years old and a boy age six. We had friends we knew in Virginia they were also stationed in Germany but further south, they grew up in West Virginia. We would go down to visit occasionally and I would go with the wife to attend their service. They didn't have an ordained minister or priest to conduct the service just one of the male member of the congregation would chose something from the bible to talk about and then when they had communion it was grape juice in little thimble cups. I didn't feel I was really attending a church service. Again, I believe in God and Jesus Christ, but I felt I just didn't have that deep commitment of spiritual faith.

When we came back from Germany we were assigned to Holloman AFB, New Mexico. We didn't care for the climate and desert like surroundings so Brian volunteered to transfer to McChord AFB, in Tacoma, Washington. So again Brian came ahead and found us a house to buy in Lacey, Washington. Brian came back to help pack up our things and he drove the moving van and I followed in our car to Washington State. By this time I realized the boys were nine and seven years old and neither one had made their First Holy Communion. I talked to Brian about this and we decided we needed to start going to church. I found a Roman Catholic Church near our home called Sacred Heart and we started to go to services there. Again, I believe in God and Jesus Christ, but I felt I just didn't have that deep commitment of spiritual faith.

In August, 1983 the church bulletin was announcing registration for religious education classes and they were also looking for teachers. I was aware that in 1972 the Roman Catholic Church was going through major changes in how they performed the mass and included the congregation in participating. I decided to enroll the boys into the Sacramental Preparation classes and to volunteer to be a teacher. I felt that with all the changes the church went through I could learn along with my sons. I was accepted to be a teacher and I have been there ever since. So over the years my faith was quietly developing, our religious director would have instructional workshops on how to prepare lesson plans, the learning styles of individuals, and faith formation classes. I received several certificates in completing faith development courses. Again, I believe in God and Jesus Christ, but I felt I just didn't have that deep commitment of spiritual faith.

In 1987, our religious director, Diane Koval, came to me and asked if I would be interested in creating a new class and curriculum for children who never been baptized as infants and still haven't been baptized by the time they were seven or were baptized in another faith but now they or their parents want to become Roman Catholic, this was called The Rites of Christian Adults (adapted for children) or RCIA. I found that the Catholic Church developed this program/process in 1982 and now the dilemma was their parents are converting what does the church do with these older children. I thought about the challenge and told Diane I would be glad to do it. Over the years working with parents and their children ages seven to eighteen years old preparing the children to receive their full sacraments (Baptism, Confirmation and Holy Communion) all on the night of the Easter Vigil. Each year at the Easter Vigil seeing each child rising up out of the baptismal pool dripping wet and being accepted by the congregation of the church is very heart warming. But, Again, I believe in God and Jesus Christ, but I felt I just didn't have that deep commitment of spiritual faith.

Well, here is the event that changed that feeling. The end of October, 2009 I elected to have knee replacement surgery on both of my knees. I felt at the time if my mother could have it done back in the "80's" then I could do it also. Three years before the operation my doctor scheduled me to have a cardiogram and stress test done. They didn't find any cholesterol buildup in my arteries but being I was diabetic and I put on high blood pressure medication. A week before the surgery I went through and EKG and blood work and everything seemed fine and the surgery was a go. My surgery was scheduled for 7:30 am and I had to be at the hospital at 5:30 am. so Brian drove me over. When I was waking up from surgery I could hear my sons calling to me and talking to me with me barely answering and drifting back to sleep. When I really woke up I find I am in ICU with only my right knee completed and an incision with staples in my left knee and hooked up to a temporary pacemaker and I was in ICU for three days. Standing next to my bed is a cardiologist asking me to sign paperwork to give him permission to perform an angioplasty. I said to him, "wait a moment I'm just recovering from one surgery and I'm not ready to go under for another. I need to know what happened to me." Eventually I find out that while I was having the knee surgery I went into cardiac arrest and I died on the table. After the three days

I was transferred to the cardiac floor so I could be monitored while I was convalescing. The therapist came up the next day to get me up and get my knees moving and a nurse comes running in because the bells were going off and my blood pressure was dropping so needless to say I was rushed back into bed and the therapist didn't try to get me up anymore. The next day after this the cardio team takes me down to a room to perform a cardiogram. The results they were not able to see any blockage. So I signed the papers to have angioplasty and I was taken down the following morning, again they didn't find any blockage. So the determination was my heart stops beating once in a while so the decision was made to have a pacemaker inserted into me. With all of this going on I didn't have a moment to really reflect on the ramifications of what had happened to me during my knee surgery till I was transferred to a convalescent home for therapy on my knees to get me walking again. While I was in the home they have a priest that performs services and comes around to the rooms. I asked to speak with him and explained to him what happened during my surgery. My question to him was why did this happened and how could I deal with this. We prayed for awhile and he counseled me that it would take time for me to understand what God wanted for me. Twenty-three days after my surgery I was released to go home to start outpatient therapy to strengthen my knees. When I would talk to people about my surgery and that I died on the table they would ask if I saw the light. I would answer no I didn't see any light so I have decided that "God Wasn't Ready for Me". After my convalescent I went back to teaching my religious classes and found I was gradually developing a deeper relationship with God. For many people it doesn't take a tragedy or dying on the table during surgery to have a deep relationship with God but for me I'm a stubborn little Polack so God had to do something drastic to get my attention. At the time I didn't know what plans God had for me but I now have this quiet deep commitment of spiritual faith growing in me to pass on to others. I didn't know how I could help others to come to a spiritual relationship with God until I was invited by Linda Eastman to be a contributing author to The Power of God series I realized this was a chance to share my story of how I was able to create a deeper relationship with God.

Notes:

_____

_____

_____

_____

_____

_____

_____

_____

_____

_____

_____

_____

_____

_____

_____

_____

_____

_____

_____

_____

_____

_____

_____

ABOUT THE AUTHOR

Ramona Monique Pinckney, MSN, MA, MBA

Ramona Monique Pinckney is the founder and CEO of Women's Speaker Network and seeks to inspire, encourage and empower women everywhere. She is certified in Women's Issues and Diversity and has over 20 years experience as a registered nurse and developed a passion for people and women's issues over the course of her career lead to the creation of Women's Speaker Network.

Ramona holds many other degrees which include a Bachelor of Science in Nursing, a Bachelor of Science in Biblical Studies, a Master's in Computer Resources and a Master's in Business Administration from Webster University and a Master of Science in Nursing from Armstrong Atlantic State University.

She is board certified with the American Nurses Credentialing Center and is currently employed as an Adult Nurse Practitioner for the medically underserved.

Ramona has a strong faith in God and credits Him with all of her accomplishments. She is dedicated to fulfilling the plan for her life that God has designed. It is her lifelong dream to help others to overcome the trauma of physical, emotional and sexual abuse.

She also is a member of the *Professional Woman Network* and has served as chair of a *Women's Empowerment Conference*. Ramona also actively participates on local health committees in her community. She is available as a keynote speaker and workshop leader for groups, organizations both locally and nationally. She continues to seek opportunities to grow in knowledge and kindness.

Contact:
Ramona M. Pinckney
P.O. Box 2251
Beaufort, SC 29901
ramonapinckney@ymail.com
www.empowermentlivinginstitute.com
(888) 471-8029

SIX

POWER, PRAISE AND PRISON

By Ramona Pinckney

Acts 16:25-26

"About midnight Paul and Silas were praying and singing hymns to God, and the other prisoners were listening to them. Suddenly there was such a violent earthquake that the foundations of the prison were shaken. At once all the prison doors flew open, and everyone's chains came loose."

God's Power to Release you from Prison

In Acts 16 we see where Paul and Silas travelled to Europe to preach to the good news of Jesus. While they were there, a young girl was possessed with a spirit that yelled "these men are servants of the Most High God, who are telling you the way to be saved" (16:17). This girl spoke the truth, but it was for the wrong purpose and Paul commanded the spirit to come out of the girl. This poor girl had "owners" who became furious that the spirit was made to leave this girl. Once this young woman was free of this spirit they could no longer exploit her and sought to punish Paul by demanding that he and his companion be placed in prison. But, when the power of God is present one is freed from physical or psychological prisons. The young woman was released from a psychological prison and exploitation by others because of the power of God.

I also was once in prison. No, not a physical one, but a psychological one. I grew up in Bronx, New York in a dysfunctional family living in the inner city. Everyone seemed to live for the moment and without hope for a future. As a product of my surroundings, I lived a life of hopelessness and despair. My greatest desire was to be rescued from my mental anguish and self-imposed prison. My only point of reference of a better life was what I saw on television and of course out of my reach. Not equipped with the life skills needed to escape my surroundings, I became just another statistic of inner city life.

At eight years of age, I was molested by my cousin. Evil's embrace taught me that safety did not exist, not even in the home. I became a teenaged mother at the age of 15 and attempted suicide twice. For many years, depression, isolation and hopelessness were my closest companions. There was always a louder voice inside me that said "give up," "what's the use," "no one cares." But, there was also a quieter voice saying "just maybe," "keep trying," "God loves you." Holding onto God's love kept me going. I don't know how I knew that He loved me, but I just knew. Still, I desperately wished for someone to come and rescue me from myself and my personal prison, but no one came. Can you relate to my experience?

If you feel hopeless, read Psalm 31:23-24.

If you have suffered abuse, read Psalm 119:28.

If you are experiencing mental anguish due to the abuse and/or neglect by others, read Psalm 31:9.

The answer to these questions lies within you. One day I realized that there is a freedom that cannot be contained by physical walls. I could be free spiritually and mentally through the power of God and so can you. The Bible teaches us that true freedom is trusting in God. Paul and Silas prayed and sang while in prison because they rested in the assurance that God was in charge of their situation. There are many that live in a psychological or mental prison due to past hurts, unforgiveness and bitterness.

Consider these questions:

Are you in a spiritual or mental prison?

Do you feel you tired and overwhelmed?

Do you feel lonely or misunderstood?

Do you feel as if your life is a constant struggle?

Do you feel as if your circumstances will never change?

Who or what do you trust in?

Do you believe that God loves you?

Maybe you had a rough childhood or suffered lost as an adult. For many of us, life has not worked out as we expected. The disappointments, betrayals and burdens of life have become more than we can bear. Sadly, many of us feel as if there isn't anyone we can turn to. They were freed because they believed and trusted in God. There is no safer place to be than putting your trust in the Lord. Knowing that God is almighty and all powerful gives us an assurance that He will take care of us no matter the situation. We too can sing praises to God even in difficult circumstances because truly we know that he cares for us.

God's Power to Release Us

God has the power to change our life and any circumstance because He is all powerful. You do not have to live in a prison of emotional, mental and physical despair. Society has created a way to physically confine those who have been found guilty of a crime; however, there are many who are placed in psychological confinement through no fault of their own. Low-self-esteem, depression, addictions and self-hatred are just a few of the byproducts of mistreatment from others. Paul and Silas were punished and imprisoned unjustly like many of us.

Paul and Silas were placed in physical prisons, but were released because of the power of God. Despite their circumstance they sang hymns and prayed because they knew that they could never truly be imprisoned by anyone. They knew a living God that continues to reach beyond walls, heartache, disappointments, failures, betrayals, mistakes, depression, or any unclean spirit that seeks to possess that which He has created. God's healing and saving power are available to those who call on Him for "Everyone who calls on the name of the Lord will be saved (Rom. 10:13, NIV)."

Answer the following questions with a simple yes or no. What must you do to turn it into a yes?

Do you know God?

Do you believe in prayer?

Do you believe that God can save you and heal you?

God's Power will keep you

There is no greater power than Jesus. The grave could not even hold Him because on the third day He was raised to everlasting life. No pain or prison can hold you either when you call on His name. When you have lost all hope the power of God will come in and raise you up for it is the same power that raised Jesus from the dead. You may feel like your life is over and giving up, "but if Christ is in you, then even though your body is subject to death because of sin, the Spirit gives life because of righteousness. And if the Spirit of him who raised Jesus from the dead is living in you, he who raised Christ from the dead will also give life to your mortal bodies because of his Spirit who lives in you (Rom. 8:10-11)." The power or God can deliver you from the chains that bind you.

Who are what are you trusting in? People will surely disappoint you. We have to learn to live a life of contentment and know that God is all that we really need. Eve lived in the Garden of Eden and had all of her needs taken care of by God Himself and still it wasn't enough. This is where sin enters in. Our action tells God that He is not enough, but He is all that really matters. What is your prison? Is it depression, low self- esteems, addictions?

Prisons can be physical or psychological. Ironically, some who are confined behind prison walls are free because they are "free" in their mind and spirit. Many who are living outside of prison walls are confined by crippling emotions often brought on by the abuse, neglect and harm by others. You can be released from the prison and chains that bind you by confessing Jesus as Lord. No matter what your circumstance, God can bring you out. He will save you, deliver you and give you a new mind and a new life. Do not look to others to save you because they cannot save themselves. God's love is greater than any wrong that you may have done in the past.

The Power of God's Love

No sin is too great to keep you from God's love. "No, in all these things we are more than conquerors through him who loved us. For I am convinced that neither death nor life, neither angels nor demons, neither the present nor the future, nor any powers, neither height nor depth, nor anything else in all creation, will be able to separate us from the love of God that is in Christ Jesus our Lord (Rom. 8:37-39)." Jesus came to Paul while he was on the Damascus road to kill Christians. God saved Paul and He will save you. You can take your burdens to Him and leave them there. They have become too heavy for you to bear. Paul and Silas knew they did not have a way to be released from their prison so they decided to pray and sing hymns in their circumstance. This is what their story illustrates. We are to sing hymns and pray to God although it looks like our circumstance has not changed, but God is working it out for us and He hears our prayers. He will keep you no matter what your circumstance.

He will lift you up when it seems as if all hope is gone. He is a sustainer. He is faithful. There is no one greater. You may feel as if all is lost and your situation is hopeless. You may even feel like giving up, but the same power that raised Jesus from the dead is the same power that will raise you from a life of misery and despair. He is glorious, Holy, righteous, majestic and wonderful. There are not enough names to describe God. Ten thousand lifetimes are not enough to talk of His goodness. We can never fail in Him. All that is required is to call on Him. Knowing of Him is not enough, but you must call on Him for yourself for anyone who calls on the name of the Lord will be saved.

Trust in His Power

Paul and Silas did not question why they were in that circumstance. They knew they had a purpose and when there is purpose there is hope. No one can stop your destiny. Whatever God has predestined for your life, it will come to pass. No one can stop you from your purpose-except you. You are the only one who can stop you from reaching your purpose due to unbelief. The power of God will keep you from giving up. The promises of God will keep you from committing suicide. The awesomeness of God will remind you how Great God is compared to your problems. No one will love you and stand by you like Jesus. When everyone else abandons you God will be there. He is the beginning and the end and He will never leave you. Your family may forsake you and friends may abandon you, but He sticks closer than a brother. There is no one like Him in all the earth.

The Power of Praise

Your praise to God will release you from your prison. If you have breath in your body, you have a reason to praise the Lord. The Bible says "let everything that has breath praise the Lord (Ps. 150:6.)" Paul and Silas did not wait for the manifestation of the open prison doors, and praised God before they were released. They knew no matter what happen they were in the care of the Lord. We can learn from them. We can praise God in the middle of a terrible circumstance. No matter what the circumstance, God is still good. He is our Father and our heart cries Abba Farther. What three things can you be grateful for? Do you always worry and complain? What situation or circumstance are you hoping will change?

He is great and mighty from the majestic mountain to the flowing river. There is no other like Him. When you have lost all hope, look to the Lord and know that there is hope. He specializes in those who have been wounded and rejected. There is no safer place to be then in His arm. His grace and mercy are all encompassing and everlasting. Circumstances of life have tried to rob you of a life full of abundance and joy, but just know that the God loves you. He tells us "for I know the plans I have for you," declares the LORD, "plans to prosper you and not to harm you, plans to give you hope and a future (Jer. 29:11, NIV)." Do not listen to the lies of others. Do not even listen to the negative voices in your own head. If you are still living, it is because God has a purpose for your life. Just like Paul and Silas, some of us have been unjustly put into emotional and psychological prisons by others, but it is our praise and prayer that can deliver us. God is all powerful and all mighty. Bring your burdens to Him for only can save you and keep you. Do not put your hope in man because "the life of mortals is like grass, they flourish like a flower of the field; the wind blows over it and it is gone, and its place remembers it no more (Ps.103:15, NIV)."

No chains or prison walls can confine you when you have a song in your heart and laughter in your spirit. God will give you a peace that surpasses all understanding (Phil 4:7, NIV)." In Him, you will find peace, you will find joy. From everlasting to everlasting is His love towards us. It does not matter what you have done. God desires are to have mercy upon His children. Trust in Him and believe in Him. Neither money, success nor any other thing can give you the peace and security of God.

Prayer of Salvation

Knowing who you are in Christ and your purpose will enable you to walk in what God has called you to do. Stop seeking the approval of others because they do not have the answer. Your life is in the hands of God and He will take care of you. He will be there even when others walk away and abandon you. Put your trust in Him and He will grace you with the strength you need to endure. He is an awesome God. He is full of wonder, majesty, praise and glory. If you don't know Christ as your personal Savior, please say this simple prayer. Dear Jesus, I confess with my mouth that you are Lord and believe in my heart that God raised you from the dead. Because I confess with my mouth and believe in my heart, I will be saved. Read Romans 10:10.

ABOUT THE AUTHOR

QUENTIN NEWHOUSE, JR., PhD

Dr. Quentin Newhouse, Jr. Is the President of Q. Newhouse Structured Coaching Strategies, Inc. a Life and Organizational Coaching organization in Montreal, Canada. He is a career educator with more than 35 years of university teaching and administrative experiences, including Campus Dean. Dr. Newhouse was the first Project Director of the Bowie State University (MD) Alchohol, Tobacco, and Other Drug Prevention Center. He also served for two years as a Director of an inner-city after care program for 7-22 years old children.

Dr. Newhouse has owned two businesses and has corporate experience working with Safeway. He worked as a Social Science Statistician for the US Census Bureau. He has received awards, including Who's Who in America, Who's Who Among African Americans, and Stanford's Who's Who. He is a published author with two spiritual poem books, a non-fiction children's book about his adopted cat, and an upcoming children's book on a little boy who hates to be late.

Dr. Newhouse completed a Doctor of Philosophy degree in Experimental Social Psychology and a Master of Science degree in General Experimental Psychology, from Howard University, in Washington, DC. His doctoral dissertation focused on four years of adjustments in academic achievement for more than 300 fatherless African American boys. He completed a Bachelor of Science degree in Psychology from Marietta College in Ohio. Dr. Newhouse is a member of the American Psychological Association, Canadian Psychological Association, International Coaching Federation, Canadian Obesity Network, and the Professional Woman Network.

Dr. Newhouse is committed to promoting the health and well-being of people and families. He welcomes the opportunity to network with The Professional Woman Network.

Contact:

Q Newhouse Structured Coaching Strategies, Inc.,
1365 Avenue Beaumont, CP 65518 BEAUMONT
Montreal, Quebec, H3P 3H8
www.qnewhousecoachs.com
(438) 333-1590

SEVEN

FOUR TIMES CLOSER TO GOD

By Quentin Newhouse, Jr., PhD

This testimony chronicles the testimony of my wife, who experienced four near death experiences, and is so modest, that she did not want this story to be told to the world. I convinced her (sort of) because it is a testament to her courage, fortitude, and will to survive. I have always been inspired by this story and felt compelled to share this story with others. I experienced the third near death experience with her, and totally believe her story is one of faith, hope, and courage. The next time you have a minor pain, read this story. I am convinced that you will shake your head, stop complaining and praise God for whatever your state of health. My wife has never complained about any of these past and present pains and always smiles, rarely shows her obvious pains, has a positive attitude toward life, and continues to help others. These are true accounts told in my wife's voice.

"As a nurse, I have seen more than my share of suffering, misery, and pain. I try never to make a big deal of it, but my husband said he was inspired when he heard about the number of surgeries I have had. I have had 11 surgeries under general anesthesia and a total of 8 bone fractures, rods and screws.

April 7, 1990

You will never imagine what happened to me on my wedding day in my homeland, Thailand. I was on my way to get my hair done for my wedding that afternoon. I was in a car driven by my good friend. Five minutes after we had left the house, the car went down a bridge and a truck came into our lane from a different direction. She turned to avoid that truck and our car spun down the road and fell into a ditch on the side of the road in Bangkok.

The last thing I remembered was when I told my friend to slow down while we came down the bridge. The car was totalled. My bridesmaid was also in the back seat. She had a broken nose. The driver got a chest injury, but was still conscious. I was told that I passed out and was full of blood flowing from my head. A taxi driver who passed by pulled me out from the window of the car.

At the hospital, they found out that I had sustained chest trauma, lung contusion, lumbar spine fracture, head laceration, a fractured left foot and right collar bone fracture. It took me total of 3 weeks in the hospital where I did my nursing training to recover. I had the best Orthopedic spine surgeon in the university teaching hospital. He operated on my back and after 6 hours, put a long rod in to hold on my broken spine which is called a burst fracture. The doctor explained to my family that my shattered spine was like powder. He had to take another piece of bone from my hip to make a graft to repair the missing part of my spine. He told my mother that it was so close to my spinal cord. There were even some predictions that I might be paralyzed from my waist down.

I was in ICU for one week. I was so sick and full of wire, machine and tubes from everywhere in my body, a friend recalled. I had a tube for breathing from my mouth, a tube for feeding from my nose, a drain from the operation site on my back, and a tube from my bladder. I had an Intravenous line from my chest (central line) to give powerful medication to keep me alive and hooked up with my arms monitored I spent a total of three weeks in the hospital.

I was half conscious. I remembered being suctioned by nurses through my breathing tube. It was very uncomfortable . I had to be turned by 3 persons every 2 hours. They had to be very careful because of my spinal surgery. I kept looking at the clock in the ICU. I was trying to figure if it was day or night. I could not talk because of my breathing tube. I was slightly conscious of what was going on because I was kept sedated while in the ICU unit. My care required nurses and doctors checking me 24 hours a day. Friends and families were frequently visiting me. In Thailand , the rule then was 5 minutes per visit. My mother made a visiting book so friends could write something encouraging for me.

I was the first person in my nursing class to get married. The school had finished by the end of March and my wedding was a week after that ! Being 22 years old, I was so excited about getting married. I had known my fiancé since the end of my high school year. There were about 400 guests expected. Since the wedding had to be cancelled, the food was sent to feed the children in the orphanage. I received tons of presents in my hospital room. So many friends who showed up at the wedding that afternoon at the church came to the ER to visit me. I was unconscious . My clothes were stained with blood.

My mother, who was also a nurse, sat by my side everyday and every night. Whenever I opened my eyes, she was there. When I could eat, she would put a straw in my mouth so that I could drink more milk. She said that I needed high protein to get stronger faster. My favorite aunt also visited me every day. She sat in front of ICU knitting with her crochet in a vigil, praying for me to get well and greeting my visitors.

Twenty one days later, I was discharged from the hospital. I was able to walk a short distance before needing a wheelchair. The wedding was the same day of my discharge. In Thai culture, a woman cannot live with a man without being married. My cousin did my makeup and my hair while I was still in the hospital. I was quite the bride as she tried to hide a bruise from my face .my loss of 20 pounds, and the fact that my wedding dress was now so loosely fit. I could not walk on high heels, so my mother got me a pair of flat white shoes. I could not walk the whole isle, so the

wedding march was cut in to only half an isle. I was happy to finally get married. This time, there was no reception after and there were about 80 guests, mostly my grade school friends and family members. I rested and recuperated for 3 months.

In July I was able to join the graduation ceremony. At that time The King of Thailand gave diplomas to each graduate.. We took so many pictures. My parent were thrilled. I was the eldest of their 4 children and the first to graduate from a university. As long as I could remember, my parents had always said to me that it was my responsibility to be a good example to my younger siblings. I was happy that I had done what I was supposed to do-graduate from a university.

Chulalongkorn University was rated the best and oldest university in Thailand. My mother also went to the same nursing school 25 years earlier. Both of my parents had their pictures taken years before me when they got their university diploma from the same king of Thailand.

I worked for 5 months as a nurse in Thailand before moving to Montreal, Canada with my husband. I thank God for helping me surviving this serious, big accident. My aunt told me later that she had asked 10 churches to pray for me while I was in the hospital.

June 17, 2006

The second incident occurred after having been in Canada for 16 years and working as an ER nurse for over 10 years . At that time, I was divorced from my first husband and a single parent with two young children.. I often biked my way to work and it had been fun and relaxing. After the one hour trek to work,   I would take a nice shower and be refreshed for my 8 or 12 hour shift. On that night , after putting my 2 children to bed, I rushed out as usual. Having been a single mother for 6 years, I had a lot on my mind. While I was worried for my children 15 and 9, I know I needed to double my income, since I had just bought a new house just a year earlier. I did many overtime shifts to cover my expenses and pay my new mortgage.

It was about 10:45 PM when I bicycled across the street from one sidewalk to the next. It was quiet and I could hear no car coming. As I rode half way across the street, I felt a light on my face. It was a car coming in my direction. I was going to stop and give the driver a bad look. "Are you really going to hit me, I thought", but I decided to hurry to reach another side of the street. Oddly, the car did not slow down. I felt the car hit my back wheel very hard and speed away ! I flew in the air and landed on the road. I could not believe I was in a car accident again for the second time ! In the back of my mind I wondered if my rod that had been placed in my back from the first accident would be affected.

I could not get up. I felt pain in my left hand , my right foot and my buttocks.

A car passed by and stopped to call 911. She was also a doctor who was on her way to work her night shift at another ER. Within 5 minutes. I heard a sound of a police car, fire truck and an ambulance. The paramedic recognized me. He was surprised to see me as a patient instead of working in the Emergency Room. The ambulance scooped me up on the backboard , put me on hard neck collar and rushed me to the trauma center hospital. This time, I broke my right ankle , my left hand and my left pelvic. It was painful everywhere, but miraculously, my spine and rod from my first accident were intact.

I spent the night in the ER and had many x-rays and CT scans done. My friends from my ER came to visit me after their shifts. One ended up staying with me all night. In the morning, I was transferred to a traumatic ward. I had 2 casts, one on my left hand and the other on my right foot for my ankle fracture. Four days later, I was wheeled into the operating room. The doctor had to operate on my right ankle . He had to put one screw in to hold my broken ankle bone. I stayed in the hospital for a total of 10 days. I was transferred to a rehab hospital by wheelchair. After three months during the summer, I was discharged to my home with my 2 crutches. After 2 years of physical therapy, I was able to let go my crutches and walk again. I went back to work as an ER nurse.

One night In the midst of my recovery, Friday August 11th, 2007 to be precise, I was bored and playing scrabble online all evening. The children had left to be with their father and the house was totally empty and quiet. I was alone with my cat and my dog. They must have missed the children, too. Both of them were sleeping next to me in the room. I love the game of Scrabble and had been playing in one particular site for 8 years. I had played so many games of Scrabble that evening. One particular player, Scribbled, who played so many games with me , somehow that night, connected with me and we fell in love . It was strange, but it felt right. We met in person a month after in Vermont and I rode 2 hours on a Greyhound bus with him to Montreal. The day after he arrived in Montreal, he asked me to marry him. I said yes, and we got married two month after in Syracuse, New York. I thank God for the second accident. Not only had God saved me again, but this time let love fall down in my lap, (through Scrabble), which was the prayer I had prayed for. Being home recovering, I had spare time to play Scrabble. When I was working , I only had time to sleep , taking care of children and prepare to go to work the next day.

February 2010

Ironically, my third near death experience happened with my second husband. While flying to my father's funeral in Thailand, the plane dropped suddenly about 2000 feet while flying over Alaska. I sensed the plane wobbling and told my husband to fasten his seat belt, and he did. Literally seconds later, the pilot announced "seatbelts now". There was no time to react and people were screaming and bouncing through the ceiling. Both my husband and I had flown many times and agreed that on this particular flight and on this particular day, we were going to die. One could hear the wings bending in the turbulence and the angle of plane placed it literally below us.

I remembered how it was in the plane crash movies. Wow ! but that was real ! We prayed and prayed with prayers such as "God, how horrible it would be that we would die on our way to a funeral". I even suggested that my husband put our names on a piece of paper so that our bodies would be recognized after the crash. We held hands, kissed once passionately , and thanked God that at least we would die together. After praying, the plane righted itself and flew another 9 hours to Japan.

The flight attendants who were trying to make lunch when the accident occurred were among those who were injured by flying plates, cups, and other objects. We were not able to eat because the kitchen was destroyed and several of the flight attendants required medical attention. Ironically, the movie shown through this ordeal was the one of meatballs and other food raining from the sky. The pilot made an announcement that anyone with medical experience should volunteer to help. My wife raised her hand, but was not needed. There were many injured passengers with bloody eyes, bruised heads, broken hands and legs and assorted injuries. They were escorted from the plane to local hospitals by ambulances. The airline company that flew us to Japan was so scared by the incident, all 4 connecting planes scheduled to fly to Thailand that night were cancelled.

We prayed again because my family was waiting for us to conduct my father's funeral in Thailand. We walked past McDonald's at the airport to get food. We heard some disgruntled passengers get special treatment and new flights to their destinations. Although there were more than 300 people who were sent to Tokyo hotels for the night without connections to their destinations, we were able to get tickets for the next day to go to Thailand. We arrived successfully and attended the funeral. Again, God saved me as well as my husband from sure death.

February 17, 2012

The fourth incident occurred this year after having a rod in my back for 23 years. I was suffering from left hip and lower back pain for no apparent reason .I had seen many doctors and had done many tests. After all those long investigations, I was told by the orthopedic spine surgeon that I needed another surgery to repair my spine! My spine was suffering from what I had experienced 23 years earlier. I had 4 levels of herniated discs some pressed on the nerve, causing some weakness and changes of sensation on my leg with severe low back pain.

All of this recent pain seemed to stem from the first rod that had caused my lower back to be flat instead of the normal curve that would absorb the shocks for my body. The surgery I had to go through lasted 10 hours instead of 6 hours as planned. I lost a large amount of blood and got needed blood transfusions. The surgery occurred with me face down for a long period of time.

Most of the devices that are normally attached to a patient were actually surgically implanted within me so that they would not fall out during the surgery. I have many scars from that process. As a result of being on my face for 10 hours, my right eye was sealed close for several days. Now, 6 months after the surgery, there is still a slight difference in my vision. The next morning I could not breathe because my lungs were collapsed and had too much fluid in my body. I had a weakness in my right thigh for another week as a part of the complications. After two weeks in the hospital, I was transferred to a Rehab Center. One night I was not feeling well and had my blood checked. My hemoglobin count was down to 70 (before surgery was 140) and it was 90 one week earlier. The nurse requested that I be transferred from the Rehab Center to the Emergency Room for a blood transfusion. Thirty seven hours later, after all investigations, I received two bags of blood to raise my hemoglobin to 100. I was returned to the Rehab Center for recovery. I was in the rehab hospital for another 5 weeks. I had to learn how to move with a wheelchair and graduated to a walker. I was discharged home with 2 crutches and now 6 months after, I was told by my doctor that I may probably need another spinal surgery to free my nerves in the back. It should be easy to understand that I do not wish any more surgery, but as was the case with my other four near death experiences, I am in God's hands and care."

Perhaps now you know why I have been so emphatic about telling my wife's story. It is awe inspiring to me up to today. God uses others to show us His mercy and grace is always sufficient in our times of trouble. As a reader, I pray you draw strength as I have from this powerful testimony of the power of God to heal and to save, no matter how severe the situations.

Notes:

ABOUT THE AUTHOR

DONNELL SEYNI

Donnell Seyni **is an entrepreneur, inspirational speaker, author, and personal coach.**

She is the founder of Iamazing Group LLC. Her philosophy is to address the spiritual-man (inner self) before the soul-man (mind, will, and intellect). The results will be the transformation of the physical-man which is accomplished by discovering God's provisions through biblical principal, planning how to apply God's word in your life with the use of practical tools and lastly, becoming, which is walking out your God given vision.

She specializes in the areas of developing Life Vision (movie clips of God's provisions for your entire life (your world) which includes: you, your family, career, physical and emotional health and all your relationships; dual faith relationships, specifically in saved/unsaved mismatch; spiritual exploration such as your beliefs, values, fears and loves and what they say about you; and Donnell assists individuals in the transformation of ordinary mundane and tired lives into extraordinary inspired lovers of life.

Donnell offers life experiences as a testament to her Provision Heiress mentality founded on the Bible which is God's word to his children, who are heirs/heiress' to the world. The Bible contains all the revelation and historical inherited provisions (all the substance needed to sustain us for this journey we call life).

She represents a living example of a non-traditional college graduate, a marriage legacy from a dual faith relationship, a mother from a non-traditional family nucleus, evidence of faith applications and Christian love, which she utilizes to empower others. She has a special anointing to connect with women who may find themselves in the same crossroads that she has encountered.

*"**My Passion as a Life Coach** is to better others and move them to the forefront of a particular area which I have mastered.*
***My Purpose as a Life Coach** is to enable you to identify and create resonating ideas for lasting change in every aspect of your life. I will assist you in awakening the dormant areas of your life by illuminating the foundational principles that govern the way you see, hear and feel what is going on around you.*
***Together** we will embark on a journey in the exploration of your authentic self and define your vision for success. "*

Contact:
Iamazing Group LLC
donnellseyni.com

EIGHT

ABRAHAM AND SARAH'S DAUGHTER

By Donnell Seyni

I suddenly open my eyes after being shaken by my mom. I felt like I had just fallen asleep and indeed I had because she worked third shift at the mill and I stayed by myself at night. So to actually see her up and dressed meant she hadn't left for work yet. I remember her words like it was yesterday and knew I had to protect my family if necessary. "Donnie, some people are saying bad things about me and you might hear a word you're not familiar with like 'Lesbian,' but do not worry. Let me know if someone says something or tries to hurt you." My mom always protected me and other kids in the neighborhood. There was always food to eat and a strong correction for any adult misleading a child. Mom always said, "As adults we should put aside our own issues for our children." I was ready for anything! After all, I was a big girl and who cares what people say about my mom and me; together we could face the world! Oh, but not the church; I walked there alone and I prayed alone.

Father to the fatherless, defender of widows–this is God,
whose dwelling is holy. –Psalms 68:5 NLT(2007) bible.cc.com

My mom was a straight gangster, she shot Papa Sammy and called a cab. Marrying Sammy kinda shifted our reputation in the community and the chaos doubled in the house. He was a Vietnam Vet with a metal plate in his head which potentially caused a seizure disorder. This combination under the influence attributed to an awfully mean alcoholic. My mom had the cab waiting this time she'd packed papa's belongings. They were arguing as normal; he got loud, yelling, saying he wasn't leaving. Mom did not tolerate being disrespected, especially in her own house, so she shot him!

Then as usual mom got all upset and bent out of shape about her actions and then walked Papa Sammy to the cab, apologizing all the way. I remember I had to pick him up from the hospital. Not sure of the story he told the police but they decided not to bother my mom this time; after all, they knew her well. It was one of many encounters with the police we had throughout the years.

From birth my mom has taken care of me; I was her Donnie Girl and she was my Mommie. She had been running from the police for many years due to the fact my real mother wanted me back after abandoning me in the hospital. I was pretty sure that the police knew who I was but mom had lots of friends in high places according to the FBI, and back in the 60's if children were reported to be lost or stolen and were known to be in better situations they weren't removed from the caring individuals.

I awaken to a bump in the road to discover I was in the back seat of a moving car with mom. It seemed like we had been moving forever as I drifted in and out of naps. I had a feeling this trip was far different so I chose to look around. I got on mom's lap and looked out the back window and was disappointed when I saw this big container behind us which she referred to as a U-Haul. It contained everything we owned.

She was a beautician by trade and gangster by night and very well known. People would come near and far to have her to style their hair and do their makeup. She had other ladies wash and condition her clients before they could even set foot in her chair. She was loved and celebrated and always carried a pad and pen to track all her finances. It was very important to keep good records, a skill that really helped us in bad times as Mom became the neighborhood loan shark.

Mom awakened me once the car stopped so that I could see our new home in Greensboro, North Carolina, but what was special about this home was there were children living there not like the hotels and motels. We had a small mattress and a kitchen table, and that's when I realized that Mom was smoking and drinking; at least this was my first recollection of her taking part in such activities and my new home becoming a party house. It was also the first time that Mom needed my help, so I would put her to bed at night; her head would be slumped down or she would lay it in her plate. I would put the alcohol up but not without drinking the orange one. I love the taste of orange. There were many nights that followed the same routine. We finished the house nicely and gay, straight, male, female, married, single, young or old, black, white, "niggers", and "crackers", and all took advantage of the invitation by design, of course. Soon I would be off to school, leaving the neighbors to help Mom.

I will bring them to my holy mountain of Jerusalem and will fill them with joy in my house of prayer.... my Temple will be called a house of prayer for all nations. –Isa 56:7 Bible.cc.com NLT 2007

I remember my first fight and how the police finally took Mom to jail. As Mom lay sleeping on a beautifully upholstery green and white Louis XIV couch with the high back and engraved marking and claw-like feet you could hear her snoring in unison with her chest rising and falling. I hated to disturb her because she worked a double shift and third shift is rough enough (and doing hair on weekends) and when she gets angry someone is going to pay the price! But I would rather wake her than the neighbors "Mommy, mommy, you awake?" I repeated it, but this time a little louder. "Huh", she said, "what's going on, why are you not outside in the lounge chair?" she asked. "Well, Karen stopped by after the school bus dropped her off and started teasing me, so I grabbed her by her hair and threw her down on the ground". "Are you ok" Mom asked, "I'm tired but ok". "Let's go talk to her mother and get this straight", mom said.

When Mom raised up she stood 5"7 , one hundred and eighty pounds and looked African but with a straight nose and small lips and very nice hair tucked under either a white or black turban. Her black features weren't like the blacks in our neighborhood because her mom was from Barbados (and never worked a day in her life) and her dad worked for the railroad and owned liquor houses in New Jersey and Philadelphia. So labor for mom in the mills of North Carolina was strenuous; but it was only necessary because of past events that got her here.

As we walked to the neighbor's apartment, I begin to explain what happened. All the kids in the neighborhood knew that I was very ill I sat in the front yard everyday so I could watch my school mates come home. I had been out of school for the entire semester with a rare case of a childhood disease. I had been blind and practically on my death bed for months so to give a classmate a beat down was pretty impressive to all the kids in the neighborhood. I had officially earned my gangster status.

We reached the back of my classmate Karen's house and immediately Mom knocked and called for her mom, who was in the kitchen. They were pretty good friends so to have us all fight made little or no sense at all.

Karen's mom came to the door and called me everything but a child of God for beating up her daughter. Not surprisingly, this language is the norm and Jesus characteristics weren't displayed a lot but nightly prayer and blessing the food was a must.

Before I realized it Mom knocked down the kitchen door and began to beat on Karen's mom and then dragged her outside by her hair. She yelled for me to get her axe, instinctly I knew that would not have the best outcome so I ran next door to get my Auntie Von (neighbor) to help me get Mom off the lady. All the neighbors started to come out of their apartments and Auntie Von finally got mom to let Karen's mother go and she crawled back to her kitchen and locked the door. Later the police come and took Mom into custody. Boy she cursed them exactly how Karen's mom acted toward me. It's amazing with mom how often the word "Nigger" was used as well as so many other curse words with our friends, guest and enemies but mom never used such language when we were alone. She always addressed me in such a manner that molded me in to the woman of integrity and deligence I am today. It was inferred that this environment we were currently living in called for such shenanigans. My mom would beat Karen's mom every time she saw her till the lady finally moved.

By the time I was in middle school, Mom was smoking a pack of cigarettes a day and sometimes she had actually broke the seal of the next pack. I remember that her smoking habit was getting worse and it meant more work for me. A daily store run after school was part of my usual routine. It took me about fifteen minutes if I took the shortcut and thirty if I had to go the long way when it was dark. It was best to go the long way after dark because the street lights were my saving grace from child preditors.

Smoking wasn't the only habit that increased in Mom's life; she was drinking more as well. Seagram gin was her favorite and our house was stocked with half gallon bottles nicely tucked beneath the kitchen cabinets so much so that we had a constant stream of company always enjoying the spirits that kept our home's atmosphere filled with laughter, dancing which normally grew into the escalation of altercations. When our guests would finally leave I was left to clean up the mess of cups, bottles, ash trays, and plates. Mom never let you drink without eating. Cleanup was always extended to mom herself; however, she normally fell asleep in a plate cleared of food with occasional chicken bones stacked on one side. I would carefully remove the plate and empty the bones and gently shake her after letting her nap for an hour after our guests left; mom would be at least able to move and lean on me until we got to the bedroom then I would undress her, wash her up a bit and put her to bed.

This routine continued for years. "I'm never smoking another cigarette," mom said, "good riddance", which was her favorite phase and I use it to this day. Yo-ho no more long walks to the store for me! Well, it's amazing how people trade one vice for another; now instead of cigarettes I was picking up candy bars. Mom was eating them by the pound especially Babe Ruth and if the corner store was out of them, I was picking up Butterfingers. As it turned out candy bars and gin happen to be the perfect combination to receive a lasting visit from Type 2 Diabetes. The onset of the disease did not surface immediately. It slowly caged mom's arteries from her groin down to her ankles. The doctors performed one of two bypass surgeries mom would later need. Instead of after school activities I was learning to give insulin shots.

The neighborhood celebrated my mom, more so after her surgery. Never did a college student starve nor did any child that mom suspected their parents were skimping on food monies. She was offered a job in our apartment rental office. She took it since her days were now free and disability income was in a waiting period. Plus working with the rental tenant's files gave mom access to all the tenants' personal information; particularly to the ones that would be best to approach in need of special services she provided.

She was a genius at keeping up with who she loaned money to and how much she was expecting in return. Depending on who you were and where you worked, the interest she collected was between 25-50% on the dollar. A legal institution such as a bank would never lend to the people in my neighborhood. Mom understood that people always needed money and things that make you laugh. She would always say "As bad as I am God is so good to me."

God's law was given so that all people could see how sinful they were. But as people sinned more and more, God's wonderful grace became more abundant. –Rom 5:20 NLT(2007) Bible.cc.com

Mom did need additional help collecting on debts. The honor system worked for a while, but it got really tricky when monies where loaned to individuals and not families. That's when mom started changing her friendships to include some of the more shady characters in the neighborhood. Some of those cats, I would never let close to me or give them eye contact. I would get chills just from seeing them at a distance not to mention in my house. Why they were friends of mom was a question I never asked her. But, before I could put my head around what was going on, the parties at my house that normally occurred on the weekend became a constant 24/7 gig with a dark, almost eerie atmosphere of smoking, drinking and music. Lots of dealing went down in my house. But God was there.

I can recall one of the scariest nights of my life and it happened to be the second time that the house was raided. I had no idea that Mom was stashing alcohol and drugs in my car.

I was usually on campus which was 5 minutes away by car, but was called home to help out because Mom was expecting a boat load of guests and she had no help. The alcohol had to be measured for profit, which meant watering it down with out changing the color or the taste. The beer had to be loaded from the fridge to the coolers at just the right time, and there was to be no interruption in the music. Mom kept her pen and pad ready because some clients ran tabs and some paid cashed. Plus rule #1- never allow the money to be funny, meaning any disputes were never with Mom and money, everything else was open to discussion.

There was this loud noise and people screaming as I exited the bathroom to see police everywhere in plain clothes which meant they were wearing khaki pants and black matching tee shirts that read NARCOTICS. I counted them "1..2..3...," On their side were holstered big hand guns. They proceeded to remove the cooler full of beer and half gallon bottles of liquor.

Their leader was addressing mom by her first name – Evelyn. I thought wow, I missed something; they are on a first name basis. The conversation was around drugs not so much the alcohol, drugs I thought, do we sell drugs? Mom, with her cool straight stance leaned over and pulled one of the kitchen stools over and sat down and replied. " I have the best defense attorney in the city on retainer, I will be out on bond before you can write down my last name".

There was a shift of power in the entire room; and the leader replied "I won't be taking you downtown but this pretty girl here." He was referring to me. What? I interrupted the silence that weighted the room like a blow of steam in an empty sauna. Now, all the cards were on the table and the question on everyone's mind was - who would be first to fold? Well, I had prepared myself for the worst, jail. I was engulfed with fear, but to my surprise they both went out back and had private conversations and then the police were gone. I hurriedly packed my butt up for college where I belonged.

Therefore…. pray for each other so that you may be healed.
The prayer of a righteous man is powerful and effective.
–James 5:16 NLT(2007) Bible.cc.com

After that horror, I pleaded with mom and prayed constantly to leave the neighborhood and even presented her with a budget proposal that showed the negative the income and expense of the business and showed positive cash flow with just her disability income and Social Security income from Papa Sammy. She was now 63. I knew she understood the numbers but was enveloped in that life style. It wasn't until after that last quintuple bypass surgery and renal failure on the operating table that mom built a relationship with the most important person – Jesus!

"… Woman, thou art loosed from thine infimity"…"And ought not this woman, being a daughter of Abraham, whom Satan hath bound, lo, these eighteen years, be loosed from this bond?… ""
–Luke 13:12-16 KJV (Cambridge Ed.) Bible.cc.com

Although mom and I lived in a questionable environment, there was no questioning her obedience to those she loved or her friendship to those she liked. She took me in and raised me as her own, just as she fed the neighborhood kids and counseled many relationships particularly the homosexual ones.

"just as Sarah obeyed Abraham and called him lord. You have become her daughters by doing good and by not letting anything terrify you"
–I Peter 3:6 NSV(2008)Bible.cc.com

Mom fought alcoholism, diabetes and kidney disease head on. She became an advocate for the other patients in her dialysis unit if treatment was questionable. After a leg amputation and several mini-strokes, mom refused dialysis. Her last words were "Jesus what's the report?"

Upon hearing those words, I called the Red Cross, who contacted her estranged son in Europe and we agreed to bury her close to me in Greensboro, North Carolina. She had no other known relatives.

Finally resting contently in 2001, I found her commitment to Jesus card in her bible, and assuredly included in her obituary for all to see.

Think It Over...

Where are you going?
Where have you been?
How did you get here?
What are your plans?
How much time do you have left?

You answer - "Oh, I'll make it. I'll get by."
        "It'll work out all right."

Take a look back - What do you see?
    hard times, broken promises,
    some good times, disappointments,
    lies, sin... a messed up life.

Looking back is rough, looks hopeless...
    the future doesn't look good either
    more disappointment, more failure, more sin.

UNLESS

You listen to God as He calls you...
    "Come, though your sins are as scarlet,
    they shall be as white as snow..."

He loves you...He wants you...

He wants you to know His Son Jesus...
He died for you...for your sins.

If you will turn to Him
    ask Him to forgive your sins
    ask Him to be your Savior
        He will.
    He will save you
    He will forgive your sins
    He will make you God's child
    He will give you a new life.

Prayer:

*Lord, I know that I am a sinner. I deserve to go
to hell. I thank You that Jesus died on the cross
for my sins. Right now, I want Jesus to come into
my heart and forgive my sins and save me. Thank
You for hearing me and saving me.*

Signed: *Evelyn Montgomery*

Now, look back at the questions...

Where are you going?	Heaven
Where have you been?	Lost
How did you get here?	Jesus
What are your plans?	Live for God
How much time do you have left?	Only God Knows

ABOUT THE AUTHOR

ANN RANSOM, M.ED

Ann McCullough Ransom, a Portsmouth, Virginia native, has been blessed to garner wide-ranged experiences in many diverse professions: news director for WRAP Radio, shift supervisor for Arbitron Ratings, prayer counselor for Christian Broadcasting Network, sales consultant for Johnson Products (Ultra Sheen), New York Life Insurance, and Kay Jewelers and realtor with Century 21 Nachman Realty. She received a bachelor's degree in English from Norfolk State University in 1974. And in May 2012 one of her longtime desires became a reality; she received a master's degree from Regent University.

Furthermore, Ann has completed training from the Professional Woman Network in women's issues which include health and wellness, self-esteem and assertiveness, and leadership. In addition, she has received biblical training from Evans Smith Bible Institute and Regent University School of Divinity. Moreover, she attributes the prayers and lessons learned early in her life from her maternal grandmother for laying a solid foundation for her desire to have a personal relationship with God.

Ann has participated in church leadership conferences, youth revivals and women's day workshops. Also, she has served as an advisor for church youth groups and as a school based mentor for Big Brothers/Big Sisters. Ann is currently employed as a Special Education teacher for Portsmouth Public Schools.

Contact:
E-mail: annhransom@cox.net
Phone: (757) 673-6172 (VM) (757) 434-8022 (C)
Mailing address: 108 Snead Fairway, Portsmouth, VA 23701.

NINE

WAITING ON THE LORD

By Ann Ransom

"By all stretches of the imagination, you should already be paralyzed." Those were the words from my neurosurgeon as she relayed the results of my MRI to me. At the time, I was four years into a relationship that was not going well. In fact, I was ready to pack up and move on when I received this most disconcerting news. Hearing those words did not connect with my thoughts, which were of leaving to get the peace of mind that I felt I desperately needed. But as we all know too well, the Lord's plan is always different than ours. And as His Word declares, "his thoughts are not our thoughts and his ways are not our ways." Shortly thereafter, I realized that I was being prepared for what I now call my time of "waiting on the Lord." Waiting on the Lord, for me, has been a continuous learning process in which I have learned "to lean on, trust in, and rely on" the Lord to renew me spiritually, physically, mentally, and even financially. I believe that we all come to that place in life sometimes when we just don't know what to do. However, as I have gone through numerous trials, tribulations, hard times, or whatever you want to nickname them, I have learned that I can depend on God to see me through each and every one. Regardless of how dire or traumatic a situation has seemed, the Lord has never left me nor forsaken me. Waiting on the Lord has gotten me through sickness, financial crises, unemployment, underemployment, bereavement, isolation, divorce, depression, distress, disillusionment, misery, pain and beyond. At any rate, all I can say is that I know God is real and He does answer prayer. From experience, I have learned that all one has to do is wait on the Lord every day in every situation without fail.

Whether in times of spiritual droughts, relationship issues, career/ education decisions, or sickness/health concerns, we who claim Jesus as Lord and Savior, will find ourselves waiting on God to help us through our dry places and hard times.

❖ Waiting on the Lord in Sickness

"But those who wait on the Lord [who expect, look for, and hope in Him] shall change and renew their strength and power; they shall lift their wings and mount up [close to God] as eagles [mount up to the sun]; they shall run and not be weary, they shall walk and not faint or become tired (Isaiah 40:31)." **(Amplified Bible)**

The summer of 1992 is one that will remain prominent in my memories because following symptoms of numbness in my hands, the results of a MRI revealed that I had four herniated discs of my cervical spine. After a physical examination and being given the news, I was told "to get my business in order" and to prepare to have surgery on my neck. At the time, I walked several miles each morning and came back and did sit-ups. When I told my doctor this, she replied that God was on my side because while doing a sit-up, I could have gone down and not been able to get back up. The severity of my condition was just that grim. While looking at the images, she informed me that she had called the office where I had had the MRI done. She stated that she had to specifically ask if I had actually walked in for the procedure. Next, she declared that she could not believe it and she explained that with the degree of deterioration I had I should have been paralyzed. In addition, she was amazed that I had taken the news concerning my condition so calmly. As she continued to describe what she would have to do, I felt a peace come over me as I realized that I would not have to go through it alone.

Needless to say, the preparation and surgery which was to take up to six hours, took nearly twelve hours to complete. At least that's what family and friends told me later. The surgery was on a Thursday morning. I vaguely remember coming out of surgery; but, I do remember opening my eyes that Sunday morning to find that I was in intensive care. In addition, I recall that same afternoon I walked down the corridor holding on to the railing with the assistance of a nurse. And to my amazement, I was discharged the following day. Next was the difficult part, recuperation.

My doctor told me that I was to do absolutely nothing, not even to lift a plate. Once I got home, during the first couple of months I could not go downstairs unless I was going to the doctor. To my dismay and sometimes embarrassment, I even had to have someone bath me, brush my teeth, feed me, and put on my gown. Anyone who is an oldest child can relate to being independent and used to doing "stuff" for ourselves. Initially, this was a bitter pill to swallow because I felt so helpless and I had never liked to be dependent on anyone to do anything for me. Now, on the other hand, I will go out my way to help someone else with almost anything that they may stand in need of. But somehow, for whatever reason, I felt that I could not accept that help in return. However, on my first morning home, a friend was washing my face when she asked why I was crying. I told her that if anyone had told me that I would be in a situation where I could not do for myself, I would not have believed it. Her response to me was, "If it were me, I know that you would be doing the same thing for me." And she was right.

During my time of convalescence, I realized that God will slow us down to get our undivided attention. You may have ninety-nine things going on at once and juggling them all pretty good, or so you think. But sometimes God's plan requires us to be still in order for us to listen for His instruction. One of my favorite scriptures is **Jeremiah 29:11** because whenever I am trying to figure out what to do next, I am reminded that the plan is God's and not mine. *("For I know the thoughts and plans that I have for you, says the Lord, thoughts and plans for welfare and peace and not for evil, to give you hope in your final outcome.")*

My recuperation period following the surgery required no physical therapy and lasted four and a half months. Several years later, I had to have a similar surgery on three other discs in my neck. That recovery time took nearly two years and months of physical therapy. To me, it seems as if I have experienced my greatest spiritual growth throughout the times that I have experienced physical trials. Although during these instances, I have also had bouts of sadness, frustration, depression, and anxiety, I realized that these periods were part of my waiting on the Lord.

❖ **Waiting on the Lord in Times of Challenge**

"The young lions lack food and suffer hunger, but they who seek (inquire of and require) the Lord [by right of their need and on the authority of His Word], none of them shall lack any beneficial thing (Psalm 34:10)."

One of my long time dreams has been about teaching in my own classroom. For over fifty years, I have had a desire to become a teacher. Although I have worked as a substitute teacher off and on for many years it was not enough. As a result, during one of the most challenging times in my life, following the death of my mother and the hospitalization of one of my siblings due to a brain aneurysm, I decided to go back to school to pursue a master's degree in education. At the same time, I still had the responsibility of being the only caregiver for some other members of my family.

In August 2009 I enrolled in a graduate program for the third time. Looking back, this was one of the best decisions that I could have made. To say it was not easy would be to put it mildly. Needless to say, there were times when I wanted to give up due the stress of trying to study, to take care of my family, to keep a roof over my head and not starve to death in the process. Also during the course of my studies, there were times that I found my health failing, my spirit low and my confidence waning as I endured the hardship of trying to cope with so much. This was definitely another phase of waiting on the Lord to bring me through and to bring me out. Consequently, I realized once again that I found renewed strength during my time of waiting. This year I completed the requirements for a master's degree in Special Education and a certification in Autism as finished with 3.66 GPA.

Going through this period of challenge, once again prayer as well as scripture, guided me through these times:

"I can do all things through Christ which strengthened me
(Philippians 4:13)."
And
"I am more than a conqueror through Him that loved us
(Romans 8:37)."

❖ **Waiting on the Lord with Expectancy**

"I waited patiently and expectantly for the Lord; and he inclined to me and heard my cry (Psalm 40:1)."

Throughout my life, most people who know me would call me a "go-getter." In fact, my friends and family would say that I always have a lot of irons in the fire. Even I must admit that I may sometimes take on more than I might need to. But then again, I know that it's not me doing anything on my own, I do it only by the grace of God.

At the same time, there might be someone who has witnessed me in a moment of anxiety who might conclude that I am an impatient person. Thinking about it, there may have been times when that person would be right! Nevertheless, I thank God and as the song or saying goes, "I wouldn't take nothing for my journey."

Some years ago a friend said to me, "To whom much is given, much is required." At the time, I had quite a few things going on in my life and I was questioning why I was experiencing such trying times. Back then I did not understand what he meant and I did not realize that it was biblical (Luke 12:48). However, as my life has evolved, I am more aware of what he was trying to tell me and I accept the challenges that come with the "much is given" part. Also, I have learned and continue to learn to wait on the Lord to guide me through the "much is required" part. Thus, I have discovered that "waiting" is not always an easy place to be. Furthermore, I have found that during my most challenging times, waiting on the Lord was the best and only option. What's more, I surmise that it doesn't matter what you are waiting for or how long you may have to wait. The key to waiting in any situation is how you respond during the process. And to that I say, wait expectantly.

Prior to my first neck surgery, my preparation included having some professional photographs taken of myself. During my recovery time, those pictures were on the walls and a nearby dresser in my room. Each time I woke up throughout the day and before I closed my eyes, I viewed those pictures as I waited expecting God to heal me and make me whole again.

When I finally made the decision to go back to school to become a teacher, I was reminded of a poem by Langston Hughes about a mother telling her son about the hard times she had experienced in her life. I remember reading that same poem to my son when I returned to college a couple of years after he was born. The irony is I no longer identify with that mother's statement that life had not been "no crystal stair." Today, I live expectantly waiting on God's plan to give me "an expected end." In addition, I have a broader perspective of what it means to trust God. Therefore, I know that I have come this far by faith, leaning on the Lord and I live each day expecting his new mercies. I recognize that I am clearly in the right place, at the right time, and walking in the plan that God has for me.

"Through Him also we have [our] access (entrance, introduction) by faith into this grace (state of God's favor) in which we [firmly and safely] stand. And let us rejoice and exult in our hope of experiencing and enjoying the glory of God. Moreover [let us also be full of joy now!] let us exult and triumph in our troubles and rejoice in our suffering, knowing that pressure and affliction and hardship produce patient and unswerving endurance."
(Romans 5:2-3)."

Many of us may have learned that challenges are a part of life and in most instances they cannot be avoided. However, when challenging times do come, there is something that you can do. You can pray and wait on God to guide you through those rough times.

"For nothing is impossible with God **(Luke 1:37).** *"*

Notes:

_____

_____

_____

_____

_____

_____

_____

_____

_____

_____

_____

_____

_____

_____

_____

_____

_____

_____

_____

_____

_____

_____

_____

ABOUT THE AUTHOR

JANET STEVENSON, BA (HONS), CERT FE

Janet Stevenson is founder and owner of Train2Grow Consultancy and Achieve Insight Coaching. She is a professional Training Consultant and qualified Teacher, Coach and Counselor. Her passion is to help people grow, become more fulfilled and achieve success in every aspect of their lives.

Janet specializes in personal development and has empowered, trained and coached individuals and groups to set and exceed goals, find fulfilment, and realize their dreams both personally and professionally. She is a licensed Springboard trainer - a personal development program for women - and runs Leadership for Women, 'Kickstart' and 'Empower' women's programmes.

Other seminar topics include Leadership, Management, Counselling, Coaching, Mentoring, Building Better Relationships, Doing Business Across Cultures, Train the Trainer, Interpersonal Skills, Influencing, Assertiveness & Managing Conflict, in addition to the women's programmes above. Janet's training style is highly participative, using brain-friendly techniques, and her coaching style has been described as "life-changing, intuitive and insightful". Her clients are from both the private and public sectors, and include banks, hospitals, universities, councils, as well as small businesses.

She has been published in Training Journal and Executive PA magazine, and is a contributing author in The Power of a Woman and Madame CEO. She is a Master Practitioner of NLP and Non-Verbal Intelligence, a member of the Institute of Leadership and Management, member of the British Institute for Learning & Development, member of the Academy of Professional Coaching, member of the International Coach Federation, member of European Mentoring & Coaching Council & member of the Professional Woman Network.

Contact:
Mrs. Janet Stevenson
info@train2grow.co.uk
www.train2grow.co.uk
www.achieveinsight.co.uk
Tel + 44 1293 614624 or +44 7801 479801

TEN

THE POWER OF FORGIVENESS

By Janet Stevenson

What do we mean by forgiveness? According to www.
thefreedictionary.com, *to forgive* means (1) to cease to blame
or hold resentment against someone or something, (2) to grant pardon
for a mistake, wrongdoing.

When we seek God's forgiveness through faith in Jesus Christ, he
goes beyond pardoning or ceasing to hold resentment against us. He
washes us clean and makes us whole: *'As far as the east is from the west,
so far has he removed our transgressions from us'* – Psalm 103:12. He also
gives us his Spirit, filling us with his love, joy and peace, enabling us to
truly forgive and love those who have hurt us.

This chapter tells the story of abandonment, deep injury and
suffering, but also of divine freedom and release through the power
of forgiveness. Names have been changed to protect the identity and
families of those involved.

Twins Mirela and Gabriela were born prematurely into a poor Romanian family in the spring of 1979, unwanted from the start. Their mother was married to an alcoholic who drank every cent they had. Saddled with one child already, the last thing she wanted was another mouth to feed. She tried to abort her pregnancy ... but God had other plans. *'For you created my inmost being; you knit me together in my mother's womb ... All the days ordained for me were written in your book before one of them came to be'* – Psalm 139:13 &16.

After the girls were born, their mother abandoned them in hospital. Racked with guilt, she returned several days later to the hospital to take them home but no-one knew where they were. After a search, they were found in a tiny room, drenched in their own vomit and urine, and both suffering from a kidney infection. Only God knows how they survived.

Their earliest memory is of being taken on a walk by their mother. It was an exhaustingly long walk and they repeatedly asked where they were going. She told them they were visiting a friend. Eventually, they were met at the door of a large building by a woman, who locked them in a room with her. Realising their mother had gone they screamed after her, but were told to shut up and were beaten until they did. Just three years old, distressed and bewildered, they were abandoned at an orphanage for unwanted children.

As the months passed, they had to learn to 'get on with it' and to compete for survival with the other children in the orphanage. It was the best part of a year before their mother returned to visit. They pleaded with her to take them home but she deserted them again, leaving the girls distraught and confused. "Why was she going away? Why wouldn't she take us with them?" they cried.

The subsequent, rare visits from their mother were extremely painful because they poured salt on the aching wounds of abandonment and rejection, and they began to feel bitter towards her. *'Being unwanted, unloved, uncared for, forgotten by everybody, I think that is a much greater hunger, a much greater poverty than the person who has nothing to eat'* - Mother Teresa.

They did not dare tell her of the beatings, hunger and abuse they suffered for fear of punishment from orphanage staff. They – like thousands of other Romanian orphans – were undernourished and distressed mentally and physically. But God saw their misery.

When they were about seven years old, they were transferred to an orphanage for bigger girls, where they were to stay until they were 15. Here there was a pecking order, with the more senior girls bullying the younger ones and treating them like slaves. While the conditions were awful, at least they felt less isolated and made some friends.

'Religion that God our Father accepts as pure and faultless is this: to look after orphans and widows in their distress' – James 1:27

Ceausescu, the brutal and repressive Communist Romanian leader, had neither religion nor compassion. In fact he had a burning hatred for Christianity, imprisoning priests, pastors and church leaders in his efforts to indoctrinate people into atheism. Having commandeered the country's revenue to repay foreign debt, Romania was in abject poverty. Orphanages were hugely underfinanced and desperate places to live. However, in December 1989, Ceausescu's government was overthrown and he was assassinated. As the appalling treatment and conditions of orphans subsequently came to light, the West was shocked, and many charities responded by providing food and medicines. However Mirela and Gabriela said they saw little improvement, with staff seeing to their own needs first.

The increasing freedom allowed an Austrian missionary to begin visiting the orphanage where Gabriela and Mirela lived, telling them about God's love, mercy and forgiveness. For the first time, they felt accepted and loved by God, and looked forward to the missionary's visits. Although she did not yet know God in a personal way, Mirela remembers praying one day, "Please God make my mother come to see us", and within five minutes, her mother arrived – a miraculous answer to prayer!

As they became older, they were occasionally allowed 'home' for a few days. It was an unhappy place where they felt deeply unloved and unwanted. During one of these visits, their mother took them to a market. She pointed out a drunk begging in the centre of town and told them he was their father. They wanted to go and say "hello" but she pulled them away. It was another deeply painful experience, and their mother's refusal to allow them to speak to him simply intensified the anger and hatred they felt towards her.

At the age of 15, the girls left the orphanage and returned home. Their mother started to attend church around this time, searching for some meaning in her life, though she did not yet know God in a personal way. Ever since her childhood, she had battled with her own demons of abandonment and rejection. Life had been a relentless struggle and, even now, violence and arguments remained a constant feature. Home was a desperately unhappy place. Not surprisingly, Mirela and Gabriela detested living there, and life seemed utterly hopeless.

'For I know the plans I have for you,' declares the Lord, *'plans to prosper you and not to harm you, plans to give you hope and a future'*
– Jeremiah 19:11

Then one day the Austrian missionary came to invite them to study at a Bible school in Bucharest. Gabriela and Mirela were stunned and deeply moved by this, and grabbed the opportunity with both hands. While there, they learned more about God's love and forgiveness, as well as a little English through listening to an American preacher.

When their year of study was finished they returned home, where violence and arguments continued. This time they ran away – first Gabriela and then Mirela – back to the Bible school. They were offered board and lodging but had to find work. While they were there, Gabriela was baptized. She understood intellectually that she was a sinner and that Christ had died for her, but she still had not turned to him in repentance and faith. Meanwhile, Mirela was opposed to God and had suicidal thoughts running through her head.

They struggled through their teens with a knot of bitterness festering inside, taking various jobs to survive. While working in Bucharest, they met two Englishmen who were to become their husbands. Despite the men being twice their age, the girls believed they would love and care for them. Against the advice of the Bible school, they had a double wedding at the age of 19 and shortly afterwards moved to England.

Married life proved difficult. Gabriela found herself living with her husband in his parents' home; Mirela was miles away in a flat, alone all day while her husband was at work. Separated from each other, they felt isolated and unhappy. Within six months of each other, both became pregnant and had a child. However, their husbands showed them no love, treating them instead like subservient skivvies. This caused lots of arguments and the marriages eventually floundered – first Gabriela's and then Mirela's.

They were now both single parents. Gabriela's daughter had epilepsy and she was very worried about what a forthcoming MRI scan would reveal, so she went to see a pastor for prayer and to dedicate her daughter to God. The results of this and a later MRI scan were clear, and Gabriela knew that God had miraculously healed her daughter! She remembers a vivid dream of queuing before God to be judged, and she knew she needed to repent and seek his forgiveness.

Instead Gabriela met a young man she fell deeply in love with. They were together for four years until one day he upped and left, saying he didn't love her any more. She was in utter despair, and could not stop crying. As the weeks went by, she lost weight. Mirela was frantically worried, but Gabriela felt she had nothing left to live for.

Then a voice from deep inside her said, "What about God?" Gabriela cried out, "If you are truly there, I need your help!" and suddenly she knew God's overwhelming presence. Falling on her knees, she confessed her sins and asked God to forgive her. Her tears stopped and she was filled with his peace and joy. There was no longer any doubt that God was real, and that he had washed her clean.

Gabriela had not spoken to her mother for two years. Now, convicted of her sin, she asked her mother during an online video call to forgive her for all that she had done. As she did so, she sensed all the hostility and rage inside simply melt away. *'Forgiveness brings freedom ... from being controlled by the past ... from the inner conflicts of bitterness and hate'* – Jeanette Vought.

Hungry to learn more about God, Gabriela would go regularly to her sister's – who had a TV – to listen to Christian programs. God then led her to a church where a loving couple nurtured her and encouraged her to grow in her new-found faith. Despite having a God-shaped hole in her heart and having witnessed an astounding change in her sister, Mirela showed no interest in him.

But one August night, Mirela struggled to sleep, haunted by past memories and all that was wrong in her life. She felt suicidal, so turned on the TV to distract herself. It was tuned in to the Christian channel Gabriela had been watching earlier. The preacher spoke of God's love, urging her to turn to him before it was too late. Suddenly, Mirela found herself on her knees, tears rolling down her face, asking God to forgive her. She felt like a new-born baby, enveloped with love, washed clean and with an indescribable peace within.

The first person she told was Gabriela, who was ecstatic with joy. Yet Mirela faced the challenge of her mother. For years, she had disguised her true feelings, hiding how much she hated and blamed her for the past. In repentance, she asked her mother to forgive her, and her bitterness evaporated. *'Forgiveness is the key which unlocks the door of resentment and the handcuffs of hatred'* – Corrie Ten Boom. Both Gabriela and Mirela recognised their mother had had to make many heart-breaking decisions, and had let go of the resentment they once had towards her.

Mirela now joined her sister in going to church, where they continued to learn and grow in their faith. They started to pray earnestly for their mother, who was living and working in Italy, caring for an elderly gentleman. One day, his daughter took her to a Baptist church, where she heard the good news of Jesus Christ and gave her life to him. At last she found freedom and forgiveness, healing and restoration!

When she called Mirela and Gabriela to tell them, it was obvious a profound change had happened in her life. In place of anger and swearing were joy and humility. Now the sisters were completely reconciled to their mother, as well as to each other, bound together by the love of Christ. As they describe it, "Jesus is in the middle of us, binding us together. The more we serve him, the more love we know."

Today, Mirela and Gabriela are growing, active and vibrant Christians. The complete transformation of their lives is testament to the power of forgiveness. While their eyes shine with the love, joy and gentleness of God, they recognise forgiveness is an ongoing challenge. *'Forgiveness is not an occasional act; it is a permanent attitude'* – Martin Luther King.

May Mirela and Gabriela's testimony bless and inspire you. If you feel God prompting you to forgive people for past hurts and offences, then I encourage you to work prayerfully through the steps below.

Steps to Forgiving

- **Reflect** Look deep into your heart and identify all those who have hurt you in some way.

- **Begin with the person who caused you the most emotional trauma** Write down what this person said or did to offend you.

- **Be honest with yourself** *'None of us wants to admit that we hate someone … When we deny our hate we detour around the crisis of forgiveness',* Lewis B Smedes, *Forgive & Forget: Healing the Hurts We Don't Deserve.*

- **Notice what your body is telling you** As you feel the intensity of your resentment, observe what is going on in your body, e.g. shallow breathing, tensed muscles, raised heartbeat, etc. According to medical practitioners, unforgiveness affects our health adversely.

- **Are you ready to forgive this person?** *'There is a time for everything'* – Ecclesiastes 3:1. *'There is a right moment to forgive'* – Lewis B Smedes.

- **Recognise that God's forgiveness of us is tied to our forgiveness of those who've wronged us** *'For if you forgive men when they sin against you, your heavenly Father will also forgive you. But if you do not forgive men their sins, your Father will not forgive your sins.'* – Matthew 6: 14-15.

- **Turn to God** Ask God to forgive you for holding resentment and bitterness and for his help in forgiving your offender. Thank him for his promise in 1 John 1:9, *'If we confess our sins, he is faithful and just and will forgive us our sins and purify us from all unrighteousness.'*

- **Forgive your offender** If it's appropriate to write or speak to the offender in person, plan carefully how to do so in a sensitive and non-threatening way. If it's inappropriate to do so – e.g. if the person has died or you are no longer in contact, or for your own protection – then write down what you would say to the person face to face. In both cases, describe how you feel, avoiding blaming statements like, *'You made me feel ...'* but rather, *'When you ..., I felt ...', 'and I now forgive you for ....'* Say it out loud and repeat it. Allow yourself to experience your emotions fully without suppressing them and without standing in judgment of the offender.

- **Recognise that forgiveness takes time** Having forgiven, you may or may not experience release and be ready to move on. *'Forgiving*

... is a process, sometimes a long one, especially when it comes to wounds gouged deep' – Lewis B Smedes. If your cuts are deep, consider seeing a therapist to support you and help you work through the issues.

- **Keep a journal of your progress** This is a helpful and healthy way to express and process what has happened. What have you learned from it? What are you grateful for? *'You will know that forgiveness has begun when you recall those who hurt you and feel the power to wish them well'* – Lewis B Smedes.

Finally, let's remember that Satan *'is a liar and the father of all lies'* - John 8: 44, and he *'prowls around like a roaring lion looking for someone to devour. Resist him, standing firm in the faith'* – 1 Peter 5: 8-9. Therefore, it is helpful to be reminded that forgiveness is not:

- **Denying feelings of anger and resentment** *'Genuine forgiveness does not deny anger but faces it head-on'* - Alice Duer Miller.

- **Understanding what happened** *'Understanding may come later, in fragments, an insight here and a glimpse there, after forgiving'* – Lewis B Smedes.

- **Forgetting** We often say "forgive and forget" but forgetting is not really possible. However when we forgive, God alters our perspective on the past.

- **Condoning what is wrong** Forgiving the sinner does not mean excusing or overlooking the sin. The offender may need to be brought to justice under the law.

- **Leaving yourself open and vulnerable to repeated mistreatment** Take steps to protect yourself. Forgiveness does not mean remaining in a situation that puts you at risk of further harm or is abusive.

- **Expecting the offender to show remorse and repent** *'Sincere forgiveness isn't colored with expectations that the other person apologize or change'* - Sara Paddison. Nor does it mean that reconciliation will follow.

- **Taking the easy way out** Forgiveness can be tough, and it takes courage to confront your pain.

May the grace of our Lord Jesus Christ be with you as you seek to forgive those who have offended you.

ABOUT THE AUTHOR

TAMERA SWAN MASON

Rev. Tamera Swan Mason was born and raised in Baltimore City. She was educated in the Baltimore City Public Schools before attending the University of Baltimore where she received a Bachelor of Science from the School of Business and a Master of Public Administration from the Yale Gordon College of Liberal Arts. She continued to study in many areas, and eventually became an ordained New Thought Minister. Her ministerial degree was obtained from the University of Metaphysics in conjunction with the University of Sedona, specializing in metaphysical counseling and training. For many years she was the administrator and occasional speaker at the Unity Center of Christianity, a New Thought Organization As a member of the Professional Woman Network she received several certifications dealing with women's issues Tamera has combined her knowledge of women's issues with metaphysics in assisting her to enhance her counseling activities.

She has authored two books; <u>How to Start and Operate a Home-Based Business</u> and <u>Mail Order Mania,</u> eight articles that appear in the Professional Woman Network publications and several independent articles on business topics.

She offers her services as a workshop facilitator in the areas of Board Leadership Training, Small Business Management, and women's issues. She presently contributes as an adjunct professor, teaching business subjects at a local college.

Five years ago she started a mail order company called White Swan by promoting her own line of personal care products for women. Her products are known as "Wild Rose" because of their unique rose fragrance.

Married with three children and seven grandchildren, Tamera advises women to follow their dreams. There are many challenges that women face in life that will take them away from their timetable of accomplishment. The women who ultimately succeed are the women who continue to strive and <u>never give up</u> no matter how long it takes their dreams to come to fruition.

Contact:
Tamera Swan Mason
White Swan
PO Box 303
Randallstown, MD 21133
www.readingforlifemd.com
www.whiteswanproducts.com
410-521-4249

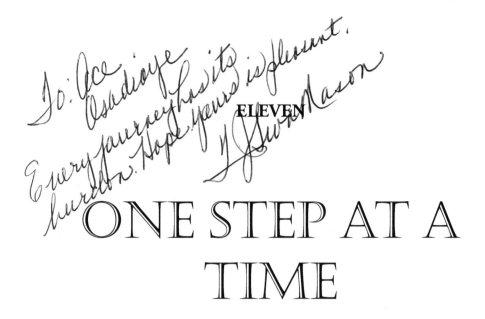

ELEVEN

ONE STEP AT A TIME

By Tamera Swan Mason

Many years ago I found a copy of a little book called The Daily Word that provided daily inspirational messages. This book was published each month by The Unity Center of Christianity. In reading these daily thoughts prepared by ministers and teachers of the philosophy, I felt these messages were just for me. They always seemed to answer a particular question or provide a new outlook for a pressing problem. Down through the years these lessons, as I like to call them, have had a remarkable influence on my daily life. They have opened my consciousness to a new way of thinking and looking at life.

As a young girl my sisters and me went to Sunday school and later to church. I began to wonder why we did the things we did. Why do we go to church, and why on Sunday? Why go to work Monday through Friday and not on Saturday and Sunday? As a child when I asked probing questions I often got an annoying look, and no real answer. At least not the answer I was looking for. At some point most children would stop asking questions and simply accept the status quo. But, I wasn't one of those children. I wanted to understand why. Even now as I continue to question the whys and wherefores, I continue to come up with additional questions. I suppose I will never really understand the universe in which we live. I guess I will have to go on accepting everything the way it is, at least for now.

As I continued to question, I noticed many years later that my questioning was what eventually led me on my spiritual journey. Who were these people who came years ago; Jesus, Buddha, Krishna, Mohammed? What were the lessons they tried to bring to their world? In studying all of them I saw that they all, in their own language and culture, were trying to teach love, understanding, discipline, brotherhood, etc. They tried to teach all the good attributes that man needs to live in a harmonious and decent environment.

As stated above my journey began with the reading of The Daily Word. In digesting the principles that were taught in this little book, I began to find the philosophy fascinating. So much so, that I enrolled in Unity's correspondence course and when available took courses in the local Unity Center. When I was able, I made various trips to the Unity Center of Christianity in Unity Village, Missouri. These were exciting and rewarding trips. At some point, I don't remember the exact year, the correspondence course was discontinued. Later, Unity's educational department no longer allowed classes to be taken for credit from the minister in the local Centers. I was interested in taking classes towards becoming a licensed Unity teacher. When the correspondence course and the local classes for credit were discontinued, all classes had to be taken at Unity Village. This put a crunch on many individuals who were unable to make the necessary trips to finish their studies. I was at this time a divorcee with three children and unable to complete the lessons that I started. This was quite a blow and I felt like "a loss sheep" so to speak, a sheep without a shepherd. But as God would have it, he put me in a position to utilize the skills I had acquired thus far.

During my years of study I could see how miraculously God works. My daily routine of meditation in the silence was the main factor that kept me going. When you meditate on a continuous basis day after day you begin to recognize and see how life unfolds and falls into place. For many years I facilitated an hour of silent meditation every Wednesday night at our Center.

Some would say this is simply mind over matter. But I know when you constantly go to God for guidance and direction that is exactly what you get, guidance and direction. Others would say with this constant vigil, you are on your way to becoming an enlightened one. I was indeed enlightened to the power of the universe, enlightened in understanding how God works. I cannot go out and chart the course of heaven and earth, but I do fully understand without a doubt that God's plan for all of us will be revealed to us if we are open and receptive to his guidance. His plan for us will be revealed to us if we acknowledge his presence and stay close to him. When your understanding is quickened your attitude changes from one of doubt, fear and judgment to peace and assurance. You find that you are more trusting and less likely to be judgmental. You begin to see things in a different light. I realized that we are all God's children and that each one of us has a place and purpose in life. It is unfortunate that we do not always recognize God's plan for us as we are living it. For if we did, we would always give 100% to wherever we find ourselves at any given moment. God indeed has a plan for our lives. For some this recognition and understanding takes a lifetime, for others it is quick and automatic. It simply depends on your level of acceptance.

Some would say that we have free will and that God's plan, whatever that might be, may not always be their plan. I would agree that we have free will. We are not puppets. But our free will allows us to recognize and make the right choices within God's plan.

Each time the Center was without a minister, I found myself time and time again being voted into office as the Center's administrator. My job was to manage and run the Center until a new minister was found. I could have chosen not to accept this position. But I recognized that God had a plan for me and that I was exactly where I was supposed to be. Why, because, I thoroughly enjoyed serving in this capacity. When things run smoothly, when confusion and discord move out of the way, the fact that I know that God has a hand in what is going on. That I found The Daily Word, took classes in the local center, or I traveled to the home office was no accident. This was all in God's plan to assist me with where I find myself today.

God knows what you want and need long before you ask. The Bible tells us that He goes before us making our path straight and preparing a place for us. I can attest to this 100%. When individuals pray for a solution to a problem, they often tell God how they want the problem solved. They tell God when, where and how to solve it. They present God with a whole host of details and are very disappointed when it doesn't work out that way. Then they will be the first to proclaim that prayer doesn't work. Many people go to God but many do not understand that prayer really works or how to pray effectively. Again, dear friends, God has a plan and His will may not be my will and I needed to understand that fact. I never imagined myself in those early days as a minister. I can look back now and wonder what would have become of me if I had followed some of the ideas that I had for my life. What you want to do when you pray is to end your prayer by saying, "not my will but your will be done," or "this dear Father or something better." This opens the door for spirit to come in and do its perfect work. This is not to say that you do not ask God for what you want, but what God's plan for you may be greater than you could ever imagine. I can also attest to this. When I pray for a solution to a problem it is never the solution I had in mind. However, the solution that God gives us is always in the best interest of all the parties involved.

As human beings, the "ego" is often afraid of "leaving it up to God." This shows a lack of faith that God knows best. To be so utterly trusting in the power of God in the world in which we live takes practice, practice, practice. This goes beyond mere blind faith, but faith unending, faith that one never questions. Until our faith is on solid ground, the world around us will intercede every time. I am still working on this.

Our local Center has undergone several episodes of unsteadiness and upheaval. On one occasion our minister retired and there were others in the Center who felt they should have the position. This minister had been at the Center for many years. Most of the ministers who came after this individual never stayed more than five years. We have had five ministers in the thirty years that I have been associated with this Center. One minister retired, two left for greener pastures and two were fired. As mentioned earlier, I served on the Board of Directors on several occasions. Each time a minister left, I found myself in the position of the Center Administrator until a new minister was installed. It wasn't until recently, as I looked back at my life and realized that every time the Center was in distress I was there to smooth things over, to calm the congregation and to keep the Center operative. Under my direction the Center grew on several occasions. We instituted various activities such as overnight retreats, bus trips, guest vocalist, trips to Unity Village, an annual afternoon tea, religious plays, picnics, and a book signing for local religious writers.   Our annual Sunday afternoon tea was not only a fund raiser but a big hit. We partnered with other like organizations and churches in the community and joined the community association. These were just a few of the many activities that were initiated during the time I was in charge. Our congregants felt good about being a part of the Center. There was never any time that I could not get volunteers to help out.

During the years that I was at the helm, I worked tirelessly for the Center. I tried to set an example not only for our congregants but to teach my children these metaphysical principles that I had put into place. As I look back now on these events, I have to smile. I must have been the Center administrator for at least five times for about a year and a half between each minister. The last time was the first time I received a salary-- minimum wage. But that didn't matter because I understood the necessity of what I was doing and loved every moment of it.

Jesus' basic theme was Love. I try to see love in everyone with whom I come in contact. This can be very difficult. How can I love the murderer, the rapist, the serial killer? I learned that as children of God we are "our brother's keeper." We have a responsibility to every human being on this planet to express love and goodwill even if it is not returned. We must honor and respect life. Many; unfortunately, have not been taught these principles and have gone astray. That's why the examples we set and the attitudes we carry should always be positive and uplifting. But how can you be positive and uplifting to someone who destroys the lives of children, or whose mental capacity has been so altered that it allows them to do horrible things? When these situations present themselves, I simply have to remember that they are also God's children. Even though they have committed heinous crimes, not only against their victims but also against themselves, they are still human beings. Then I remember that God forgives even if man doesn't.

Sometimes when going about my daily routine, I meet an individual who appears hostile and unpleasant, and who obviously is not faring very well. Usually this attitude has nothing to do with me. I usually look them straight in the eye and repeat silently, "God loves you, and so do I." This method of silent communication always works. What you are saying to this person is, if you are having a bad day, look on the bright side it could be worse. You will be surprised how this always gets a smile.

God always gives us strength to move on, to go forward in the face of adversity. Many women find life disappointing, hard and unpleasant after divorce, especially when there are children involved. They find their lives static and at a standstill. Just because man has rejected you does not mean that God has done the same. Staying close to God allowed me to move forward after my divorce and continue to enjoy friends and family in a spirit of love and friendship. Certainly rejection is never easy but knowing that God is in charge and that life takes many twist and turns has enabled me to look forward to a new adventure rather than bury myself in sorrow as a result of the old. Time and time again we are challenged and tossed into unpleasant situations. But like the saying goes, if life gives you a lemon, make lemonade.

There will be times when doubts will creep into your mind. When worry about your children, your job, your finances or any situation that you feel may destroy or impede your health or your wellbeing becomes a factor, simply go to God. I know this works; I have been there many times.

I have learned not to just listen and intellectually accept these teachings but how to live them and incorporate them into my daily life. This is where you exercise real spirituality. When you know, really know from your heart and not from your intellect that God is in charge, you begin to relax knowing all it well. This was a very hard lesson to learn. When everyone around you is in sorrow and worry, you are calm and relax. Sometimes it may look as if you don't care. But I know and have learned that a calm and peaceful attitude allows God to move through me because my consciousness is not cluttered with negativity. There was a time when that old friend "worry" would visit, and he would paint a very vivid picture of what could I have done better, what should I have done, what would happen if, etc. I don't allow him to visit anymore. Why? Because I know there is no reason for me to get upset when God is in charge.

I give thanks constantly because I know that all good stems from God and that I need only to keep an attitude of thanks and forgiveness to clear away the cobwebs of distraught. We are constantly bombarded daily with unclean and unkind words and thoughts. I find this helps me to feel as if I am providing a barrier for such things to enter my consciousness. I sometimes wonder if this is one of the reasons why we have convents and monasteries for those who wish to only concern themselves with religion.

As I continued with my growth and development I later enrolled in The University of Metaphysics in conjunction with the University of Sedona in Sedona, Arizona and received a Bachelor of Metaphysical Science degree. As an Ordained Metaphysical Minister I utilize my training scholastically as well as practically. I utilize metaphysics as part of my counseling activities to assist my clients, as well as in my personal life.

I often remind myself how far I have traveled in understanding these principles intellectually which is great, but until that understanding becomes an integral part of heart and soul; until it becomes a part of the feeling nature, you cannot truly say you understand. Then and only then, did these principles espoused by the master thinkers become a reality for me. My progress through this spiritual journey, learning the theory and putting these principles into practice has been one step at a time.

But no matter how far I have traveled there is still a long laborious road ahead of me if I am to follow God's plan to do my part and fulfill my purpose. Each day as I sit in the silence and commune with God I am aware that He is with me always. I am aware that all that I learn, all that I do, and all that I could ever be, come forth from the spirit within.

When I travel from this earth, I want them to say as Jesus proclaimed, "Let your light so shine before men that they may see your good works and glorify your Father which is in heaven." I want them to say my light did indeed shine, she did good works, and she was a wonderful, true and faithful servant.

And so it is!

Rev. Tamera Swan Mason

ABOUT THE AUTHOR

KATHY L. MOORE

Kathy L . Moore is on the Ministerial Staff at St. Matthew P.B. Church in Huntsville, AL, where she serves under Pastor E. Bernard Birgans and she teaches Sunday School and works with the youth. She was licensed at New Hope Memorial Baptist Church in Elizabeth , NJ under the tutelage of Pastors Steffie and Harriet Bartley. Kathy's mission is to empower and encourage women and young ladies to embrace their self worth to become the person God has called them to be. Kathy utilizes the wisdom, knowledge, and skills she has obtained through studying and meditating on the word of God, and her life experiences to fulfill her mission. She uses the teachings and examples of Jesus Christ as the cornerstone of her ministry. Kathy has served in various capacities in the Ministry: Women, Youth, Finance, and Outreach. Kathy believes that education is a key factor in establishing self-worth. She has created and presented several workshops to Christian and secular audiences: Self-Esteem; Team Building; Leadership; Effective Communication. She also believes that we came to serve and has volunteered with the American Red Cross as an HIV/AIDS Educator, and is a former commissioner with the Elizabeth, NJ Board of Education. Kathy was Blessed to receive a BA in Political Science from Rutgers University, and a MSM from Florida Institute of Technology and desires to use the knowledge obtained to help those in her community and fulfill her mission. Kathy believes there is power in words, and if we would just use our mouths to encourage, uplift, and empower, we can make a difference and" We can do all things through Christ Jesus, which strengthens us." Philippians 4:13.

TWELVE

FORGIVE TO LIVE

By Kathy L. Moore

In my experiences dealing with forgiving those who have indirectly harmed or offended me, I realize that forgiveness is not optional it is mandatory. One of the most powerful statements of forgiveness shown was by Jesus on the cross; He asked Father God to forgive those who had participated in the crucifixion. I daily think that if Jesus, the Savior of the world, our Redeemer, our High Priest, our Mighty Intercessor, could forgive His offenders, who am I not to forgive those who have harmed me. I also think about, if God did not forgive me for the many sins I have committed against Him daily, where would I be. In this chapter we will discuss what forgiveness is and is not, some causes of unforgiveness, my journey towards forgiveness and steps to forgiveness. As I share my journey of learning to forgive, I hope you will be inspired to allow the Power of God to teach you to forgive to live.

What is Forgiveness?

To show forgiveness to someone is to look past the harm someone has done to you or someone you love. It means that every time something comes up, you are not constantly reminding the person(s) of the hurt they put you through, that you are still resenting what they did to you. Colossians 312- :13: (12) Put on therefore, as the elect of God, holy and beloved, bowels of mercies, kindness, humbleness of mind, meekness, long-suffering, (13) Forbearing one another, and forgiving one another, if any man have a quarrel against any: even as Christ forgave you, so also do ye. According to this scripture and verses from the King James Version, we are to consistently assume the qualities listed in verse 12, which is sometime hard to do. In order to truly forgive, you need the word of God embedded in your hearts, you have to pray, and sometimes fast, but in the end it all is worth the peace you feel by turning the offender over to the Lord.

Causes of Unforgiveness

Have you been praying to God for something, but it seems like your prayers are not being heard? Are you feeling spiritually destitute? Do situations continue to arise time after time that remind you of something that someone has done to hurt or offend you or a loved and certain emotions began to flow and you began to dwell on all these things. I want you to know that you are dealing with unforgiveness. Hebrews 12:14-15: Follow peace with all men, and holiness, without which no man shall see the Lord; (15) Looking diligently lest any man fail of the grace of God; lest any root of bitterness springing up trouble you, and thereby many be defiled. Unforgiveness is like a sore that is not attended to, it continues to grow and become infected, and eventually could lead to something more serious. It causes anger, division, lack of peace, and eventually leads a person to walk around spiritually dead. A person who is carrying unforgiveness around in their hearts is unhappy, mean, and lonely. These characteristics should never be associated with a child of God.

My Journey Towards Forgiveness

The Prodigal Daughter:

Proverbs 22: 6 Train up a child in the way he should go, and when he is old, he will not depart from it. My firstborn daughter and was the joy of my life. I had big hopes and dreams for my daughter, but most of all I wanted to raise her up in the foundation of the Lord, and did not want her to make the same bad choices as I had. Growing up we had a close and loving relationship, and a new addition to our family, a younger sister. When she was twelve years old, I decided to leave my job I had been at for nine years, and move to another city. I made the decision because I wanted my daughters' to have a better life. I had been at this job and desired to advance, but I knew it was not going to happen, if I stayed there. I prayed to the Lord to open up doors and He did.

I thought I was doing what was best for my children, and was excited about the new adventure. We moved to a new city, developed was blessed with a new church home, a promising career, and we made new friends. Everything was going well, or so I thought. My daughter had not adjusted to the city life well, and fell in with the wrong crowd and started to rebel against me. She started skipping school, being disrespectful, ran away from home, and caused me to lose countless sleepless nights. I prayed and fasted for her daughter, because I seen the destructive path that she was on, but it seems as if God had turned

His back on me. I began to question if God I had really heard God correctly and was I truly in His will when I moved my family to this other city.

The more I prayed, it seemed the worse my daughter became, and after almost four years of Dee's rebellion, I moved my family back to our hometown after my daughter promised that she would do better if we would only move back home. To save my daughter, I left a thriving ministry, and a career where I was on the fast track to becoming an HR Director, but I was fine with it, because my daughter meant the world to me. Once we moved back home, her behavior did not change, it only became worse.

I tried counseling, but nothing worked, her rebellion continued until age eighteen. I could not find work in my field , so I went to work for my father at his restaurant. After many unsuccessful interviews and still no promising jobs, I was praying, fasting, studying the word of God, my sister was constantly encouraging me to turn my daughter over to the Lord, and I had other friends interceding on my daughter's behalf, because I could not understand why this was happening to me, I put up a my life on hold for my child, should I not be rewarded for this. One day after talking to my minister friends, I realized that I had become angry, bitter, and resentful towards my daughter, which held me in the bondage of unforgiveness, and the root of bitterness had sprung up in my heart. I kept rehearsing how I had left a successful ministry, a promising career, and new friends. I could not find a new job, and felt depressed and angry.

Because I was tired of feeling this way, I just cried out to Lord to help me, and I remembered the Scripture Key for Kingdom Living manual compiled by June Newman Davies that had been given to me by one of my minister friends and one of the topics was about children and it said (5)" Trust in the Lord with all thine heart; and lean not into thine own understanding(6) In all thine ways acknowledge him and he shall direst thy paths. In this book she says that looking at their ungodly ways causes us to bring them into bondage of judgment. She goes on to say to start trusting God and His word, that God cannot work if we do not forgive our children for ungodly ways. She also states that they need to learn about God's grace, mercy, and forgiveness through their experiences in life and believing and trusting God's word will draw them into submission to the Lord's will much sooner". I meditated on this as well as other scriptures and when I truly turned my daughter over to Lord, instead rehashing the hurt and pain I felt that she had caused me, when I stopped reminding her of everything I had sacrificed for her, and she still did not change, when I stopped worrying about how people were looking at me because I was a Minister, and my daughter was rebelling, and truly forgave her and prayed for her deliverance, I was finally at peace. I am here to tell you that my relationship with my daughter became stronger, I was blessed to be part of a another great ministry, and I am working for a great company.

An Unthinkable Act

I will never forget the phone call I received early that morning telling me that my daughter's father had died, as a result of murder was the hardest thing I ever had to tell them. To hear my nine year old daughter let out a blood–curdling scream of pain and anguish will forever be in my mind.

This was a long journey, but through each step, God was with us. I remember feeling angry and resentful that someone had decided after be judge and jury and take someone's life. I could only think that my daughter would not have her father around to see her reach many milestones: entering middle school; making the cheerleading squad, going and graduating from high school, attending prom, going to college, not having her father walk her down the aisle on her wedding day. I had always watched criminal shows on television and seen the anguish that the families on both sides went through, and I remember saying I would never want to go through anything like this, but there was another plan for my life.

I remember telling my daughter that we would have to forgive the perpetrator and show mercy towards her because God is the ultimate judge, and no matter how the trial turned out, we had to trust in Jesus to see us through. It would be almost two years before the trial would convene, and each day was a day of anticipation. I had never felt so helpless in my life, but once again trusting in the Lord seen me through, even though it was so hard, because the perpetrator was walking around free, and our family member had been laid to rest, even though we knew he was in better place, because he was with Jesus, it still was hard to fathom why it was taking so long for the perpetrator to have their day in court.

The day finally arrives and we receive the phone call that the trial is going to convene, and we are excited yet anxious, because no matter what the outcome is going to be, two families will forever be changed, the one who's loved one was murdered, and the other whose family member committed the heinous act. As I walk into the courtroom and come face to face with the perpetrator, all types of emotions come to surface, but I hold on to Philippians 4:13: I can do all thing through Christ Jesus which strengthens me, and we would definitely need strength to make it through, I decided to fast and pray throughout this entire trial, because I knew that would be only way to have peace amidst this thunderstorm and hold on to God's promise that he would never leave or forsake me. It was hard to face the perpetrator and their family remembers who looked upon us with anger, like we had done something to them, but remembering what Jesus went through to give us eternal life, enabled me to bear it.

During the trial we had to listen to countless people testify, look at autopsy photos, and listen to 911 calls, and I tell you it was a nightmare and several days without sleep, because those images and voices you hear in your sleep, and you just want it to be over with. Finally, the trial has come to an end. Both sides have presented their testimonies and rested their case; it is now in the twelve jurors' hand. We again have to pray that God's justice will prevail. It would be another two in half days before the juror renders their decision, so yet again we had to wait, and another scripture came to my mind where God instructs us to Be Still and know that He is God, and Vengeance is mine saith the Lord, and He will repay.

We receive the call that the jury is in and pile back into the courtroom to hear the verdict, which is guilty on all charges. There is a sense a relief and sadness, because no matter the outcome, our loved one will never walk this earth with us again. Even though the twelve jurors have found the person guilty, we still would have to wait more months before the sentencing.

The night before the sentencing , the Holy Spirit spoke to me the word life, and I knew He was preparing me for the sentence the person would receive for the malicious act committed, but I still understood that the Lord did not want me to gloat. We are once again in the courtroom, and family members from the victim's side share their feelings on the impact this tragedy had on their families, and the family members from the perpetrators side shared their feelings' that the judge should give the person a lighter sentence. Before the judge hands down her sentence, she lets us know that she had never felt the presence of God in the courtroom like she did with this case, and she sentenced the person to life. Even though the perpetrator was given a life sentence, the journey has not ended for my daughter, she will have to attend parole hearings, and face the fact that she will not see her earthly father on this side again, but because she has been taught to forgive she can live. My daughter is doing well these days, and has started high school. She realizes that even though her earthly father is gone, her Heavenly Father loves, protects, guides, and blesses her daily, and she could not ask for a better Father.

As I stated before, God does not want us to gloat when justice is handed down to those who have harmed us, he still wants us to show mercy and pray for them. I believe to this day the reason the person received this harsh sentence is because we the family members trusted in God, we bore no malice or hatred toward the perpetrator, and we only wanted justice for our loved ones. I know some of you may be saying, you do not know what this person has done to me or my loved one, you do not know how badly they have hurt us, and you are right. I cannot imagine some of the trials and tribulations some of you have been through, but I do know that if you show forgiveness, and mercy towards them, and turn them over to God, you will be released from the bondage of unforgiveness and you will have that wholeness and peace that you desire.

Let Go Let God

I have not been involved in many relationships, but the ones I have been involved in I was cheated on and betrayed. After these failed relationships, I held on to unforgiveness, because I felt like I would never be in a relationship where I could totally trust someone to have my best interest at heart. I discovered that if you desire a good mate, but it seems like you keep getting involved with bad apples, could it be that you have not let go of past hurts from the person who cheated, abused, or left you and you are holding on to the anger and pain . I felt like I was not deserving of someone good, but If it God's will for you to be married, He will bless you with the right person, but you have to forgive the ones that have hurt you, to receive the person that God has for you. I am a witness to this fact, after I learned to let go and let God, I have been blessed with the love of a man that I did not know was possible for me because I was still holding on to bitterness from past relationships. He has taught me so much about forgiveness through the trials he has endured in his life.

A Season or a Lifetime

Bad relationships also involve friendships. I have been betrayed by people I have thought were friends, and it caused me to become angry, and it was so easy for me not to forgive them, than it was for me to forgive someone who I did not consider a friend. Fortunately, I have learned that some people are only in my life for a season and some for lifetime. Now that I am able to discern between the two, I have been blessed with wonderful relationships, and I have been able to let go of the past and forgive those people. I thank God they are not in my life anymore, and pray for them. I know some of you have been hurt by people in the church and those who call themselves Christians, and so have I, but I have learned that this is one of the tools that Satan uses to keep us in bondage, and we must forgive them.

Once I forgave the persons, and learned to love God, myself, and others. My betrayals are nothing compared to the betrayal Jesus suffered at the hands of His disciples. At the hour that Jesus needed those most they ran off a left Him, but He was never alone because God was always with Him. We too can take can comfort in the fact that when we are betrayed and left alone, God is with us and has promised to never leave or forsake us. No matter where your hurt has taken place: home, church, job, etc. God is with you.

Steps to Forgiveness

- Recognize that you have unforgiveness in your heart by asking the Holy Spirit to reveal to you anything that is unlike God in your heart

- Confess the sin of unforgiveness and repent

- Pray for God's mercy upon the offender(s)

- Pray and fast when it seems like you have been hurt so bad that you cannot forgive

- Seek out a prayer partner to pray with you

- Write in a journal the feelings you are having

- Read and study about the life of Jesus and His examples of forgiveness

- Read and study the Holy Bible form the Old to the New Testaments and you will experience God's forgiveness towards us, and it will help you to begin to forgive others

- Bind up the spirit of unforgiveness, and loose the spirit of forgiveness

- Place scriptures that deal directly with forgiveness in areas that you will see them (bathroom mirror, refrigerator, in the car, in your office, in your phone and meditate on them

I hope you have been inspired by my personal struggles with forgiveness. It has been a long road for me, and it is something I deal with daily. I can tell you without a doubt that if it was not for the Power of God, I would not be able to share my journey with you. Because I decided I wanted to live, I realized that forgiveness was not an option, it was mandatory. I know many of you may have suffered or is still suffering unspeakable acts at the hands of an offender, but I implore you today to cry out to God. I have shared with you steps that I have taken, and I am sure there are many more, and I hope you will implement them into your daily lives. God's promises are yea and amen, and His word will never return void. I daily have to remember that if I ask God to forgive me for my sins against Him, I must also ask Him to forgive those who I have harmed, and who have harmed me so I can forgive to Live.

I have many people to whom I am grateful for teaching me about forgiveness. My sister is one of my biggest inspirations, as well as my other minister friends of the Gospel. I hope you too will ask the Lord to bless you with people to help you on your journey of forgiveness. I would like to leave you with words from my Pastor, Elder E. Bernard Birgans "as long as you are holding on to animosity, anger, hatred and unforgiveness against the person who has harmed or hurt you, you will never be able to move on and enjoy the life that Jesus has promised you. You will not be able to enjoy this life because you are holding that person in bondage and judgment and not allowing God to move on both of your behalfs'. Decide today to forgive to live and enjoy the life that Jesus has promised us in John 10:10" I am come that they might have life, and that they might have it more abundantly.

Notes:

Thank you God, I was hurt when my students complained about me & all I have done was to help them learn so I did not want to forgive them until I read this page 141. I totally forgive Patience, Tamfu & Earnest for what he did to me.

ABOUT THE AUTHOR

JANET PFEIFFER

Janet Pfeiffer, international inspirational speaker and award-winning author has appeared on CNN, Lifetime, ABC News, The 700 Club, NBC News, Fox News, The Harvest Show, Celebration, TruTV and many others. She's been a guest on over 100 top radio shows, is a contributor to Ebru Today TV and hosts her own radio show, Anger 911, on www.Anger911.net.

Janet's spoken at the United Nations, Notre Dame University, was a keynote speaker for the YWCA National Week Without Violence Campaign, and is a past board member for the World Addiction Foundation.

She's a former columnist for the Daily Record and contributing writer to Woman's World Magazine, Living Solo, Prime Woman Magazine, and N.J. Family. Her name has appeared in print more than 72 million times, including The Wall Street Journal, Huffington Post, Alaska Business Monthly and more than 50 other publications.

A consultant to corporations including AT&T, U.S. Army, U.S. Postal Service, and Hoffman-LaRoche, Janet is N.J. State certified in domestic violence, an instructor at a battered women's shelter, and founder of The Antidote to Anger Group. She specializes in healing anger and conflict and creating inner peace and writes a weekly blog and bi-monthly newsletter.

Janet has authored 8 books, including the highly acclaimed The Secret Side of Anger (endorsed by NY Times bestselling author, Dr. Bernie Siegel).

Read what Marci Shimoff, New York Times bestselling author, says of Janet's latest book, The Great Truth; Shattering Life's Most Insidious Lies That Sabotage Your Happiness Along With the Revelation of Life's Sole Purpose:

"Janet dispels the lies and misconceptions many people have lived by and outlines a practical path to an extraordinary life beyond suffering. Written with honesty, clarity, sincerity, and humor, this book serves as a wonderful guide for anyone seeking a more enriching and fulfilling life."

Dr. Bernie Siegel says, *"All books of wisdom are meant to be read more than once. The Great Truth is one such book."*

Contact:
Janet Pfeiffer
PO Box 2773
Oak Ridge, N.J. 07438
973-697-1904
Janet@PfeifferPowerSeminars.com
www.PfeifferPowerSeminars.com

THIRTEEN

60 SECONDS WITH GOD

By Janet Pfeiffer

I felt extraordinarily blessed. In 1969, I married my high school sweetheart, the only man I had ever dated. Our families had known each other for many years and were good friends so both sides were ecstatic when we tied the knot. Within the next few years our family grew to include four precious children. Finances were tight and we had our share of marital issues but I truly felt I was the luckiest woman in the world. I was in love with and married to the father of my children and looked forward to a life-time of sharing our love.

However, after thirteen years of living as husband and wife, he unexpectedly announced that he no longer wanted me as his life-partner, citing only that we had *drifted apart. Drifted apart?* I thought. *After eighteen years together, that's the lame excuse he's offering?* The year was 1982. I had been a stay-at-home mom for twelve years and had just re-enrolled in college to finish my degree in psychology. The prior year had been a challenging one including the diagnosis of my, then, nine-year-old son with glaucoma in his right eye. Surgery and treatment over the past year yielded discouraging results and subsequent surgeries in the immediate future were imminent. In total, he had seven operations in the following nine months, all without success. Additionally, I was unexpectedly thrust back into the work-force to help support my young family. Due to the unpredictability of my son's treatments, I was unable to sustain a traditional job. I was hired and fired in a single day from what appeared to be promising employment.

Desperate times call for desperate measures so I began a home-based business which I operated successfully for the next sixteen years. However, the stress of everything I was dealing with was more than I could bear (or so I thought at the time) and as a result I developed an eating disorder as a way of coping with the anxiety, loneliness, anger, and grief I was experiencing. I was drowning in fear and pain as my life spiraled out of control.

Approximately six weeks into our separation, I awoke one morning suffocating in despair. As I swung my legs over the side of my bed, I knew they would buckle should I attempt to stand. The unbearable weight of the hopelessness resting upon my shoulders was more than my five-foot, two-inch frame could support. Tears welled up in my eyes. "I can't do this", I cried out to God. "It's too much. I have nothing inside of me anymore." Instantly, a gentle Presence filled the room. It permeated every inch from wall to wall, ceiling to floor. Strong, protective, and comforting, Presence was unlike anything I had ever encountered before. Clearly, it was not of this world but of another realm outside of the human experience. Most pronounced was the intense sensation of Love that I felt. Unlike the human equivalent, this was pure, sacred, holy, and unconditional.

I knew instinctively I was in the presence of the Divine. I felt arms of reassurance envelop me as I felt Presence convey words without speaking. "Why are you so afraid? I am here and will never allow anything to happen to you."

Instantly, a calmness infused every cell of my being, removing all anguish, and restoring my strength. I rose to my feet. Intention complete, Presence softly retreated, leaving hope and serenity in place of sorrow, which by now had dissipated into a harmless memory. I had been in the Holy Presence of the Divine and in an instant my life was forever changed. I knew with great certainty I could face and conquer whatever life put in my path for I had the unconditional and ever-present strength of God within me and around me. I went from fear to faith in under sixty seconds.

A fleeting moment in the presence of our Lord
changes one for all eternity.

It is difficult to accurately convey the magnitude of what I experienced. As lovely as it sounds, my encounter with God far exceeds what I have written. To say "God is Love" is akin to saying the Universe is big. Unless you have experienced the Father in perfect form, you cannot fully appreciate my narrative.

Each of us, at some point in our lives, knows love. Whether from a parent, spouse, friend, or child - we have all loved and been loved in return. And we have all grieved the painful loss when that love is no longer with us. For some, the loss appears as the breakup of a relationship, for another it manifests in the form of death. We learn all-too-well that this emotion of affection is only temporary and like the wind, cannot be held on to but merely savored in the moment. The anticipation of a possible loss interferes with our ability to fully appreciate the relationship present to us knowing that in one brief moment everything can change. When we experience love from a finite source it is filled with imperfections, expectations, and conditions. And an imperfect source oftentimes includes heartache and disappointment.

When I was a child I loved my dog Chips and thought I knew what love was. Then at age fifteen, I met my future husband and declared, "Now I know love!" But when my first child was born I knew emphatically, "There is no love greater than this!" But now I can say with even greater certainty - if you think you know love now, you will be in awe when you stand before the face of God, for God's Love is everlasting, without limitations, and not of this world.

"Eye has not seen, nor ear heard, neither have entered into the heart of man, the things which God has prepared for them that love Him." —1 Corinthians 2:9

Knowing God, *truly* knowing God - not in your head as most of us know Him but in your heart -transforms you. It's like knowing health. We all know being healthy means being free of disease, feeling strong, and being void of pain or physical restrictions. We know it in our head. But most people don't experience it in their bodies. Most of us have some physical ailments - allergies, back pain, headaches, diabetes or worse. We have days when we feel relatively strong and healthy - our arthritis isn't acting up or that wretched cancer momentarily rests in obscurity, providing false respite. But imagine for a moment, what it would feel like to *experience* perfect health? For anyone who has ever recovered from a serious illness, it is easy to compare the profound differences.

Being completely *healed* from physical imperfections invites an entirely new understanding of health and transforms the way in which we live our lives. Every joy is magnified and every opportunity is appreciated. There is an undeniable change in our internal as well as external being. It radiates from every cell of our existence. It is reflected in every decision we make, every encounter we have with others, and every word spoken. So it is with genuinely knowing God. God *is* Love. There is no distinction. They are one and the same.

> *To experience perfect Love, unconditional,*
> *without judgment or restriction creates a yearning for more.*

Each day, I long to be at one with the source of perfect Love. I yearn to have Divine Love reflected in me and through me so that in everything I do, in everything I say, and with everyone I encounter, I am Love manifest in form. (Just for the record, I haven't perfected this yet but I am making steady progress.) Each morning, I remind myself of who I am as I recite the following prayer…

> *"Lord, I am a physical manifestation of your*
> *presence in this world. Let all who know me come*
> *to know you through me. Help me to live my life*
> *today and everyday in a way that pleases you.*
> *For you alone are my Lord, you alone are my*
> *God, you alone are my Savior. Amen."*

Having felt the love of God in its unadulterated form, it is fundamentally important for me to bring that love to others in all I say and do.

Nothing in life matters more to me than this - to be a living example of the Father's love.

Well, this is all very lovely, you may be thinking, *but it also sounds terribly impractical. How can one bring love to those who are mean, hateful or do bad things? Some people just don't deserve to be treated with love.*

Believe me, I can fully appreciate that this can present a great challenge at times and takes a significant amount of energy. Granted, it requires little effort to love those who are kind and respectful towards us. It's quite another to be generous to one who has betrayed us, hurt us, spoken unkindly about us, treated us unfairly or made our life difficult. But herein lies the great challenge. One does not achieve greatness by only engaging in easy tasks. Only when we face life's greatest obstacles are we given the opportunity to grow. And life without growth is unfulfilling. It is, in essence, a form of death.

In Matthew 5:44 God instructs us to...

"Love your enemies, bless them that curse you, do good to them that hate you, and pray for them which despitefully use you and persecute you."

To many this sounds unrealistic, absurd, and impractical and consequently they refuse to abide by God's dictates. Instead, they pick and choose who and when to love and to what degree. Additionally, they decide when to withdraw their affections and more offensively, designate who is deserving of love and who is not. Those who refuse God's commands are living in ego (it's all about me) rather than Spirit (my life is about God).

Imagine for a moment being diagnosed with a life-threatening illness. One day you miraculously discover a cure. Or perhaps, you were born into poverty. Hard work and determination enabled you to formulate a strategy out of a life of depravation and into one of great prosperity. Knowing that there were unlimited and abundant resources for all to share in your success, would you not feel compelled to present your knowledge to others? And each time you did, wouldn't you experience immense joy knowing your generous spirit allowed you to make a positive difference in someone's life? To know in your heart that you have brought something of great value to another is truly rewarding. And each experience of pleasure perpetuates a hunger for more. You have been blessed by the initial encounter, the other party benefits, and the rewards eventually extend to all humanity.

The key is not to discriminate. Each of us deserves to be treated as God treats us. He does not deny His favor to any of His precious children. To Him, each of us is equally as deserving of His love, generosity, forgiveness, knowledge, and so on. We do not need to *earn* His blessings - they are offered freely and unconditionally. He gives simply because it is His nature to give.

When I choose to love those who persecute me, I am showing them the heart of God. I am sharing with them His goodness through me, acting as a conduit of His benevolent nature. I am presenting the opportunity for them to know God. And who's life would not be enriched beyond measure by knowing the Almighty? (Likewise, who would not benefit from experiencing perfect health? No one.)

Each challenging individual presents a great opportunity to teach through our actions, to help them come to know God's Love and to be transformed as I was more than thirty years ago.

When I live to please God, I reap the benefits. Like a child pleasing their earthly father, there is a sense of joyful accomplishment and oneness with that parent when we know emphatically we measured up to their expectations of us. A parent who insists that their child study hard and get good grades in school only has the child's best interest at heart. The parent fully understands that their demands are not popular ones but in their wisdom the father or mother continually reminds their offspring to behave in such a manner as to reward the child in the moment as well as later on in life. So it is with our Heavenly Father - He always has our best interest at heart and unequivocally knows what is best for us, now and for eternity. By abiding by His laws, we receive immediate gratification and a life characterized by high moral integrity, self-respect (as well as respect from others), improved health and relationships, and most importantly inner peace and serenity.

Having spent sixty seconds in the presence of God and being transformed by perfect Love, it is impossible for me to withhold that love from anyone. It is imperative that I be a physical manifestation of God's presence in this world. I cannot hold anger in my heart, judge others, hate or wish harm to any of His children. It matters most to me to let them feel, on some level, God's infinite Love and mercy. This one instance completely and forever changed the way I view humanity, the choices I make, and the manner in which I treat all whom I encounter. And it only took a mere sixty seconds.

Food for thought:

Think of someone in your life who you are not fond of - particularly someone who has offended or betrayed you or someone you have had a falling-out with.

- In what way can you be an example of God's perfect Love to him/her?

- What do you need to change in your heart and mind in order to proceed?

- What would you say to or do for them?

- What kind of impact do you hope it would have on their life?

- Even if they were unreceptive, would you choose to exemplify God's Love regardless?

- How would this experience bring you closer to God?

- How would your life change/benefit?

ABOUT THE AUTHOR

Wanda H. Pritchett

Wanda H. Pritchett is the founder and proprietor of W P Concepts & Associates in Harrisburg, Pennsylvania. She operates as a Senior Consultant providing services in business and organization development, project management for church building projects, mentoring and coaching, managing conferences/events, a speaker and workshop presentations. She has over thirty year's business experience. Her executive profile extends from being a co-owner in a family business providing professional janitorial services to corporate and government agencies as well as a partner in a construction company. She has served on several business association boards.

She has received education at Harrisburg Area Community College and University of Phoenix. She has been sponsored by IBM and attended their national Executive Minority Training Programs. She also has been sponsored by Met Ed and Capital Blue Cross and attended the Executive Minority Business Management and the Advanced Executive Minority Business Management Training programs from the Amos Tuck School at Dartmouth College.

She accepted her ministry calling and was licensed as an Evangelist in 2003 through General Assembly Church of God In Christ. She received ministry training from American Association of Christian Counselors, Center of Religion and Health (Hershey Medical Center), Penn State Kiesinger Health System, Marilyn Hickey Ministries and life as a businesswoman, wife and mother.

She believes God uses her in supporting the visions of leaders in ecumenical and secular circles. Her goal is to help one achieve to live their life with expectations and hope by the ultimate experience of seeing their "*visions become a reality*."

She is a co-author in the book "Power of God" and is presently working on other literary projects, conferences, mentoring and training programs.

Contact:
WP Concepts & Associates
P.O. Box 5084, Harrisburg, PA 17110
717-343-5271
whpritchett1@gmail.com
wp3200@aol.com
Website is under reconstruction.

FOURTEEN

WALKING IN UNLIMITED POWER

By Wanda H. Pritchett

*God hath spoken once; twice have I heard this,
that power belongeth unto God.* —Psalms 62:11 (KJV)

As a woman of God, I have always desired to operate with power. I just believe and have seen that when the power of God is in operation, you become a vessel that is effective and you can make a difference. This takes place when we allow the Holy Spirit to have his way in our lives. It's not something that we have naturally, it's spiritual and a process and it comes when we allow change. What is *power*? According to "the" Merriam-Webster dictionary *power* is the ability to act or produce an effect; it is the capacity for being acted upon or undergoing an effect; and possession of control, authority, or influence over others. Most of the time power signifies authority and this is the power that the world craves and seeks after.

How can we describe the *Power of God?* God's power is that ability and strength by which He brings to pass whatever pleases him, whatever his infinite wisdom gives direction, and what his purity can resolve. Power is not an act, but the ability to bring or produce something. This power from God is what the believer should desire.

To gain a better understanding one must recognize the source and demonstration of this power and what we will do as believers if we really believe and are committed. The God we serve is "omnipotent – all powerful," meaning He is the only source of power and has been since the creation of the world in which we live in.   If we really want to operate in **unlimited power**, we have to seek God first in prayer and not as an alternate source after failure, and we would not trust in idols of this day but totally trust Him.   Our prayers should be filled with worship, praise and thanksgiving, knowing that God is the one who has bestowed on us every blessing we receive.

Secondly, we would not be so willing to give Satan the victory. We would realize that Satan is nothing but a creature and God is the great creator.   God is not fighting Satan with the hope of defeating him; he is already a defeated enemy soon to expire.

Thirdly, we would not resist walking in obedience to the things God has spoken or commanded.

God does not depend on tools and instruments of mankind; all it takes is His breath, word or power.   From the beginning of time, the earliest manifestation of His power was demonstrated in the creation of the world in which we live, as well as the Exodus and throughout the Old Testament. An angel told Mary about the Messiah's birth. She was told about this miraculous virgin birth that she would participate in and would take place by the power of God. There were many miracles performed throughout the New Testament. I thank God for the power of the cross and His resurrection power that saved me. No one was good enough to step in for me but the son of God (Jesus)-- His Father's unselfish act of love. Today in the life of the committed believers this source operates daily.

I can remember the time when I was the chairwoman of a building project in 1991 (the fourth chairperson). This position for which I had no prior experience came from God. I wasn't where I should have been in God and didn't want to really be bothered. It came at a time that I consider to be the most inconvenient time, but I knew I had heard the voice of God. In the beginning of this project, my Pastor didn't have much faith and I asked him "why he asked me to take on this task." His response was, "you're the best I have right now." His response was not encouraging because he never said, "I think you can do it." However, I already knew about the assignment that God spoke to me before the Pastor asked, so I could say, "Yes." Did I have doubts "Hello!" My natural man was saying I shouldn't be doing this because I was going through a business reorganization. I thought it would appear to others that I wasn't qualified and should I even be considered to take on this church task?

In making that decision to serve, over the years it taught me to make better choices, understand what commitment meant and step up my walk of living a consecrated life. I allowed the Holy Spirit to lead me so that my service would be pleasing to God, for that was my desire. This project was a part of me for ten years; and because of the power of God operating in my life a new beautiful worship center was built.

When I think about time ten years was a long period but if it were not for God, I know I wouldn't have made it. You may be thinking anyone can do a project like this and you're right, but to you: Is it a God calling divine appointment? Is it your purpose? Or even your job to do? So often we take on tasks in the name of serving the Lord and become weary, burnt out and ready to quit. Most of the time when God wants to use you it is something that you have never done before. Secondly, it seems as if all hell is breaking loose in your life, and you have no choice but to trust God. I can tell you throughout those years, I have experienced the ability to ***walk in this unlimited power.*** Also, I have witnessed the manifestations of His power; and reaped many benefits in my life because God received the glory. His glory came through my life while serving and you too can also walk in ***unlimited power.***

I mentioned in the beginning about change. I believe there are many requirements for ***"walking in unlimited power,"*** but the three "**C's**" or characteristics that changed my life and are responsible for taking me higher in God are: **Choice, Commitment and Consecration.** Choice, commitment and consecration will allow the operation of the Holy Spirit to manifest miraculously by the effect it has on others, circumstances and events. You can't mistakenly take credit because you know for a fact that it is not doable by your own might. You know for sure you are working in a plan with an expected end. If not careful, "one" who takes credit may very well be headed towards "his or her" demise. A checking point for me occurs when I start saying I did this and I did that, promoting myself versus God.

A CHOICE TO CHOOSE

*According as he hath chosen us in him
before the foundation of the world...* —Ephesians 1:4 (KJV)

It is true God enables us and give us the authority to operate in His name but He wants all the accolades and the glory from our lives. I have chosen to obey and live for Christ. I know that God has empowered me to do so because the bible tells me.

What I love about God is that we are free mortal agents and have options. This means we have a choice whether or not we want to do something. If we want to be successful in our endeavors and walk in His power, we have to choose Christ as the role model. Ironically, He chose us first from the beginning, looking past our faults and seeing into our futures. It does not matter to God what and where our weaknesses are when we accept Him. All you have to do is accept Him by faith! The power of God is not weakened by our weaknesses. We have to recognize our limitations. This is the real basis for turning to God in depending upon His power to work in us. By turning, to Him in this manner God will receive all the glory.

When you choose to follow Jesus Christ as the great example this offers a life of freedom. Where the Spirit of the Lord is there is liberty. We don't have to worry about who we are; we just worry about whose we are and anything and everything can happen. "Oh," what joy when you know who and whose you are when you choose to serve.

*Behold, I am the Lord, the God of all flesh:
is there anything too hard for me?* —Jeremiah 32:27 (KJV)

COMMITMENT TO THE CALL

Commit thy works unto the Lord, and thy thoughts shall be established.
(Proverbs 16:3 KJV)

Everyone has a calling on "his" or "her" life some greater than others. No matter what the call is you're called to make a difference. This means you have to be committed to disciplines wherein control is gained by enforcing obedience or order. There is a separation from oneself and the ways of the world that has to take place. These disciplines become a" way of life" or "the way we live" with a mindset to drive forward or onward. This mindset allows us to fulfill our God-given purposes while propelling to our destinations. Once you know what you're call to do, the commitment to do it enables you to be successful.

CONSECRATION FOR SERVICE

Consecrate yourselves to day to the Lord… (Exodus 32:29a KJV)

The most important "C" to me is the lifestyle of "Consecration." A consecrated life is the only way to "**walk in unlimited power.**" This allows us to tap into all the benefits a consecrated life has to offer. The more we stay consecrated, the more we can move in His power and be effective. Rick Deem stated in his article "Consecration." It reads, *"Consecration is the act of setting oneself apart from the world to become dedicated as an instrument of righteousness for the purposes of God."* The act of separation is vital to the life line of our relationship with God. It is the workstation where we punch the clock "to serve" or "to provide service" unto God.

This separation takes place in the heart and prepares us for whatever God wants to do in our lives. Many men and woman of God want to do the extraordinary. However, this expectation cannot be met if they are not willing to go into intimacy and solitude confinement. This place of preparation is where He ministers to us; heals us; speaks to us; reveals things to us; purifies us; and transforms us. God has to do this with us before we can help others.

This is also the place from where our spiritual gifts flow in greater and different ways at higher levels. It is important that a believer know what "his" or "her" spiritual gifts are. You will be able to work where God qualifies you, as well as, operate in your ministry. Every believer has a ministry. Many believers are uncertain; what their spiritual gifts are "therefore," I appeal to them to seek God. I remember very well when I was uncertain about my spiritual gifts. I was sitting in a workshop at a women's conference and troubled about not knowing my spiritual gifts. God spoke in a very clear voice and revealed my spiritual gifts to me. From that revelation, I had such peace and confidence in knowing how God might use me.

We are all born with spiritual gifts. What breaks yokes and makes a difference is the anointing upon you. God will only anoint you for what He has called you to do. What is the anointing? Jean-Claude Soupin stated in the article "Carriers of God's Anointing." It reads, *"The anointing is the presence of the Holy Spirit being smeared upon someone."* This power comes from the extension of Jesus's life that imparts supernatural strength. This supernatural strength will assist one to perform a special assignment or function in the office one is appointed. There are other purposes: "preach the good news," "proclaim freedom for the prisoners," "bring recovery of sight for the blind," "release the oppressed," "heal the sick," "empower us to hear," "discern," "hold to truth," "sort out false teachers and teachings," as well as, "teach us." These are just a few of the benefits of a consecrated life.

The objective of a consecrated life is the willingness to serve God and to provide service. As believers, when we walk with God; we should be motivated to do His business first. All that we desire to do should be secondary. The power that we walk in with God is the same power that overflows into our everyday living and fortifies us to be successful at our dreams and visions. I have found that when I take care of the Father's business He takes care of mine!

In closing let's review what we need to do to *"walk in God's unlimited power."*

#1 Open your heart to change!

Let your light shine before men, that they may see your good works, and glorify your Father which is in heaven. (Matthew 5:16 KJV)

#2 Recognize where the source of your power comes from!

God hath spoken once; twice have I heard this, that power belongeth unto God. (Psalms 62:11 KJV)

#3 Trust the source of this power!

Trust in the Lord with all thine heart; and lean not unto thine own understanding. In all thy ways acknowledge him, and he shall direct thy paths. (Proverbs 3:5-6 KJV)

#4 Choose the lifestyle of Jesus Christ as the example to follow!

My sheep hear my voice, and I know them, and they follow me:
(John 10:27 KJV)

#5 Choose first to serve Jesus Christ!

No man can serve two masters for either he will hate the one, and love the other, or else he will hold to the one, and despise the other.
(Matthew 6:24 KJV)

Whatsoever thy hand findeth to do, do it with thy might:
(Ecclesiastes 9:10a KJV)

#6 Be sure you know what you are called to do!

The voice of the Lord is powerful; the voice of the Lord is full of majesty.
(Psalm 29:4 KJV)

Wherefore the rather, brethren, give diligence to make your call and election sure: for if ye do these thinsgs, ye shall never fall:
(I Peter 1:10 KJV)

#7 Make a commitment to your calling!

Commit thy works unto the Lord, and thy thoughts shall be established.
(Proverbs 16:3 KJV)

#8 Consecrate yourself daily (Separate or set apart to serve)!

Sanctify yourselves: for to morrow the Lord will do wonders among you.
(Joshua 3:5 KJV)

#9 Know what your spiritual gifts are!

Desire spiritual gifts. (I Corinthians 14:1 KJV)

Every good gift and every perfect gift is from above, (James 1:17a KJV)

#10 You must receive the baptism of the Holy Spirit!

*But ye shall receive power, after that the Holy Ghost is come
upon you: (Acts 1:8 KJV)*

AS YOU JOURNEY FROM DAY TO DAY WALK IN THIS UNLIMITED POWER!

*"It is about the greatness of God, not the significance of man, God made
man small and the universe big to say something about himself."*
—John Piper

References and Further Reading:
Merriam Webster, Inc. 2012

Deffinbaugh, Bob. "The Power of God." Let Me See Thy Glory-A Study of the Attributes of God, 18 May 2004.

http://www.bible.org/seriespage/power-god

Rickman, Mike. "Consecrate Yourself". Seven Steps to Receiving God's Miracles, 14 June 2009.
http://www.sermoncentral.com/sermons/consecrate-yourself-mike-rickman-sermon-on-holy-spirit-baptism-13602.asp

Nee, Watchman. "Consecration." New Believers Series #7 n.d.
http://www.lastdays.net

What does the Bible say about consecration?
http://www.gotquestions.org/Bible-consecration.html

Weinstein, Mary L. "Consecrate Yourself.", *EzineArticles.com*.
http://Ezine Articles.com/2486241

Bola Akin-John. "Facts about the Anointing."
http://www.elifeonline.net/elife14-November-December/akinJohn-anointing-3.htm

Feeney, Jim. "The Purposes of the Anointing of the Holy Spirit."
www.jimfeeney.org/anointing-Holy-Spirit.html

Soupin, Claude-Jean. " Carriers of God's Anointing."
http://latter-rain.com/kingdom/anointing.htm

"The Anointing of the Holy Spirit."
www.seekgod.org/message/anointing.html

Taylor, Gene. " Great Bible Examples, Volume 2."
www.padfield.com/acrobat/taylor/bible-greats-2.pdf

"Anything too hard for the Lord."
www.abundantlifecrusades.com

"Omnipotence The Almighty Power of God."
www.tecmalta.org

Matto, Ken. "Keys to Finding your Spiritual Gifts."
www.scionofzion.comkeys-htm

Wommack, Andrew. "How To Flow in the Gifts of The Holy Spirit."
www.awmi.net/extra/article/flow_gifts

Cheddie, Denver. "The Annointing."
www.bibleissues.org/anointing.html

Notes:

ABOUT THE AUTHOR

Valorie Howie Lasley

Valorie Howie Lasley resides in Louisville, KY with her husband Roderic. He has been a beacon of support for her, encouraging her to expand her horizons and follow her desire to empower others. She is the founder of The ELI, The Empowered Living Institute where her workshops are designed to inspire and empower others to ask more of their minds, to stretch themselves for a greater good.

She received her education at the University of Louisville, completing with a degree in Guidance and Counseling. She began her career with the Kentucky State Employment Department as an employment and training counselor. After five years she moved to Louisville Metro Government to work with individuals and families in need of housing assistance and social services support. She retired in February 2011 after a 22 year career.

Valorie Howie Lasley has conducted seminars with church youth groups and community center groups on the topics of self-esteem, drug abuse, and violence in dating. She has also participated with Urban Readers of Louisville, a youth group that uses creative writing as a tool of expression.

She is a Certified Diversity Trainer with special emphasis on Women's Issues. She is also a Certified Life Coach and certified Women Empowerment Coach.

She authored the book, *The Battle Is the Lord's*, a story of surviving abuse written in poetry. She has co-authored two books, *The Power of a Woman* to be published in August 2011 and *Celebration of Life, An Inspiration for Women* to be published in December 2011.

Valorie Howie Lasley is a member of The Professional Woman Network Speakers and Authors Bureau. She is also a member of the National Association of Professional Women.

Contact
Valorie Howie Lasley
The ELI
PO Box 206155
Louisville, KY 40250-6155
vlasley@theeli.org
502 718-9927
502 468-8485

FIFTEEN

LETTING GOD LEAD

By Valorie Lasley

My mother- in- law passed away recently and I was given the opportunity to write her obituary. I wanted to honor her life with my writing; therefore I had to do some research about her life. She had been a true Christian soldier. I read an article that had been written about her in the local newspaper many years before and it spoke about how she had searched for her calling from God.

She was the granddaughter of a Baptist minister and had considered full time ministry for a while. She went back to school and received two degrees in Religious Education with a two year major in social work . She had a special gift of making people know that they mattered. She recognized this gift as her calling in her Christian walk and she served well. She led by example.

She requested the song, "May the Life I Live Speak for Me" be sung at her funeral. The words in the title of that song speak volumes for a person who has learned how to allow God to lead. If we are truly following God people should be able to see it in our actions and hear it in our words.

Is there a difference between allowing God to lead and walking with God? Some may say that it is the same thing but I beg to differ on that. I believe walking with God is likened to walking with a friend, I may ask for your opinion often but that doesn't mean I am going to do what you tell me to do. I want to give the appearance of a close relationship with you but I still exercise a great deal of free will. I believe that letting God lead is so much deeper than that and it is the very thing that many of us struggle with today. We make our decision often without seeking God's guidance and then ask God if it is okay or ask Him to fix it when everything goes wrong.

Think about it. Isn't that what we do? We may attend worship services regularly, have a prayer life when we can fit it in or remember to do it, and give our offering to the church. We make Sunday God's day but what do we do the other six days in the week? It reminds me of when I was growing up at home and learning how to dance with a partner. I was almost always the one to lead. Then when I got old enough to dance with a boy, I still wanted to lead. Before we become Christians we live our lives doing whatever we want and when we become Christians we forget we are no longer supposed to lead, God is.

What It Means To Let God Lead

Letting God lead is not an easy task for many of us. We are both flesh and spirit. It is easier to operate from our flesh. We have to work harder to operate from the spirit.

Rest in the Lord, and wait patiently for Him; Do not fret because of him who prospers in his way, Because of the man who brings wicked schemes to pass. Cease from anger, and forsake wrath; Do not fret-it only **causes** *harm. Psalm 37:7-8*

This is a powerful verse that speaks to what our conduct should be toward life. Resting in the Lord means that we are to trust Him with our lives, with our daily circumstances. When we ask for His guidance we are to wait patiently for the answer. If we could trust our own decisions we would have no need of God. We should not concern ourselves with what others have nor how they get it. So many times we allow ourselves to get caught up in what someone deserves to have or not have. We become jealous of what someone has because we don't have it but we believe we deserve to have it. The above verse warns against anger or wrath. In the dictionary wrath means extreme anger. We are instructed not to get angry or even bitter about not only our own circumstances but also about someone else's. The word fret means to be worried or distressed, anxious or act in an irritable manner. The verse states that to fret causes harm. Who do you think it harms? It harms the one is worried or distressed. It can cause not only physical harm but mental and emotional harm as well. And I think it goes even deeper than that.

I am sure you have heard the phrase, "God don't like ugly." I believe that when we allow ourselves to begin worrying about what someone else has we put our own blessings in jeopardy. Maybe you have known people who get so angry about what someone else has that they sabotage the person in some way causing them to lose what they have. In these situations I strongly believe that one will have to pay in some way for what he/she has done.

Many of us are guilty of being concerned about what others have or are able to do. I know I have been guilty of worrying about building my business when it seems to come easily for others. I have learned to repent quickly at those times. I know that how God blesses someone else has nothing to do with how He blesses me. Any blessing from God for you and me has our name on it. And not only does God know who to bless, how to bless, and when to bless but He is always on time, His time. We have to accept that God's time is not our time. His time is better.

Seven Steps in Learning to Let God Lead

1. **Start the day with God.** When I awaken but before I get out of bed, I say three verses to myself. This sets the tone for my day. I chose Psalm 118:24, Psalm 23, 1Chronicles 4:9-10. Doing this puts my attitude in check for the day. I am free to begin the day with a trust that God is able and will take care of me instead of worrying about what the day will bring.

2. **Study God's Word.** Whenever you make a purchase of an electronic device it comes with an instruction manual. Most of us need to use that manual in order to operate it properly . If what we have purchased has to be put together we rarely guess about how to do it. We rely on the manufacturer's manual so as not to void the warranty. How much more important do you think it is to use God's manual in order to know how we are to live right before Him. This is not something we should guess about but something we should take seriously, otherwise we may void the warranty. I recommend daily study of God's word in a quiet place without interruptions. God deserves your undivided attention.

3. **Develop FAITH.** Firm Actions In Trusting Him. Many times people will say, "I gave that to God" and in the next moment they

begin trying to figure out what they can do about it themselves. Faith allows you to give it to God and leave it there. Faith allows you to accept what comes without questions. Faith allows you to believe the answer will come. I am not saying it is easy to have a faith attitude but it is possible.

4. **Pray and pray some more.** The Bible speaks often and clearly about the need for God's people to pray.

    Pray without ceasing. —1 Thessolonians 5:17 NKJV

    Praying always with all prayer and supplication in the Spirit.
    —Ephesians 6:18a NKJV

    Bless those who curse you, and pray for those who spitefully use you.
    —Luke 6:28 NKJV

    Not only are God's people to pray for ourselves but we are to pray for others including our enemies.

5. **Wait on the Lord.** It is easier to let God lead in our lives when all is going well. But what is the common reaction when things are going all wrong? Have you ever prayed for something and watched your prayer go unanswered. Problems just continue to come. Many times we assume that God is not going to answer our prayer so we then try to fix it ourselves. It is possible that the waiting is a test. It is not so much about the test but about how we will respond to it. God may want to see if we will continue to wait on Him and if we trust Him to supply our needs. When we fail to wait on the Lord we are in disobedience. God never tells us to fix things

ourselves but we are instructed in His Word to wait on Him. *Wait on the Lord; Be of good courage, and He shall strengthen your heart; Wait, I say on the Lord.* Psalm 27:14 NKJV

6. **Be thankful and speak it.** If God has done something in your life to bless you tell someone what He has done. And display an attitude of thanksgiving. Just the fact that God wakes us up in the morning deserves a prayer of thanksgiving. Look around you, there is always someone in a worse situation than you. Take the time to recognize your blessings all during the day, write them down if you need to and speak them aloud at the end of the day. Becoming more aware of your blessings helps you to grow in your faith and recognize the fact that you can trust God to meet your needs.

7. **Don't drive looking in the rear view mirror.** Stop focusing on the past. Bad things happen to people, get over it and let it go. If you drive looking in the rear view mirror it becomes difficult to see what might be in front of you. You can only see what is behind you and you deny yourself the possibility of a better future. That is one change you have to make in order for God to operate in your future. God's people are instructed not to live in the past because we have become new creatures in Him.

Brethren, I do not count myself to have apprehended; but one thing I do, forgetting those things which are behind and reaching forward to those things which are ahead. —Philippians 3:13 NKJV

Exercise 1

Be completely honest with yourself. Think of a specific time in your life when you prayed for guidance to make a decision. What was the decision that you needed to make?

_____ \

_____

Were you patient in waiting for the answer?

_____

Was the answer what you wanted it to be?

_____

If not, did you then take steps to make things happen as you wanted? If so, what steps did you take?

_____

_____

_____

Did you make things better or worse?

_____

If worse, did you then pray for God to fix it?

_____

It is better to trust in the Lord than to put confidence in man.
—Psalm 118:8 NKJV

Exercise 2
List 10 things that you are thankful God has provided for you.
1. _____
2. _____
3. _____
4 _____
5 _____
6. _____

7. _____

8. _____

9. _____

10. _____

Exercise 3

List the top 8 things you need to let go of in your past. If you have less than 8, congratulations. List as many as you can.

1. _____

2. _____

3. _____

4. _____

5. _____

6. _____

7. _____

8. _____

Exercise 4

Pray for more patience to wait on God and more faith to believe that He cares for you and is able to meet your needs. Thank God for the things He has provided for you. Ask God to enable you to let go of things in your past that still hinder you from being able to move forward. Be blessed.

8 Verses to Strengthen You for God's Leadership

1. Trust in the Lord with all your heart, And lean not on your own understanding; In all your ways acknowledge Him, and He shall direct your paths. Proverbs 3:5-6 NKJV

2. Surely He scorns the scornful, But gives grace to the humble. The wise shall inherit glory, But shame shall be the legacy of fools. Proverbs 3:34-35 NKJV

3. I shall instruct you and teach you in the way you should go; I will guide you with my eye. Psalm 32:8 NKJV

4. Cast your burden upon the Lord, And He shall sustain you; He shall never permit the righteous to be moved. Psalm 55:22 NKJV

5. In you, O Lord, I put my trust; Let me never be put to shame. Deliver me in your righteousness, and cause me to escape; I incline Your ear to me, and save me. Psalm 71:1-2

6. Great peace have those who love Your law, and nothing causes them to stumble. Proverbs 119:165

7. If any of you lacks wisdom, let him ask of God, who gives to all liberally and and without reproach, and it will be given to him. James 1:5

8. For where envy and self-seeking exist, confusion and every evil thing are there. But the wisdom that is from above is first pure, then peaceable, gentle, willing to yield, full of mercy and good fruits, without partiality and without hypocrisy. James 3:16-17 NKJV

References

The Holy Bible

Scripture taken from the New King James Version.

Copyright ©1982 by Thomas Nelson, Inc.

Recommended Reading

Joy for a Woman's Soul: Promises to Refresh the Spirit

The One Year Walk with God Devotional: 365 Daily Bible Readings to Transform Your Mind

Notes:

_____

_____

_____

_____

_____

_____

_____

_____

_____

_____

_____

_____

_____

_____

_____

_____

_____

_____

_____

_____

_____

_____

ABOUT THE AUTHOR

CLARA PAGE

Clara Page is a retired Social Worker, Business Administrator, qualified Mental Retardation Professional (QMRP), AND Program Specialist for people with Developmental Disabilities.

Her education includes an Associate in Science, a Bachelors in Social Work (BSW) with a minor in Education. A certificate in Business Administration and Secretarial Science.

She is a public speaker, and the author of one book, The Little Book of Christian Plays for Adults and Children. She is a member of the Palestine Negro Business and Professional Women's Club and a Volunteer for (CASA) Court Appointed Special Advocate for foster children.

Was married to the late Walter Page, Jr. for thirty-eight years, a mother of four children, grandmother of eight children and great grandmother of one precious baby boy. She enjoys reading and studying the Bible and other books, especially Christian literature. She also enjoys writing and staging Christian presentations and traveling.

She is an active member of the Pilgrim Hill Baptist Church where she is a Sunday School Teacher, Usher, Program Coordinator and Church Clerk.

Contact:
Clara Page
P. O. Box 54
Palestine, Texas 75803

SIXTEEN

GOD'S AWESOME POWER

By Clara Page

What is Awesome? Awesome is inspiring awe; Great, Excellent; a mixed feeling of fear and wonder. God is Divine. He is an awesome God. God is perfect, all wise, and all powerful. "For the Lord our God is God of gods and Lord of lords. The great God, mighty and awesome, who is not partial and takes no bribe, who executes justice for the orphan and the widow and who loves the strangers, providing them food and clothing." He looks beyond our faults and see our needs. He is our father.

What better words to describe the Creator of the universe, and his great power. Deuteronomy 7:21 says, "Do not be terrified by them, for the Lord your God, who is among you, is a great and Awesome God.

Our God is awesome in Power: Our God is a Healer, He is greater, He is stronger, He is higher than any other. We serve an awesome God. His power is unlimited! That is to say, He is unlimited in His power, but we put our own human limitations on Him when we fail to completely surrender to the work of the Holy Spirit.

Mark 10:27 says, "And Jesus looking upon them saith, with men it is impossible, but with God all things are possible.

Power: We cannot describe the power of God because he is so powerful and great that our little minds Cannot even to begin to describe it or take it all in. He is an awesome God with awesome power. God has moved in my life. I praise Him and thank Him for his power. God's power is within each of us. It is up to us to reveal it, and use it for his purpose.

The power of God is everlasting. God has revealed Himself in the greatest Book in the world, "The Bible," which is adequately enough to give us a vast idea of His power to do anything possible that is thought to be impossible by man. With His Power, He created the world, and His Power has sustained it. There is no other power above his. He continues to replenish our earth's needs in spite of the destructive power of Satan and man because He is God, and has all power over Satan and man. His power is unlimited.

Jeremiah 10:12 says,
"But God made the earth by his power; he founded the world by his wisdom and stretched out the heavens by his understanding." (NIV).

It is God who sits above the earth in His Kingdom and watches over all the inhabitants of the earth. It is God who stretches out the heavens like a curtain, and spreads this out like a tent to dwell in.

Whom shall we seek for Power? Whom shall we compare Him to? No one else but God. We lift up our eyes to God, and see that he has created all things. He brings out His host by number; and calls them all by name, by the greatness of His might and the strength of His mighty power; not one is missing.

Jeremiah 32:17 says,
"Oh Sovereign Lord, you have made the heavens and the earth by your great power and out stretched arm. Nothing is too hard for you. (NIV).

We see evidence of God's awesome power when he met with Moses at the Red Sea. He knew Pharaoh and his Army were fast approaching the children of Israel. God told Moses to stretch out his hand over the Red Sea; and the Lord caused the sea to go back by a strong east wind all that night, and made the sea into dry land, and the waters were divided. So the children of Israel went into the midst of the sea on dry ground, and the waters were a wall to them on their right hand and on their left. Then the Lord said to Moses, "Stretch out your hand over the sea, that the waters may come back upon the Egyptians on their chariots, and on their horsemen." And Moses stretched out his hand over the sea; and when the morning appeared, the sea returned to its full depth, while the Egyptians were fleeing into it. So the Lord overthrew the Egyptians in the midst of the sea.

Then the waters returned and covered the chariots, the horsemen, and all the army of Pharaoh that came into the sea after them. Not so much as one of them remained. So the Lord saved Israel that day out of the hand of the Egyptians, and Israel saw the Egyptians dead on the seashore. Thus Israel saw the great work which the Lord had done in Egypt. Exodus 14:21-31.

We see the demonstration of God's power in these verses. There is no other power like the power of God. Who can open and close the waters? No one but God. His power never cease. His power never decrease. His power is always at work.

God's Power has no Boundary. There is no limit to the power of God. He does whatever he wants to. He has all power over heaven and earth, and all that dwells there in. His power is everywhere. Always at work. Everywhere at the same time. Our God is an awesome God. He never fails to out do our expectations. He is Sovereign. He is the greatest. He is supreme in power.

Mark 10:27 says, "And Jesus looking upon them saith, with men it is impossible, but with God all things are possible."

We access the power of God through grace by waiting on Him. Without the power of God working in us there is no victory. There is no overcoming. Feel the power of God when you are praying or meditating. 1 Chronicles 16:11 says, "Look to the Lord and his strength; seek his face always." (NIV) Never cease. Remember, God's power is everywhere. There is no boundary.

The Power of God and Creation.

> "*In the beginning God created the heaven and the earth.*"
> —Genesis 1:1.

> "*In the beginning was the word, and the word was with God, and the word was God. All things were Made through Him, and without Him nothing was made that was made.*" —John 1:1-3. NIV.

These verses offer us our first glimpse of the power of God.

"He comes only to steal and kill and destroy; I have come that they may have life, and have it to the full." —John 10:10. NIV .

God creates and gives light and Satan with his limited Power, steals and destroys. Satan is always roaming around to see whom he can destroy. We see Satan at work, but his little power cannot compete with God's awesome power. He replied, "I saw Satan fall like lightning from heaven." Luke 10:18 (NIV) Like lightning crashing down from the heavens, Satan falls before Christ's power. What awesome power. There is no other like it. There is no other that can compete with it. God's power is always at work on our behalf.

Stay alert. Be on the watch at all times for Satan. Be prepared with the word of God to send him on his way. Ask God for strength. He has the power to give us strength.

1 Peter says, "Be self controlled and alert, your enemy the devil prowls around like a roaring lion looking for someone to devour." Be sober, be vigilant. God do not want us to have fellowship with Satan. God's awesome power can keep us. God with his infinite power is always near.

Think of the Greatness of God's Power:

1 Chronicles 29:11-13 says, *"Yours, O Lord, is the greatness and the power and the glory and the majesty and the splendor, for everything in heaven and earth is Yours. Yours, O Lord, is the kingdom; you are exalted as head over all. " "Wealth and honor come from you; you are the ruler of all things. In your hands are strength and power to exalt and give strength to all." "Now, our God, we give you thanks, and praise your glorious name."* NIV

God's power is great, and is over all. He has the power to show us that he is God; He is in control of the universe; He is in control of our lives. He is the King of kings. How great thou art.

When we look around and see how vast the universe is that God has made. We should see that God is truly all powerful. The power of God is amazing and it has always been a wonder for me. I often look at the clouds and the sky, the sun, the moon and the stars, and I am so amazed by God's power. As I read and study the Bible, I see many scriptures on God's power.

1 Corinthians 6:14 "By his power God raised the Lord from the dead, and he will raise us also."NIV Jeremiah 10:12-13 "But God made the earth by his power; he founded the world by his wisdom and stretched out the heavens by his understanding." "When he thunders, the waters in the heavens roar; he makes clouds rise from the ends of the earth. He sends lightning with the rain and brings out the wind from his storehouses." NIV

These are just a few scriptures on the power of God. Take the time to search the Bible for more scriptures that will increase your knowledge about the power of God.

The seasons of the year change from winter to spring, from spring to summer and summer to fall, and it repeats itself year after year. The seasons in our lives change. We do not stay the same. We do not stay young. We age from day to day. This lets me know that there is a greater power; God's awesome power is at work in our lives. He helps us to grow spiritually and strengthen our faith as we trust Him with our lives.

God has the power to walk on the water. Matthew 14:25-26 says, "During the fourth watch of the night Jesus went out to them, walking on the sea. When the disciples saw Him walking on the sea, they were terrified. " it's a ghost," they said, and cried out in fear." NIV

Matthew 28:18 says, "Jesus came and spake unto them, saying all power is given unto me in heaven and in earth." NIV

God and Jesus are one. They share the same power. He has the power to save, and the power to judge. Psalm 62:11 "God has spoken once; twice have I heard this; that power belongeth unto God."

God has all power. Great power. All power belongs to God. KJV Psalm 115: 3 "But our God is in heaven; he hath done whatsoever he hath pleased." KJV God does whatever he pleases. We cannot tell God what to do. We cannot fit God into our plan the way we want to because whatever his will is, this is what he will do. Why? Because he has all power. 1Chronicles 29: 11-13 "Thine, O Lord, is the greatness, and the power, and the glory, and the victory, and the majesty; for all that is in the heaven and in the earth is thine: thine is the kingdom, O Lord, and thou art exalted as head above all. Both riches and honour come of thee, and thou reignest over all; and in his hand is power and might; and in thine hand it is to make great, and to give strength unto all. Now therefore, our God, we thank thee, and praise thy glorious name." KJV

We praise God because of his power, who he is, and who we are. We give Him honor because of his power and strength over all things.

God's Power is Eternal: God's power is everlasting. There is no end. It will last forever. Isaiah 26: 4 says, "Trust in the Lord forever, for the Lord, the Lord, is the Rock eternal." NIV

His power extends across the universe. He never cease to demonstrate how powerful he really is. 2 Peter 1:11 says, "For so an entrance will be supplied to you abundantly into the everlasting kingdom of our Lord and Savior Jesus Christ." KJV

Psalm 65:6 says, "Which by his strength setteth fast the mountains; being girded with power." KJV Psalm 90:2 says, "Before the mountains were brought forth, or ever you had formed the earth and the world, even from everlasting to everlasting, thou art God." KJV

God is everlasting. There is no changing or altering that God is everlasting and has all power. I am a living testimony of the awesome power of God. I know he has the power to save because he saved me when I was sinking deep in sin. When I was sick he healed me; physically and spiritually. We can contact the Divine power by regularly talking to Him in prayer and meditation, studying the Bible, giving thanks, praise and worship. We must acknowledge Him as our Lord and Savior Jesus Christ and depend on his Holy spirit and everlasting power. Without Him we can do nothing. We need God in our lives.

I serve an awesome God with awesome power. I serve a perfect God. He is perfect, all wise, and all powerful. The ruler of the universe. He is also merciful, kind and just. He is our father in Heaven."

FAITH:

We must have faith in God to experience his power. "Faith is the substance of things hoped for, the evidence of things not seen." (Hebrews 11:1) KJV

Faith is a present act that is oriented toward a future hope. Faith is intangible, but manifests itself in tangible results. Scripture tells us that, "Without faith it is impossible to please God." (Hebrew 11:6) KJV. God is the object of our faith and only "The fool hath said in his heart, there is no God." (Psalm 14:1). God has given each of us a measure of faith (Roman 12:3). It can remain stagnant or it can grow. Do nothing with faith, and even that you have will be taken away. However, if used, like muscle, it will grow and become strong.

In a world filled with anxiety, brought on by challenges, expectations, conflicts, problems, fears, strengths, hopes, and dreams, faith is essential for survival. We must posture ourselves to strengthen our faith through constantly saturating our consciousness with the Word of God until it penetrates and fills the hollow places of our souls. God's power is great, and with Him all things are possible.

PRAYER:

1 Thessalonians 5:7 tells us to "Pray without ceasing." Prayer is the opportunity God provides us to become intimately close with Him. In our daily conversations with God, through prayer, we develop a personal relationship with God. Prayer is the greatest power on earth."

It is communication between the soul and the heart of God. This personal contact with God's powerful presence is an exclusive privilege granted to all. Prayer gives us hope in hopeless situations, and empowers us to depend solely on God for strength. We need a daily prayer life to show our dependence on God and his great power. God will answer our prayers according to his will. He knows what we need better than we do, and before we even ask.

True prayer and closeness to God will help us always remember the greatness of an omnipotent, omniscient God, and how great he is. There should always be that assurance that the Holy Spirit is with us. The Holy Spirit assures us(reminds us we belong to God); He prays for us (strengthening us in weakness); He regenerates us (makes us alive spiritually); He convicts us (He points out our sins); He guides us (He shows us how to live). He is omnipresent. He is always with us.

God has the power to forgive our sins. He has the power to give us eternal life. God has the power to give life, and to take life. The power to redeem anyone; and make our souls pure. God's power helps us to grow spiritually; and overcome the obstacles of life. God has the power to strengthen our faith, and to give us deeper faith. There is no limit to the power of God. We need to praise God for his power; his awesome power. We serve an awesome God with awesome power. He reigns in Heaven and Earth. He is rich in mercy, and he loves us. His Grace is sufficient for all. Amazing Grace. We do not earn it. He gives it.

God has the Power to Perform Miracles: John 9:1-3 says, "And Jesus passed by, he saw a man which was blind from birth. And his disciples asked him, saying, Master, who did sin, this man, or his parents, that he was born blind? Jesus answered, neither has this man sinned, nor his parents: but that the works of God should be made manifest in him." KJV

The story of the blind man has three important elements of a miracle story: The situation of need, the miracle, and the attestation (to bear witness) of the miracle. The blind man was in desperate need, and he had no idea what was about to happen to change his life. Jesus said that his blindness would make way for the power of God to be demonstrated. The power of God is awesome in all situations. No one could heal the blind man; only the power of God.

Exodus 16:11-15,35 "And the Lord spoke to Moses, saying, "I have heard the complaints of the children of Israel. Speak to them saying, 'at the twilight you shall eat meat, and in the morning you shall be filled with bread. And you shall know that I am the Lord your God." "So it was that quails came up at evening and covered the camp, and in the morning the dew lay all around the camp. And when the layer of dew lifted, there, on the surface of the wilderness, was a small round substance, as fine as frost on the ground. So when the children of

Israel saw it, they said one to another, "What is it?" For they did not know what it was. And Moses said to them, "This is the bread which the Lord has given to you to eat.

And the children of Israel ate manna forty years, until they came to the border of the land of Canaan." NJKV God had the power to feed a million people for 40 years. He still uses his awesome power to feed more than a million people today. God provided water for a million. Exodus 17:6 says, "Behold, I will stand before you there on the rock in Horeb; and you shall strike the rock; and water will come out of it, that the people may drink." And Moses did so in the sight of the elders and Israel." How great Thou Art. There is no other power like God's awesome power.

God continues to demonstrate his awesome almighty power today. He feeds the hungry, provides water for the thirsty, heals the sick and bring back the lost.

God Uses His Power to Deliver Us When We Are In Trouble: Think of Daniel when he was in trouble. The power of God was at work on Daniel's behalf. There was a plot against Daniel because he prayed three times a day. Daniel 6:10-15. Daniel 6:16, 21,22 "So the King gave the command, and they brought Daniel and cast him into the den of lions. But the King spoke, saying to Daniel, "Your God, whom you serve continually, He will deliver you."

Then Daniel said to the King, "O King live forever!" "My God sent His angel and shut the lion's mouth, so that they have not hurt me, because I was found innocent before him; and also, O King, I have done no wrong before you." Read Daniel 6:17-20. NKJV

Only the power of God could save Daniel because he served God and believed in Him. Read Daniel 3: 16-17,21 for another demonstration of God's awesome power.

Think of a time or times you felt that you have been falsely accused and thrown into a lion's den or fiery furnace, and the power of God delivered you.

The Power of God's Love: "For God so loved the world that he gave his one and only Son, that whoever believes in him shall not perish but have eternal life." (John 3:16). There is no other love like the love of God. His love is unconditional. God's love saved the world from sin. It is incomparable.

Through scriptures we have seen the glimpses into God's word concerning His revelation of His absolutely unlimited and awesome power. The power of God is incomparable.

My Prayer: Our Heavenly Father, help us to understand and believe your Word, to stand steadfast without wavering, to be the kind of servants you want us to be. Not by our might but by your power. Help us to be guided by your Holy Spirit and always lean and depend on you. Show forth your mighty power in our lives that we can let our light shine before others that it might guide them to the Throne of Grace. I will always give you all the praise, glory and honor. In the name of your Son Jesus Christ I pray. Amen

Notes:

_____

_____

_____

_____

_____

_____

_____

_____

_____

_____

_____

_____

_____

_____

_____

_____

_____

_____

_____

_____

_____

_____

ABOUT THE AUTHOR

DR. SITHEMBILE STEM MAHLATINI

Dr. Sithembile Stem Mahlatini is a Professional and OrganizationalDevelopment Professional with a vision. Her goal is to assist individuals and organizations in balancing personal and professional life by adding value to lives through her coaching, training, books and speaking. In addition to being a Professional Woman Network Author, Speaker and Coach, she is a licensed Psychotherapist, a Life-Career Coach and a Certified Speaker, Trainer, Coach with Susanne Jeffers "Feel the Fear and Do it anyway" and the John C. Maxwell Team. Her goal is to empower, educate, and engage others so that they believe and achieve more in life than they ever thought possible. Be sure to join her during her live radio shows Let's Praise Him on www.visionsfm.com. She is also on local television channel presenting "The DrStem Talkshow" and the "The DrStem TalkRadio" on blog radio.

Originally from Zimbabwe, Dr. Stem is President and Founder of Global Coaching & Counseling Services and Founder of Women & Youth Empower Seminars WYES. She holds a B.A. degree in Liberal Arts, a Master of Social Work (MSW) degree, and Ed. D degree in Organizational Leadership. She uses her personal and professional experiences as the framework for her message, which simply stated is "Each New day is an opportunity to change your life, your organization and bring out the new you"

She has co-authored 7 books with Professional Woman Network and self-authored3 including her Memoir "Beyond the Tears-A story of hope & encouragement. A soon to be wife and mother, Dr. Stem is a messenger and champion of Hope. She is the Voice of Hope.

With an exuberant passion and dedication to empowering and inspiring others, Dr. Mahlatini is available as a Key Note Speaker or break up group facilitator at your next conference, or as a staff trainer at your next staff meeting. She serves small & large organizations, professional associations, civic & public organizations, school systems & youth groups on a local, national and international basis.

SEVENTEEN

ALL THINGS ARE POSSIBLE WITH FAITH, HOPE AND TRUST

By Dr. Stem Mahlatini

All things are possible for God. –Mathew 19v26

On that day, when evening had come, he said to them, "Let us go across to the other side." And leaving the crowd behind, they took him with them in the boat, just as he was. Other boats were with him. A great windstorm arose, and the waves beat into the boat, so that the boat was already being swamped. But he was in the stern, asleep on the cushion; and they woke him up and said to him, "Teacher, do you not care that we are perishing?" He woke up and rebuked the wind, and said to the sea, "Peace! Be still!" Then the wind ceased, and there was a dead calm. He said to them, "Why are you afraid? Have you still no faith?" And they were filled with great awe and said to one another, "Who then is this, that even the wind and the sea obey him?" –Mark 4: 35-41 NRSV

Writing this chapter is therapeutic and a great relief for me, as I trudge through the storms of my life, the challenges, the emotions and the confusion and anxiety of when it will all make sense. It is one thing to work as a therapist talking to others about coping with the storms their lives while my own life has been my greatest challenge.

I recently published my memoir "Beyond The Tears" highlighting the hope and courageous moments in my life and my mother's life. My hope was that writing the book would make it easier to deal with my now midlife crisis. At 47, I honestly thought I would be happily married with children, good job, a home and a happy life. I believed by this time my father would leave my mother alone to live her life and enjoy her grandchildren whom she loves so much. I thought I would have savings to cover my expenses for at least six months if I need to take a break. Not so.

I am however, despite it all, grateful for my life because I do have a very successful business as a Psychotherapist, life career coach, speaker, trainer and author. The rest is still the same; mother still struggles with her abusive very strained relationship with my father, I am single no kids, still live in an apartment, very little savings and not a lot of faith and hope at times. The lack of faith, hope and trust are what I lack most of the time. I write this chapter to help put at ease fears and thought that might be getting in the way. I write this chapter to strengthen our minds, so that we can increase faith, hope and trust in our daily lives.

As many of you have heard before "All things are possible for God, who has created us and walk by our side every single day of our lives". Why then do we doubt? Why then do we fail to trust the one creator whom I call God, who created earth, heaven and all humans? We have no faith, we fear and we create excuses for God, why? God only asks us to have faith and be brave enough to mindfully rebel against the doubts and fear of our human nature. It is true that sometimes it is hard for us to believe and let our human reason submit to the power of faith and trust in the Lord. It results always easier to try to create and find our own ways and explanations. However, with a humble and trusting heart, we must overcome any fear, knowing that God sees us through the darkness of hard times. His infinite love will guide us becoming the light that empowers us not to give up.

You see it all starts with Faith. When you have faith, you believe, you know without doubt that all is well, everything will work out according to God's plan. It is easier to let go of all fear, anxiety or doubt when you have faith. It is easier to have hope and trust when you have faith.

To increase my own faith I read a lot, I also love watching inspirational movies, and also watch other motivational, inspirational speakers online or on television. I also love inspiring and empowering others through my writings and speaking engagements. I recently started writing uplifting passages on Facebook for my fans to read. I call the posts "Dose of Motivation, Inspiration & Empowerment" The following five listings are some of the posts I have posted and had a lot of responses from fans.

1. Dose of Motivation, Inspiration & Empowerment

Our heavenly Father is interested in every detail of our life. If we want Him to work in a specific area--whether relationships, finances, vocation, habits, or something else--we must be willing to let go and give over to Him whatever He asks of us. We may think we have no hold backs that come between us and the Lord, but He knows our hearts. It's difficult to be completely compliant if we're holding onto something too tightly. The Lord wants our attachment our hold back to be exclusively to Him so we can live freely with no influence from the outside world.

You may have a lot of things that God has blessed you with, but the moment any of it has a hold on you, His work in your life will be blocked. But when you open your hands, gripping nothing, you will be totally free as the Holy Spirit's power flows through you. Is there anything you feel you could never give up? Think about whatever fascinates you, and honestly consider whether it also holds you confined. I challenge you to release that relationship or situation to the Lord right now so He can give you victory and the freedom you've been yearning.

2. Dose of Motivation, Inspiration & Empowerment

God wants us to look at every obstacle, every block in our lives through the lens of His unlimited strength and resources. Anything that appears to block His plans is an opportunity for Him to demonstrate His supreme power. Just because we do not see anything happening, that doesn't mean He's inactive. He is busy working it out for us. The bigger the wants we pray and yearn for, the longer we wait and the deeper the pains along the way.

Only those who have Faith, Hope and Trust will reap the rewards and enjoy the blessings.

Always remember that ***God is at work on the other side of our obstacles,*** arranging the details and bringing His plans to completion. When the spies returned to Joshua, they reported that the people of Jericho were scared to death. Having heard about the Jews' deliverance from Egypt and the parting of the Red Sea, they were engrossed by fear of the Lord.

The stage was set for the conquest, yet by that point, Joshua had done nothing. Sometimes we think we need to be involved in the solution to our problem, but **God is not limited** with regard to whom or what He can use to accomplish His will. In this case, He worked in the hearts of the enemy by instilling demoralizing fear.

For Christians, great obstacles need not be reasons for discouragement. Although much of the Lord's activity is silent and invisible, we can be sure He is dynamically working out His will for our lives. When the pieces of His plan are in place, He will move us on to victory.

3. Dose of Motivation, Inspiration & Empowerment

"Jesus told him, "Don't be afraid; just believe." Mark 5:36

Faith is not something that is increased by things such as miracles or divine coincidences happening outside of you. Because you are One with God, your faith is complete. When you release your false beliefs, your old values, you uncover those things which are blocking you from seeing that your faith has always been there, from reaping the rewards of your faith.

It is not the miracles, the proof that you are alive that increases your faith. It is your complete faith which creates and brings you the miracles in your life. The more evident this reality becomes, the greater the number of miracles and divine happenings which you bring to yourself. Your faith will be tested, not because you are being punished, but so that you will see how strong your faith truly is.

4. Dose of Motivation, Inspiration & Empowerment

"May the God of hope fill you with all joy and peace as you trust in him,
so that you may overflow with hope by the power of the Holy Spirit."
—Romans 15:13

Have you ever experienced a lack of peace that kept you from moving forward? I have. You and I may not know our future, but God does. Through the Holy Spirit, God directs our steps by the presence of peace or lack of it.

Our heavenly helper works in our lives much like a referee does in a basketball game. As long as the players stay within the boundaries of the court, they are free to move about. But when there is trouble on the court or the ball goes out of bounds, the referee blows his whistle. The sound of the whistle stops the game until the referee restores order and puts the ball back into play.

Likewise, you and I have a heavenly referee—the Holy Spirit. When there is a lack of peace in your life, that's your signal to stop moving ahead. The Holy Spirit has blown the whistle and called for a time out to redirect your path.

Sometimes your ball gets kicked out of bounds by unexpected adversity. Other times, you can step out of bounds by giving into temptation and sin. In each of these circumstances, the Holy Spirit will blow the whistle to gain your attention. If we are wise, we'll wait on our heavenly referee to restore our peace and put the "ball" back into play. That happens as we confess our sin, seek His face, and follow His instruction.

However the Spirit leads, it's important to note that stepping out of bounds doesn't mean God will call "game over." Our heavenly referee is always working to restore your life and mine.

Let's say this prayer in meekness; "Dear Lord, make my path clear and give me the courage to follow it. In Jesus' Name, Amen"

May the God of hope fill you with all joy and peace as you trust in him, so that you may overflow with hope by the power of the Holy Spirit." Romans 15:13

5. Dose of Motivation, Inspiration & Empowerment

"Because you are my help, I sing in the shadow of your wings. I cling to you; your right hand upholds me." Psalm 63:1-11 I know there are many times I have failed to cling to God, by clinging to his promises, by clinging to the testimonies. The one fact I know for sure is that, every one of us will experience moments of apprehension, and denial or trying to hide from it will do no good. When fear arises, ask yourself the following questions:

- Where does it come from? (You know it isn't from God.)

- Has God ever failed me in the past?

- Does He promise to meet all of my needs?

- Does He keep His promises?

If we read the Bible, we'll find countless stories of God's faithfulness. For example, Paul lived through hardship, persecution, pain, and all kinds of terrible circumstances. The apostle wrote these well-known words: "God causes all things to work together for good to those who love God, to those who are called according to His purpose" (Romans 8:28).

This testifies to the fact that for those who trust in Him, God turns every difficulty, loss, and separation into something good. His Word is a lamp that will give us clear guidance when circumstances are bleak. It offers the best direction we will ever find. When we meditate upon it, pray over it, grapple with it, and incorporate it into our lives, His light chases away the darkness. The psalms, in particular, are helpful in dealing with fear.

God, the supreme ruler of this universe, is in control of your life. Don't make the mistake of thinking He isn't, simply because He does not operate according to your will and schedule. If you read your Bible and meditate on it, you will find genuine strength in His promises. All things are possible to those who believe, now I know that, now I am not afraid. Many of us are even afraid of the success bestowed on us, some want more and fail to see the wealth and blessings they have received thus far.

6. Dose of Motivation, Inspiration & Empowerment

"Therefore do not worry about tomorrow, for tomorrow will worry about itself. Each day has enough trouble of its own." —Matthew 6:34

Fear obviously produces anxiety, but it also creates chaos in our lives and even affects those around us.

Fear stifles our Thinking and Actions: It creates indecisiveness that results in stagnation. I have known talented people who procrastinate indefinitely rather than risk failure. Lost opportunities cause erosion of confidence, and the downward spiral begins.

Fear Hinders us from Becoming the People God Wants us to be: When we are dominated by negative emotions, we cannot achieve the goals He has in mind for us. A lack of self-confidence stymies our belief in what the Lord can do with our lives.

Fear Can Drive People to Destructive Habits: To numb the pain of overbearing distress and foreboding, some turn to things like drugs and alcohol for artificial relief.

Fear Steals Peace and Contentment: When we're always afraid, our life becomes centered on pessimism and gloom.

Fear Creates Doubt: God promises us an abundant life, but if we surrender instead to the What are you afraid of--loss, rejection, poverty, or death? Everybody will face such realities at some point. All you need to know is, God will never reject you. Whether you accept Him it's your decision.

The Bible tells us that God will meet all our needs. He feeds the birds of the air and clothes the grass with the splendor of lilies. How much more, then, will He care for us, who are made in His image? Our only concern is to obey the heavenly Father and leave the consequences to Him. The Lord is not slow; He's patient.

7. Dose of Motivation, Inspiration & Empowerment

"Commit your way to the Lord; trust in him and he will do this: He will make your righteous reward shine like the dawn, your vindication like the noonday sun." —Psalm 37:5-6

Job was a man who certainly knew trouble and temptation, and yet he boldly claimed, "Though He slay me, I will hope in Him" (Job 13:15). That is commitment. Job had lost his children, his fortune, and his health, but he refused to abandon faith in God

The stricken man was determined to hold on because he trusted the Lord to do right. **Unwavering commitment** to trust the Lord in all situations is a cornerstone of unshakable faith. From the vantage point of that foundation, we can focus our eyes upon God alone. It is easy to be distracted by circumstances and allow them to dictate our emotions.

But if that's the case, then when life is good, we're happy; when times are tough, we're frustrated; and when hardship pours in, we're downright miserable and looking for escape.

Unlike Job, we are fortunate to have Scripture, which reveals God's nature and promises. And it is a wise believer who claims those promises when enduring hardship. For His Word tells us that our Father is always good, always just, always faithful, and always trustworthy. When we take our eyes off the turn of day-to-day activity and focus on honoring Him and following in His way, we find a consistent peace that carries us through both plenty and poverty.

In order to hold on to God through any trial or temptation, promise yourself to commit; trust and follow Him all of your days. Lay claim to His promises: The unchanging Lord and Savior (Heb. 13:8) is committed to caring for you in all circumstances (1 Peter 5:7) and will never leave or forsake you (Heb. 13:5).

It is when we make this decision to Totally Completely live our lives according to the Bible that temptation comes, that life becomes difficult. This as Bishop T.D Jakes says" It hurts because you are about to birth a 9 pound baby" You see when we pray we forget that the rewards will come after we act on what we have prayed for.

We have to do what we need to do and leave the rest to God. This is surrendering. When we surrender, we are showing that our Faith, Hope and Trust are greater than the nay sayers in our life, greater than our own self-doubts. Surrendering means we are not going to worry because worrying shows we still do not believe and trust the Lord will work it out.

I hope you will join me DrStem Mahlatini or the DrStem Talkshow page on Facebook to get more Doses of Motivation, Inspiration and Empowerment.

Remember, God has ways of shaking the world when He is at work. The shaking is what constitutes the storms in our lives. Individual lives are often shaken when a family experiences crisis or a marriage begins to unravel. If we have built on the fragile cornerstones of human wisdom, pride, and conditional love, things may look good for a while, but a weak foundation causes collapse when storms hit. While adversity affects everyone, we can have peace in knowing that God always has a greater purpose when He allows upheaval in our world. Hard times can also shake believers out of apathy and self-focus, reminding us not to trust in ourselves or the temporary structures of this world. There is only one secure foundation: a genuine, deep relationship with Jesus Christ, which will carry you through any and all turmoil. No matter what storms are raging all around, you'll stand firm if you stand on His love.

We make all things happen in our lives by first surviving the storms of life. We survive by affirming who we are in the midst of the storm, by increasing our faith, hope and trust. To make sure all things are possible for us to survive the storms of life one needs a strong sense of where we are going with our lives. We have to remember who is besides us when the storms of life are raging around us. God is the all mighty who will calm the storms at the right time and in the right order. Our steps are ordered by him. Let us renew our faith, build onto our hope and trust, remembering that "It will all make sense" one day.

All things are possible with Hope, Faith and Trust. For now I say to my storms "Peace Be Still". All is well.

The following questions will help you see where you are with your faith, hope and trust for your life.

- When it's all said and done, are you happy with your life?

_____

- Are you doing what you believe in, or are you settling for what you are doing?

_____

- What is the one thing you'd most like to change about your life right now?

_____

- What is that burning desire in your heart?

- If not now, then when?

ABOUT THE AUTHOR

Liz Howard

Liz Howard is Founder and President of L. Howard Enterprises, LLC. L.H.E provides training, seminars and workshops to individuals and organizations with an emphasis on assisting women realize their personal and professional goals. Liz has presented the workshops "Eliminating Self-Defeating Behaviors", "Moving From Pain To Purpose", and "Overcoming Obstacles (Transition and Change)" to various groups in Arizona and Nevada. Liz has been certified by The Professional Woman Network , an international consulting firm, as a Diversity Trainer with special emphasis in Women Issues. She is also a Certified Professional Coach, and co-author of "Life Is an Attitude! The Power of Positive Living, "Releasing Strongholds! Letting Go of What's Holding You Back", "The Power Of God", and "A Victim No More! Overcoming Shame, Toxic Relationships and Abuse (Spring 2013).

Liz is also a dedicated voice for over 500,000 children in the U.S. foster care system And a current member of the Foster Care Alumni of America and once a ward of the state of Illinois herself, she is well aware of the issues that plague kids aging out of the system with few skills to survive and even fewer mentors to guide them.

Liz' knowledge and experience has been enhanced by her lingering drive for higher education and her work with the various organizations with which she has helped. She is a graduate of Robert Morris College in Chicago, Illinois, attended the University of Phoenix (Human Services) and Bethany University (Psychology). Liz has worked with the Women's Resource Center in Las Vegas, completed the Mentor and Youth Ministry Training Course sponsored by Victory Missionary Baptist Church in Las Vegas, and is a Certified Competent Leader, and Communicator within the Toastmasters International Leadership Program. She was also a participant in the 100 Women In White Conference at Reconciliation Apostolic Ministries in Las Vegas and has been an ardent supporter of Azusa World Women's Ministry (South Mountain) "Each One Reach One Conference."

Liz has been a minister's wife for over 20 years and has firsthand experience in family life issues, counseling and relationship management. She and husband Kenneth are parents to five wonderful children Kenny Jr., the twins (Kristin and Kyle), Kristofer and Kaila, in addition to two beautiful grand daughters.

Contact:
L. Howard Enterprises, LLC
P.O. Box 336166
No. Las Vegas, NV 89033
702-610-4488
www.lizhoward.org
Email: lhowardenterprises@gmail.com

EIGHTEEN

THE LORD'S MERCY

By Liz Howard

It is of the Lord's mercies that we are not consumed,
because his compassions fail not.
They are new every morning: great is that faithfulness.
—Lamentations 3:22-23 KJV

The word mercy in the above text is a Hebrew word meaning loving kindness, favor, or to be kind.

The word mercy is used 262 times in the King James Version of the bible and 124 times in the New International Version of the bible. Mercy is visible in some form in almost every book of the bible. It is the reason the bible exists in the first place. God loves us with an everlasting love and wants more than anything else for his creation to be in fellowship with him. His compassion is far reaching and his grace amazing. There is no one like Him! Throughout scriptures and in our own lives we can see that many times God has had compassion on us when reprove would have been in order.

Ephesians the second chapter discusses how we were dead in sins and how we walked according to the lust of our flesh. In other words, we did what we wanted to do when we wanted to do it. But when trouble came we promised God we would change if he just got us out this time. I think we mean to do better, but somehow we get caught up again and again especially when we take our eyes off Him. In the fourth and fifth verses the apostle Paul tells us that God is rich in mercy, for His great love wherewith he loved us, even when we were dead in sins. This is not to say that we should remain in sin and keep committing the same mistakes over and over this is not what grace and mercy is for. We will have to give an account for everything that we have said and done, however there is help for us when we need it.

Your Mercy Message
What does Lamentations 3:22-23 mean to you?

_____

1. How have you seen God's mercy in your life today?

_____

In the Garden of Eden when Adam and Eve had eaten of the forbidden fruit they were ashamed of disobeying God and of being naked. They tried to fix things themselves by sewing together fig leaves to cover their nakedness. When God came to fellowship with them they tried to hide themselves. God called out to them even though he knew exactly where they were hiding.

Why do we try to hide from the very source of our help when we get into binds? He already knew what we were going to do, and he knows that we are in trouble. Don't allow the adversary to talk you into hiding when God promised to be a present help in the time of trouble. Run to the Savior where you can find the hope, healing and power you need to overcome anything that presents itself in your life. I have vowed to be open and just tell God, (since he already knows anyway) that way I can get the help I need.

Your Mercy Message

What "leaves" have you sewn together to fix an issue, that you know you need to turn over to God?

What do you find yourself battling over and over again?

How comfortable do you feel coming to God with your "real" issues?

Eighteen Years

And he was teaching in one of the synagogues on the Sabbath. And, behold, there was a woman which had a spirit of infirmity eighteen years, and was bowed together, and could in no wise lift up herself. And when Jesus saw her, he called her to him, and said unto her, Woman, thou art loosed from thine infirmity. And he laid his hands on her: and immediately she was made straight, and glorified God.
–Luke 13:10-13KJV

Have you ever had a problem that you carried for many, many years thinking that there was no answer or help for it? Perhaps you were molested, mistreated, abandoned, abused, or just did something that you are not so proud of. This is one of my favorite passages in the bible. The scriptures do not tell us much about this woman; it does not even give us her name. I think this is because she not only represents one woman, but many of us. I often wonder when I hear the story if she had a family, or was she alone. Regardless, she still had an infirmity that had lasted for 18 years.

Sometimes the infirmity is sorrow, distress and emotional pain which can open the door to physical illnesses as well. She was in the right place at the right time. Jesus saw her. When he saw her he had mercy on her and called her to himself. She came to him and he laid his hands on her, and healed her. No more would she have this infirmity, no more would she be bowed over, and bound by this burden she had carried for 18 years.

I cannot imagine being bowed over for 18 years, but I have struggled with abandonment issues for many, many years. Recently while I was talking to God about how to regain emotional balance, he began to deal with me about what I was really afraid of. I gave a bland list of things like: my husband, kids, brother or other family member being really ill and passing, failing him, and things like this. Again, he asked me "What are you afraid of?" I really dug deep and said, "I am afraid of being abandoned again, was I as in my childhood". By now I am really broken and crying out to God.

"Now, let's talk about this" he said, and He has been renewing me and healing me of these fears ever since. It has not been easy, but his mercy! Each day I have to renew my mind with his word, so my thoughts don't wonder to the wrong unhealthy places. I am not fearful like I was before, and when the wrong thoughts arise I begin to pray for my mind and reject the lies of the enemy. I thought I had dealt with all the issues of foster care and how my brother and I ended up there in the first place. Somehow the root of the issue was missed, while I tackled the vines that grew from it. The point is that like the woman in the passage, we cannot do it on our own, we need help. It is okay to need help. Jesus called her to him, to the source of assistance to meet her need.

Your Mercy Message

What might your infirmity be?

If you feel like you have to fix yourself, why do you feel that way?

Are you willing to reach out for help? Why or Why not?

God's Mercy in Your Life

O Give thanks unto the Lord; for he is good: for his mercy endureth for ever. —Psalm 136:1 KJV

This entire Psalm speaks about the mercy of God enduring forever. It speaks of his great wonders, and marvelous works. It tells of his wisdom in creating the heavens and earth. It tells of him who made great lights, and brought Israel out with a mighty hand. To him who gives food to all flesh, for his mercy endures forever.

What can you think of to give God thanks for in your life?

Have you shared something that God has done for you? If not, why not?

There have been so many times that God has shown compassion to me in my life. This is one vital reason I keep a journal, one to record his great works and words that he speaks to me either in prayer or through a messenger and two so I will never forget the large or small things he keeps doing for me.

Your Mercy Message

Do you keep a journal?

Try keeping track of one week worth of events that reveal God's mercy in your life.

Write you findings here.

_____

_____

_____

_____

_____

What other passages of scripture can you think of that reflect the mercy of God? Write them down as reminders.

_____

_____

_____

_____

_____

How do you handle times of difficulties? By writing down reminders we create our own history of God's work to look back on as proof of what he can do.

The Lord's mercy protects us from dangers we cannot see. You may drive the same route to your office each day. However, on Thursday you feel like you should go a different way. By following the leading of the Lord he saves you from a six car accident on the freeway. Our lives would be a little easier if we followed his directions. Just like the warnings we give our children, God tries to warn us of situations to prevent us from a lot of pain. Children will be children, and sometimes we don't listen either. Thankfully God can provide us with help when we call him.

Your Mercy Message

Make a note of a time when God lead you in a different path that spared you from danger

Now note a time when you did not take heed to a warning.

The great thing about God is that he corrects us without tearing us down and making us feel small. His grace has the ability to humble us without destroying our self esteem and His favor lifts us without inflating us. Several years ago I began having a reoccurring dream and open vision that my daughter was going to get hit by a car. I would hear the car brakes and see her in front of the car but that would be it. My husband and I would constantly pray for her and the other kids. However, one day she was with my sister-in-law and her daughter when they called to say that Kaila had gotten hit by a car. They were walking past a house and a dog came running up to the fence. My daughter thought the dog was coming over the fence and ran into the street where she was struck by a car. I almost fainted when they called us. Then I remembered all the dreams I had and began to pray for her healing. When we arrived at the hospital she was in a neck brace and had a few minor scraps on the side of her face. She had no broken bones, no broken skin, and no stitches. God is amazing! I keep the photos in my journal, once again to remind me of God's faithfulness. I could tell you many more incidents where God has protected our family time and time again.

Your Mercy Message

1. Has God ever allowed you to see something before it happened?

_____

2. Do you ever get gut feelings that you do not pay attention to?

_____

3. How will you respond to warnings from now on?

_____

_____

4. Why do you think it is hard for us to heed warnings?

_____

_____

The Blessings of God

Let Israel hope in the Lord: for with the Lord there is mercy, and with Him is plenteous redemption. —Psalm 130:7 KJV

The blessings of God are all around us, we just need to slow down a little in order to recognize them. God gives us wonderful blessings each day to praise Him for and to enjoy. When we slow down we can begin to take in and take note of just how many we miss because we are in such a hurry to get through each day. When we slow down God gives us opportunities to share what He has done in our lives with someone who may really need it at the time. You never know what someone else is going through, and how your words of encouragement will help them make it through.

Your Mercy Message

1. Take note of some blessings you may have missed, write them below.

2. During your bible study take note of specific scriptures that speak to you concerning blessings.

_____

_____

_____

References
The New Open Bible Study Edition

The Hebrew/ Greek Key Study Bible

ABOUT THE AUTHOR

TONYA S. COY, CPC

Certified Life Empowerment Coach Tonya S. Coy created *Empowering Your Success LLC* to inspire, empower, and motivate others to overcome their barriers to success and to create more balanced lives. Ms. Coy employs her motto *"live well, laugh often, and love much!"* through recent successful *Empowering Your Success* workshops, including: *Issues & Diversity; Wellness & Stress Management; Life Skills for Women; and Emotional Wellness for Women.* Her motivational speaking engagements and individual/group coaching sessions entertain, educate, and empower, and she recently shared her story of personal triumph in the face of adversity in the Amazon #1 bestseller *Women Living Consciously.*

A veteran director of operations for a non-profit organization serving children and families, Ms. Coy's 15-year tenure there demonstrates both her commitment and passion for the betterment of life for many, and she "walks her talk" as she applies her excellent organizational abilities and her non-profit experience to her coaching business clients and to her life in general. She serves on the board for Heart to Hearts, Inc., a non-profit health and wellness organization for women, and volunteers for Susan G. Komen for the Cure.

Certified by the Institute for Professional Excellence in Coaching (iPEC) as a Professional Coach and Energy Leadership Index Master, and by The Professional Woman Network as a Diversity Consultant, Ms. Coy is currently working toward two certifications as a Nutrition & Wellness Consultant and Weight Management Consultant through American Fitness Professionals & Associates (AFPA.)

Ms. Coy holds an M.S. in Human Resources Management from DeVry University's Keller Graduate School of Management, a B.A. in Technical Management and an Associate's Degree in Telecommunications Management, both from DeVry, and an Associate's Degree in Computer Systems and Networking Technology from Mercer County Community College.

Ms. Coy is the proud mother of two children, David and Jasmin.

Contact:
Tonya S. Coy
Empowering Your Success, LLC
P.O. Box 7284, West Trenton, NJ 08628
(609) 851-8036
www.empoweringyoursuccessllc.com
tonya@empoweringyoursuccessllc.com

NINETEEN

FINDING MY MOTIVATION THROUGH GOD

By Tonya S. Coy

It was October 19, 2011 and I had just celebrated my 44th birthday. My wish was to lose weight. I was 185 pounds and my clothes were getting smaller by the minute. I swore every time I washed them, the dryer was shrinking them. At least, that is what I told myself. I was unhappy, frustrated and convinced I would never get the weight off. Then one day, I sat on my bed and screamed out loud, "Enough is enough!" The wheels started churning in my head and at that moment, I decided to return to the gym. I was going three times a week and feeling good. By November, I had lost 10 pounds. Boy, I felt like I was on top of the world! I was so excited and dancing around my room with joy and a huge smile on my face. I started feeling better about myself and inspired to continue on my weight loss journey. Unfortunately, it didn't last long. On November 22 while I was at work, I received a dreadful call, "Tonya, come home…your house is on fire." As I went through different stages of emotions, I no longer cared about losing weight and working out. I found myself back into my old eating habits and by January, I was twenty pounds heavier. The weight I had lost was back plus some additional pounds. I did not realize it until I went to JC Penney to buy clothes since I had lost everything in the fire. As I was trying on pants and putting my thighs into the pants legs, they felt like they were suffocating and looked like watermelons in a pea pod. I was no longer in a smaller size but instead two sizes larger. I sat in the dressing room with a stunned look of disappointment. As a result, I continued on my eating journey of bad foods which tasted delicious.

Every year, I always told myself by the time the summer began I would be slimmer and treat myself to a shopping spree at NY and Company for new clothes as a reward. But the years kept creeping by, and two months before every summer, I found myself still struggling with my weight. For a while, it looked like I wouldn't keep that promise to myself. Until one day, I was searching the Internet for weight loss success stories and came across Livestrong.com which was developed by the Lance Armstrong Foundation. According to the website, it believes everyone should feel empowered through food, fitness, and inspiration to pursue their best life because eating well and staying active are critical components in preventing cancer and fighting other illnesses. This seemed like a great fit for me because it was similar to Weight Watchers but instead of tracking points, it tracked calories and it was **FREE**. As stated by Livestrong.com, it provides expert content in the diet, nutrition, fitness, wellness and lifestyle categories that informs and empowers. Its content offering includes:

- Investigative and engaging feature content created by leaders in healthy living;

- Practical, solution-oriented short form content created by experienced freelance professionals;

- Entertaining, instructional video series and short form video content;

- Expert input, personality and soul throughout the site via Q&A series and content formats with social media portability; and

- Relatable, knowledgeable editors who interacts with the community and develop content based on the members' needs and interests." (Livestrong.com)

With all of this useful information, I still could not get myself motivated to start. I had fallen into a deep black hole and could not climb my way out. I mentally struggled with the thought of having to buy clothes in a larger size but yet was not compelled to do something about it. I took a long look in the mirror and discovered my biggest issue was me. My self-esteem and confidence were at a low and I felt like an ugly duckling. However, my family and friends would say I looked fine. To me, I did not feel great. As I was dealing with these emotions, I was still grieving over the loss of Max, our family pet, and home from the fire. My emotions were on overload and I thought I was going to burst like a balloon being popped by a pin. I became depressed and wore a mask to hide my feelings of despair so everyone around me including my children could not see how I truly felt. *My soul is weary with sorrow; strengthen me according to your word.* (Psalm 119:28, NIV)

Looking back to that Sunday after the fire, I had gone to my church, True Servant Praise & Worship. It was a wonderful service. Bishop Jenkins had invited a guest speaker, a friend of his, who gave a powerful testimony about his life and the physical ailments he endured over the years to the present. Through it all, his faith in God remained strong. Listening to this man's prevailing testimony humbled me and increased my faith and trust in God, knowing that he will see me through my current struggles. I walked out of church feeling encouraged and blessed. So when the New Year began, I decided to participate in a two-day Breast Cancer walk for my 45th birthday. In accomplishing this goal, I would have to once again move forward in attempting to lose weight. I thought this would encourage and motivate me to try again. *Yeah right, I was wrong.* Even though, I felt encouraged, I still was not motivated. I couldn't believe it! "Why, am I still stuck?" I kept asking myself over and over. I spoke out loud to God asking him to help me get out of this funkiness. *Sustain me, my God, according to your promise, and I will live; do not let my hopes be dashed.* (Psalm 119:116, NIV)

As a board member and active volunteer with Heart to Hearts, a nonprofit health and wellness women organization, we participated in a health fair held by a local church on a sunny Saturday afternoon. While we were sitting in the sanctuary listening to various guest speakers talk about managing weight, staying healthy and taking care of oneself. I felt like they were looking into my soul and speaking directly to me. As I continued to listen, I started to feel inspired and took notes. I had a revelation. I pulled my cell phone out of my pocket-a-book and started searching the Internet on how I could become a certified nutrition and wellness consultant. That moment, everything started to come together... how I was going to lose weight and help others as well. I felt I had found that motivation and it was through the work of God. The American Fitness Professionals and Associates Fitness' website appeared on my cell phone screen staring up at me. It provided all the information I needed to pursue a certification. As I continued to read, I was smiling with excitement like a kid about to get a piece of candy. I couldn't wait until the day's events were over so I could go home and look more into it. I knew it was all God because He provided me with the information at that specific moment. He gave me hope and provided me with thoughts, ideas and opportunities to move forward in my weight loss and business venture. By the time the speakers were done and the people were being released from the sanctuary to visit the vendors, I had written a whole page of ideas and thoughts that had been spoken to me by God. It was awesome! We left the sanctuary in prayer and I thanked and acknowledged God for giving me the inspiration and motivation to seek these opportunities. *Trust in Lord with all thine heart; and lean not unto thine own understanding. In all thy ways acknowledge him, and he shall direct thy paths.* (Proverbs 3:5-6, KJV)

After the health fair, I headed home and sat at my Dell computer to look at the American Fitness Professionals and Associates Fitness' website. Later, as I sat alone with my thoughts, I was trying to figure out a way to pursue the certification financially and mentally. It was only one way and it was to just do it. So, I made my payment online and a week later, my study materials were in the mail. At the same time, I returned to the gym. Again, I was on my weight loss journey. *Motivation is the driving force behind our bad habits, so tap into yours and use it to form new, good habits. By identifying what you want and how you'll get it, you can shape new behaviors that, with a little practice, will become as routine as your bad habits ever were.* (Livestrong.com)

As months passed by, I was doing really well in my studies and weight loss. However, in July, I fell again into that black hole. Why? You may ask. I was going through another adjustment in my life. My house was supposed to have been ready for my children and I to return but it was not as a result of several delays. Unfortunately, I had already begun the paperwork to move out of the apartment, set up by my homeowner's insurance company, and it was too late to request for another extension. The moving process involved packing up our things, moving them into storage and temporary living with my mom and stepdad. In between, my uncle unexpectedly died. In addition to that, it was a very busy time at work. I was feeling overloaded with responsibilities and becoming mentally tapped out. I had decided to put my weight loss journey, business venture and studies on the back burner. I was extremely tired of the challenges and responsibilities I had to handle such as rent a U-Haul truck and a storage unit; prepare for a memorial; meet deadlines at work; make certain decisions pertaining to the renovation of our house, etc. So, one night, I gave it to God. My prayer "Father God, please provide me with the strength to pack our things, support my family through our loss, perform my duties at work, and handle all that may come my way." As I prayed for strength, He provided it. *He giveth power to the faint; and to them that have no might he increaseth strength… But they that wait upon the Lord shall renew their strength; they shall mount up with wings as eagles; they shall run, and not be weary; and they shall walk, and not faint.* (Isaiah 40:29, 31, KJV)

The next morning, I woke up and was ready to handle my business. With the help of my daughter's friends and our cousin, Nate, we moved our belongings into storage. With all the helping hands, we were able to complete our move in less than three hours. On Friday, the next day, my mom, Aunt Lisa, good friend DaNita and I cleaned the apartment. *You who answer prayer, to you all people will come.* (Psalm 65:2, NIV). For both days, I treated them to breakfast at McDonald's and again McDonald's for lunch, the day before, and the deli on Friday. Both days went smoothly and were fun-filled.

After moving in with my parents while my home is still under renovation, my weight continued to creep up on me. I came to the realization I could not do it on my own. As a result, I decided to seek help though LA Weight Loss. At this point in my life, I needed someone to coach me instead of going to weekly weigh-ins and attending group sessions. LA Weight Loss provided me with individual counseling and accountability. My first week, I lost 6 pounds and climbing. *The motivators you find should be specific to you and make you want something positive for yourself. Instead of 'I don't want to die, choose a statement of life' if I quit smoking, I'll have a good, long life.* (Livestrong.com) My motivator statement is *"If I lose weight, I will live a healthier life.*

I am so grateful I have finally uncovered what will work and taking the steps to gain control of my life. I understand how my thoughts have contributed to my weight gain and take daily steps to create a plan of action for myself. I am tired of living with this weight and want something new and something better for myself.

You must fully believe the fact that you are capable of losing weight, although the attempts which have been made so far have not been successful, as of yet. You definitely can move in the direction of losing weight, and keeping it off. In addition to applying positive thinking in terms of what will work for you in your weight loss efforts, it boils down to calories eaten versus calories burned and changing your eating and exercise patterns.

When I return to my home, I will continue my studies in pursuing a certification as a Nutrition and Wellness Consultant as I carry on my journey in losing weight, so I will be able to motivate and encourage others. Not only will I have the knowledge but also the personal experience giving me the tools to help someone else with their weight challenges. God is awesome! Finding my motivation through Him has provided me encouragement, guidance and three opportunities: (1) to lose weight; (2) another career/business opportunity; and (3) the ability to help others. *And we know that in all things God works for the good of those who love him, who have been called according to his purpose.* (Romans 8:28, NIV)

May you find the strength in God to overcome your challenges and move forward in your life.

Resources
Livestrong Foundation
www.livestrong.com

American Fitness Professionals & Associates (AFPA)
www.afpafitness.com (800) 494-7782

To purchase multiple copies of this book contact:
info@empoweringyoursuccessllc.com
www.empoweringyoursuccessllc.com

Empowering Your Success, LLC
(609) 851-8036

ABOUT THE AUTHOR

Sonja Senhouse Wilson (SSW)

Sonja Senhouse Wilson is President and CEO of Break Through Development Group (BTDG), an organization that seeks to empower women emotionally, spiritually and physically by discussing and addressing issues that affect women in their personal and professional daily lives.

For the past three years BTDG has been charged with the mission to free women from low self image and improve heighten self respect. BTDG has achieved this by speaking, teaching and training in the areas of self esteem, prayer life and self image. BTDG has been invited to speak in New York, New Jersey, Connecticut and Oklahoma on issues affecting women.

SSW was born in Trinidad, West Indies and raised in the United States. She is a graduate of College of Mt. Saint Vincent where she received a dual Bachelor of Arts degree in Sociology/Communications Arts while she trained in Social Work. Social Work is where she developed an understanding of and a love for women of all cultures. She is a candidate for her MBA in marketing at Wagner College. SSW has traveled the world as a professional model and has graced the pages of Vogue, Cosmopolitan, Seventeen, and Essence and Ebony magazines. She has also been featured in many ad campaigns such as L'Oreal Cosmetics and Avon.

SSW is a member of The Professional Woman Network (PWN). SSW holds membership in other professional organizations such as National Professional Executive Woman (NAFE). She is active within her church and community and serves as a role model for children and youth.

Contact:
Break Through Development Group
P.O. Box 9306
Elizabeth, New Jersey 07202
(908) 294-2465
SonjaWilson3@aim.com

TWENTY

LIFE OF GRACE... TOUCH OF GOD

By Sonja Wilson

INSPIRING AND FASCINATING
"No, there must be some mistake," I thought in my head as I looked at the nurse with bloodshot eyes, an earsplitting headache and a pounding heartbeat that felt like it would burst out of my chest at any second. How does a vibrant, healthy woman in her early forties deal with news from a routine colonoscopy test that showed positive for cancer? As the doctor, yelled across the room, "You have colon cancer," I laid motionless with tears rolling down my cheeks thinking I was given a death sentence. Too dazed to fully comprehend what was being

said, I swallowed hard and swore to face whatever was to come with faith, determination and grace. Flashing before my eyes were the many Sundays that I attended church service with my family. Many of the messages I remembered revolved around faith and trust in God. Was my faith being tested? More importantly for me was the question of grace. Oftentimes, I had heard the quote, "my grace is sufficient for you, for power is perfected in weakness." (2 Corinthian 12:9) What does this really mean? Grace as defined by Webster's Dictionary means a favor rendered voluntarily, temporary immunity or exemption, divine love and protection bestowed freely on human beings, protection or sanctification by the favor of God and an excellence or power granted by God.

Two weeks later I elected to have a left hemi colectomy performed after days of running back and forth for virtual colonoscopy, CT scan, PET scan and consultations with my internist and the surgeon who was going to perform my surgery. Simply put, I was admitted to the hospital to have a colon resection to remove the carcinoma. I didn't know what to expect as I was wheeled to the operating room but I had put all my faith in God. There was a single metal bed located in the center of the room next to a poorly hidden tray of all sorts of scary looking instruments covered by a single white cloth, which were unfortunately going to be used on me. Clad in a stylish hospital gown accessorized with faith and bravery, I was soon to emerge cancer free. I silently recited a hymn that I loved singing. "All I want to do is love you, All I want to do is love you, All I want to do is worship you, All I want to do is lay here right at your feet, As I lift my hands to heaven, Let your fire fall down on me, Rekindle the fire within me, Lord once again." I took a quick second to reflect on the faithfulness of God and allowed the anesthesiologist to guide me into a deep sleep. As I took a deep breadth, I heard a still small voice say to me, "don't fear any longer, only believe." Was this God's grace working in my life?

Barely coherent, still groggy from the anesthesia I opened my eyes slowly adjusting to the light after the four - hour surgery to see Dr. S and my family hovered over me amazed at the success of the invasive operation. The first words, I uttered was,"Dr S. did you get it all." He responded, "I got it all" kissed me on the forehead and said "you are going to recovery now. I will see you in the morning." I am convinced God's grace is His love turned inside out. Grace is the active expression of God's love. God's love is the root of grace. We are in a continuous process of experiencing more and more of God's grace when we face challenges. Our hindrances, disappointments and failures can entrap us to feel unloved, rejected, abandoned and angry but it is in these dark moments we must reflect on God's love, God's power and trust Him.

Although my surgery was a success, it was still not enough for my prognosis. The surgical pathology report showed that I was at Stage 3 and there was metastatic carcinoma in 10 out 0f 24 lymph nodes. Electing to have a colon resection, I thought I opted out of chemotherapy treatments.

My team of doctors advised that I had to have a very, aggressive treatment plan. I was concerned, apprehensive and scared Chemotherapy was not an option for me. With much resistance I sought counsel from one of the top oncologist on the East Coast. When I met Dr. A I knew instantly, I was in the palm of God's hands. He spoke softly and compassionately, "God is with you. I want a lifetime cure for you. You are at Stage 3, why settle for a 60-75% survival rate without chemo as opposed to a 90% rate with chemo." Dr. A advised chemo affects everyone differently and wanted me to speak with a patient that was already in treatment for colon cancer. We walked out of his office and into the treatment room. The room was cool and sterile. There were eight burgundy colored leather oversized recliners arranged in a circle. In the chemo suite was a large TV and lots of magazines for eating healthy. I saw patients with their own personal blankets, pillows, portable CD players, headsets and books. I assumed they wanted to distract themselves from the unpleasantness of treatment. "There is my girl" I heard Dr. A say. I spotted Fran by her captivating smile. Fran was sitting next to the window with the IV in her left arm doing knitting. Dr. A introduced us and told Fran I was a bit scared and I would be starting treatment soon. Little did I know she was battling for her life and would die three months later. Her colon cancer had metastases and spread to her liver. She was so beautiful and friendly. She confided to me that she was at Stage 4 and she had a family history of all types of cancer. I started to cry. She smiled and said, "don't be scared, don't cry you will be ok and you will not lose your hair." I found out that only 5% of colon cancer patients lose their hair. I grinned from ear to ear and squared my shoulders believing I can conquer anything.

Although Dr. A spoke English, it sounded like another language, the treatment cycle, the names of the medications, the possible side effects and all the other information was way too much for me to absorb. Oh God why do I have to have this poison going into my body. A chemo cocktail of five different drugs given to me intravenously every two weeks for a continuous 48 hour period of time over a twelve cycle period. That's equivalent to six months of torture but every-time I went for my round of treatment, I heard that still small voice again and again say, "don't fear any longer only believe."

God's love cannot be measured. He loves us unconditionally as noted in (John 3:16) "For God so loved the world that He gave His only begotten son, that whoever believes in Him should not perish but have eternal life."

We are God's greatest creation. Job knew this all too well. Job acknowledged that, "the spirit of God has made me. And the breath of the Almighty gives me life." (Job 33:4) God's spirit leads us and His grace will keep and sustains us. We like Job can and will be able to go through incredible trials because of God's grace.

God's grace was manifested in my life as I embraced His guidance by believing His holy word and allowing Him to fill me with His spirit so I could endure the pain and suffering of chemotherapy treatments.

It doesn't matter that I was a former model, a fashionista and hold an MBA. Neither good looks nor power nor popularity nor pleasure seeking can fill the God inspired desire to know him intimately. The void in our lives can only be filled with His grace and love.

To ensure that I could handle the powerful chemo cocktail I was receiving, I had to have a complete blood count prior to my bi-weekly treatments. The CBC was used to measure changes in three types of cells in my blood and was used as a standard baseline. My red and white blood cells had to meet those standards. Thank God, I met the baseline every time and I did not miss one round of my treatment. I would say that is God's grace.

It is only through our trials and our sufferings that we come in touch with His grace. It is when we feel the most distressed and our struggles seem unbearable it is then that the Lord's grace and kindness is revealed. Do you know that in failure or success, God's love and grace is always the same? In (John 9:2) Jesus and His disciples were passing through Jerusalem. They came upon a man who had been blind from birth. The disciples asked, "Who sinned, this man or his parents, that he should be born blind?" We might wonder the same thing also. We often think that illness or troubles are a sign of God's judgment. There was no question in the disciples' minds that someone had sinned; it was just a matter of who.

You see there are so many emotions involved in our situations when we experience challenges that we fear to verbalize the frustration caused from having no clear-cut answer and this can threaten our faith in the foundation of what we believe about God and His Goodness. Grace is unmerited favor. Jesus replied to his disciples and said," it was neither that this man sinned nor his parents." So could it be that illnesses and trouble come that the works of God might be displayed. This is His Grace. I am not fooled. God always knows what's going on in our lives and it has a purpose. We may be wounded but not scared, bruised but not defeated.

STAYING POSITIVE

How could I experience the grace of God if I didn't have trials? I understand the chapter of my battle with colon cancer because God blessed me through the entire struggle. He was with me and I was covered by His grace.

God is gracious, even when we are preoccupied with wrestling day after day with the same temptation, the same feeling of doubt and the same distractions. God's grace will sustain us. His grace is bestowed upon us in spite of ourselves.

I was hysterical when I learned of Fran's passing. I came to treatment and asked for Fran. We rarely saw each other after our first meeting but I knew she was scheduled to come in on Wednesdays. I was really looking forward to spending the standard six hours at treatment with Fran. We had so much to catch up on. The family, make-up tips, and places we traveled and other small talk about our health issues. I asked my oncology nurse was Fran coming in and she whispered to me that Fran was no longer with us. I cried throughout my entire intravenous infusion. There was that still small voice again. "Don't fear any longer only believe."

I had gone through six rounds of chemo. Three months was enough. I asked my oncologist to release me from treatment but he wouldn't. I believed that God had done a miracle in my life. Why did I need to continue having medication travel through my body zapping cancer cells and affecting my normal cells?

Ok, I decided to endure the duration of my twelve-cycle plan. I was going to be an advocate for a positive attitude and outcome. I tipped the fashion meter and I encouraged my co-workers to seek preventive care. Out of ten co-workers who followed my advice, one was diagnosed with breast cancer, two had benign tumors and one had a hole in the colon. I came to treatments dressed like I was ready to step on the runway for the famous fashion designers I once worked for. I wore a big smile and made a commitment to encourage the patients I was having treatment with. I was the youngest patient in my group. They were all in their late 50's, 60's, 70's and even 80's. I brought inspirational cards, bookmarks, and trays of sandwiches, coffee, water and pastries every time I came to treatment. We were on a team and we were going to win. I could tell you about Marjorie who was in remission for years when her cancer resurfaced. She was sitting next to me telling me her story. She said to me, "I am so scared, I have to have another operation tomorrow." I said to her " you'll be ok, I will be praying for you. Don't fear any longer only believe. When you open your eyes from your operation know that I did pray for you. Just believe the doctors will find no more cancer." Well, weeks later I saw Marjorie. She told me she had been looking for me because the doctors found nothing and she didn't have to continue treatment. She made it a point to tell me it was my encouragement that brought her through. Really it was God's grace through me. There are countless stories. Dennis and Paul, two elderly gentlemen were so depressed and fatigued from treatment. I helped them remember the times when they were young and energetic by encouraging them to express themselves. I listened tirelessly. That was God's grace.

It was May 2009 when I finished my last round of chemotherapy. I have been cancer free since then. I get a blood test every four months to ensure that there are no cancer markers in my body. I have gotten my routine colonoscopy, Pet Scan & CT Scan. All have resulted with a negative showing of cancer. Praise God!

GIVING THANKS

I am a walking, living testimony of God's grace. My desire for spiritual growth has intensified since this experience. The emotional and physical pain was unbearable and without God's touch throughout this experience, I would not have made it.

My surgery and chemotherapy treatments wasn't only a test of my physical limits but a test of my ability to deal with stress and the many challenges that life would throw my way. The experience although traumatic and frightening allowed me to realize that the pressures of everyday life are nothing in comparison to dealing with the scare of the BIG C=CANCER. I no longer ponder the trivialities of life; I focus on the big picture. I desire the joy of the Lord because it is my strength. I am reminded by Habakkuk 2:4 that "the righteous will live by His faith."

I am grateful and truly appreciate the gift of my life. My newfound love of life started with my overcoming my bout with cancer. This love of life continues to be fuel by the grace of God through my pursuit of excellence in all that I do, volunteerism, my love of culture, my love of adventure and my commitment to celebrate life and share hope with others.

SHARING HOPE

God revealed His grace to me by showing me
He is:
MY El Shaddai-God Almighty
MY Adonai-Lord and Master
MY Rophe-Healer
MY NIssi-His Banner
MY Tsuri-Rock
MY Roi-Shepherd
MY Tsidqenu-Righteousness
MY Shalom-Peace
MY Jireh-Provider
MY Abba-Father
MY Melek-King
MY Shammah-The Lord is there

God is love and He will give you wisdom in times of difficult decisions. He will encourage us in times of despair. He will strengthens us when we feel like giving up. He will keep us and we will be victorious. That is Grace.

ABOUT THE AUTHOR

DaNita L. Greene, CPC, ELIMP

DaNita L. Greene currently resides in the Southern Region of New Jersey and works as an Office Manager for a non-profit organization. She is the mother of an adult daughter, Nafeesah Green, whom she is awesomely proud of and adores. On June 2, 2007 DaNita heard the voice of GOD, and learned she was the "mouth-piece" of GOD and through her speaking and writing she would reveal to others "what thus saith the LORD". This revelation truly surprised her but brought much light and understanding to her great desire to always go deeper in her relationship and knowledge of GOD; as well as her love for reading and books. DaNita is a Certified Professional Development Coach & Energy Leadership Index Master Practitioner (Institute for Professional Excellence in Coaching - iPEC); and certified in Women's Issues & Diversity Training (Professional Woman's Network - PWN) and member. To date she has co-authored four (4) books which includes her most recent, "The Power of God" Book and 2013 Daily Devotional. "The Power of God" is the first installment in a Christian series published by the Professional Women's Network and will be available by Christmas 2012.

DaNita is a member of True Servant Worship & Praise Church in Hamilton, New Jersey, where Bishop E.E. Jenkins is Senior Pastor. She serves on the council of the HEELS Women's Ministry, which stands for Helping, Encouraging, Esteeming & Lifting Sisters. One of her greatest missions is to bring to fruition the ministry & coaching business GOD placed on the inside of her, to Empower, Motivate & Inspire Women from the Inside-out.

Contact:
For inquiries, you may contact DaNita via e-mail at www.destinyseekers22@gmail.com; and she can also be found on Facebook & followed on Twitter.

TWENTY-ONE

THE POWER OF 3'S

By DaNita L. Greene

T HE POWER OF 3'S

Power – having great strength or power (adj.); physical force or strength (noun); active power is that which moves the body; power may exist without exertion. We have power to speak when we are silent. (Merriam-Webster Learner's Dictionary and the KJV Dictionary)

The number **3** is GOD's number for divinity, deity, completeness, perfection... (Wiki)

In the beginning, GOD created us in HIS image and likeness, proof is in *Genesis 1:26* - "Then GOD said, let us make man in our image, according to our likeness". The words **us** and **our** were used because in the beginning was The Father, The Son (JESUS) & The Holy Spirit (aka The Holy Ghost). This is the **Trinity**-Head, **GOD The Father, GOD The Son and GOD The Holy Spirit**, all divinely existing as **three** individual entities and at the same time, all divinely one. In the Bible (NKJV), in the book of *Colossians 2:9*, it says "For in

HIM dwells all the fullness of the GOD-Head Bodily;" The "fullness" was manifested visibly in Christ, and is communicated by the Holy Spirit, for it is a fullness of which we receive by HIS mighty **Power** (The Bible Study Website). *John 1:15* says "And of HIS fullness we have all received, and Grace for Grace."

The Spirit of GOD is **Omniscient**, HE knows everything, HE is **Omnipresent**, HE is everywhere and HE is **Omnipotent**, HE is all **Power** and all authority. These Divine attributes are **3**-fold. **Power** is an action word that's very significant to GOD. It is by HIS **Power** moving, that HE created the Heavens and the Earth, it is by HIS **Power** moving, every living creature upon the earth was created and it is by HIS **Power** we move and have our being. **There is Power in 3's.**

Adam and Eve were first created as Spirit-Beings, so our original state of being is Spirit. It was only after they disobeyed GOD and ate from the Tree of the Knowledge of Good and Evil did they fall from Grace and become human-beings. It was at this time they realized their nakedness and wanted to cover (clothe) themselves in shame from GOD. The whole dynamics of their relationship with GOD had been changed by this one act of disobedience. Because of sin, in order for them to co-exist with GOD upon the earth it had to be in the form of Sprit, Soul and Body. We are **Spirit**, we have a **Soul** and we live in a **Body**, we are Spirit-beings having a natural experience upon the earth. This is the **three**-fold nature of man, Spirit, and Soul, and Body, the man consisting of neither separately, but of the whole **three** together (The Bible Study Website).

We can clearly see GOD's Glorified **Power of 3's** manifest and Bless the lives of believers through-out biblical times. The 3 Hebrew boys (*Daniel 3:8-30*), **Shadrach**, **Meshach** and **Abed-Nego** were thrown into the fiery-furnace because they refused to obey the decree of King Nebuchadnezzar to worship the gold image. They were bound and cast into the midst of the burning fiery furnace. But because of their strong Faith and belief in GOD, HE showed-up in their immediate circumstances.

Their Faith was magnified by **3** because the Bible (NKJV) says in *Matthew 18:20*, "For where 2 or **3** are **gathered together** in my Name, I AM there in the midst of them." That is why when King Nebuchadnezzar looked into the furnace he saw not **3** but 4 men loose, walking in the midst of the fire. The Son of GOD/Angel of GOD showed-up in the midst of their circumstances to deliver them out of the fire untouched, not even the smell of fire was upon them. After witnessing this Miracle, King Nebuchadnezzar began to Praise and Bless GOD, Shadrach, Meshach and Abed-Nego even got promoted by the King. **There is Power in 3's.**

Can I tell you that when we are facing challenges in our lives, if we **gather together** our thoughts and focus on the **Trinity**-Head, they will show-up in our situations and our circumstances the same as they did for the **3** Hebrew boys, and we too can emerge untouched, and healed without scars. HE will even use your adversary to elevate you, the Bible (NKJV) says in *Mark 12:36* "For David himself said by the Holy Spirit: 'The LORD said to my Lord, "Sit at my right hand, till I make your enemies your footstool." The footstool symbolizes elevation in our lives and in The Kingdom of GOD. The Spirit and **Power** of GOD is always in position to elevate us to the next level, but in order to receive elevation, we must walk in the consciousness of GOD so we are always in position to receive the things of GOD.

In the Bible (NKJV), in the book *Genesis (37-41)*, GOD Blessed Joseph with dreams of greatness and also the ability to interpret them. Joseph was the youngest of his brothers and his father's favorite. His father Israel gave him a coat of many colors and when his brothers saw this they became jealous. So when Joseph shared his dream with his brothers they began to greatly hate him. One day Joseph's brothers stripped him of his coat of many colors and sold him to the Ismaelites but they told their father that he had been killed.

A lot transpired in Joseph's life over the years after his brothers sold him, but I would like to focus on the time he was behind prison walls. GOD's favor was upon him as he began to interpret the dreams of the prisoners. He interpreted one prisoner's dream who was a **butler**, who dreamed of a vine and Joseph told him that the **3** branches represented **3** days. Another prisoner who was a **baker** came to Joseph and told him that he had a dream about **3** white baskets on his head. Joseph told him that the **3** baskets also represented **3** days. **Pharaoh** then sent for Joseph because he'd heard that he interpreted dreams and he had a dream for him to interpret. Once he shared his dream with Joseph and he interpreted it for him, it was pleasing to him. So he showed Joseph great favor and elevated and promoted him to rule over all the land of Egypt.

GOD never took his hand off Joseph, even when it seemed as if HE had. HE sent a **butler** who opened the door for him, HE sent a **baker** who prepared the way for him and HE sent a **Pharoah** who had the **power** and the finances to elevate him to his next level in life and in the Kingdom. GOD always prepares a way of escape for his people (*I Corinthians 10:13*). At times it may seem as if HE's forgotten, but HE's always working behind the scenes to walk us into our destiny. **There is Power in 3's.**

In the Bible (NKJV), in the book of Ruth, she (Ruth) convinced Naomi to allow her to continue to stay with her and move away with her, even after her husband, which was Naomi's son had died. In *Ruth 2:2*, Ruth **ask**ed Naomi, "Please let me go to the field, and glean heads of grain after him in whose sight I may find favor." And she said to her, "Go my daughter." Ruth began to glean in Boaz's field. Boaz was not only a wealthy relative of Naomi's but he was also a man of GOD. **Naomi** strategically guided **Ruth**'s steps into the path of **Boaz**, and he did notice her.

Ruth carefully followed the instructions of her mother-in-law Naomi, to **seek** out the attention of Boaz and he favored Ruth. Boaz wanted to take Ruth as his bride but because there was another relative in line before him, he had to go **knock** at his door first, to make sure he didn't want to marry Ruth. He was not interested in marrying Ruth, so Boaz and Ruth married and had a son Obed. Their union ushered in the genealogy of **Obed**, who is the father of **Jesse**, who was the father of **David**; this is **three** generations of greatness. *Matthew 7:7* says "**Ask**, and it will be given to you; **Seek**, and you will find; **Knock**, and it will be opened to you. **A**-Ask, **S**-Seek & **K**-Knock, Ruth **A**sked, Naomi showed her how to **S**eek and Boaz **K**nocked and the door was opened. **There is Power in 3's.**

In the Kingdom of GOD, there is a sowing and reaping season and this is called **Seed – Time & Harvest**. We are all seeds, and the way we live our lives are the way we sow them, we are sowing something into the atmosphere on a daily basis. In our lives, we are constantly reaping from the things we have sown, by our thoughts and the things we think, by our walk and the way we live and by our talk and the way we communicate with others. Just like when a farmer plants a **seed** into the ground, although he may not be able to see it, he knows that it is still in there. The farmer knows that there is a transformation that is taking place under the dirt with the seed and after a **time**, the crop will spring forth out of the ground and eventually in due season, it will produce a **harvest**.

In the Bible (NKJV), in the book of *Ecclesiastes 3:1*, it states "To everything there is a season, a time for every purpose under heaven and *Genesis 8:22* says "While the Earth remains, **Seed-time** and **harvest**, Cold and heat, Winter and summer, and day and night Shall not cease." **There is Power in 3's.**

GOD created marriage and in the sanctity of marriage, between a man and woman, there is an order of headship that is to be followed. **JESUS** is the Head of the Church and the husband is subject to HIM, the **Husband** is the head of the family and the **Wife** is subject to him. This is GODs divine order, it doesn't mean anyone is greater nor less than another, this order has been put in place so that we could learn how to respect authority. When this order is not in place, it allows the enemy access and/or lead-way to enter into the marriage, to attempt to disrupt the covenant made between GOD, the husband, and the wife. In the Bible (NKJV), in the book of *Ecclesiastes 4:12*, it says "A person standing alone can be attacked and defeated, but two can stand back-to-back and conquer. **Three** are even better, for a **triple** braided cord is not easily broken." **There is Power in 3's.**

With **Salvation** comes the **Baptism of Water** and the **Baptism of the Holy Spirit** (fire). We receive Salvation by repenting, which means turning away from of our sins, believing in our hearts and confessing with our mouths that JESUS CHRIST is LORD. The Water Baptism is the going-down in the water, burying the old-man (ways) and coming-up out of the water, the resurrection of the new-man (ways). Water is cleansing, and the going down in water and coming up out of it symbolizes Christ being buried and resurrected on the **third** day.

The Holy Spirit baptizes us supernaturally in our heavenly language, which creates an open portal that gives us the ability to communicate directly with The Father. The Holy Spirit also em**power**s us with supernatural **power** and ability to choose to operate in the world more in the Spirit and less in the flesh. HE is our comforter, our protector, and our guide, and HE knows All things. (*Romans 10:10* – "For with the heart one believes unto righteousness, and with the mouth confession is made unto salvation." *Matthew 3:11*, it says "I indeed baptize you with water unto repentance, but HE who is coming after me is mightier than I, whose sandals I am not worthy to carry. HE will baptize you with the Holy Spirit and fire." **There is power in 3's.**

When JESUS was crucified on the Cross, HE died for ALL of our sins; HE went to hell and served time for our sins, the sins of the world, for **three (3)** whole days. Oh but GOD, on that **third** day, HE was raised-up from the dead. HE had taken the keys of Heaven and hell back from the enemy, which was given to him in the beginning by Adam and Eve, when they sinned. HE was resurrected from the dead with All **Power** in HIS hands on the **third** day. This divine sacrifice took place because GOD so loved the world, that HE gave HIS only begotten Son (*John 3:*16). What are you willing to sacrifice for the sake of Love today? In the Bible (NKJV), in the book of *Luke 18:33*, it says "They will scourge HIM and kill HIM. And the **third** day HE will rise again;" and in the book of *Matthew 16:19*, it says, "And I will give you the keys of the Kingdom of Heaven, and whatever you bind on Earth will be bound in Heaven, and whatever you loose on Earth will be loosed in Heaven"; and in the book of *Revelations 1:18*, it says "I AM HE who lives, and was dead and behold, I AM alive forevermore. Amen. And I have the keys of hades and of death." **There is Power in 3's.**

*I Pray This Book Em**power**s You To Supernaturally Encounter The Father, The Son & The Holy Spirit In A Way Like Never Before, In The Mighty Name Of Jesus – Amen & Amen

*"EM**POWER**ING QUOTES & AFFIRMATIONS"*

*Meditate To Empower Yourself While On The Path To Your Destiny

❖ God's Grace Provokes An Attitude of Gratitude

❖ God Favors Me

❖ Faith Not Only Pleases God, It Moves The Hand Of God

❖ God Takes Great Pleasure In Prospering Me, For It Is He Who Gives Me Power To Get Wealth (*Deuteronomy 8:18*)

❖ God You Created On Purpose & With Purpose

❖ Today I Expect The Promises Of God To Manifest In My Life

❖ In Life We Are Forever Student and Teacher

❖ Faith Is Confidence In God & Fear Is Confidence In The Enemy

❖ With God's Vision Comes His Provision

❖ God Does All Things Well & You Are Proof Of It

❖ Faith Is An Action Word, Faith Without Works Is Dead

❖ God's Word Is Incorruptible Seed, Plant It In Your Heart

❖ Poverty Is The Enemy To God's Prosperity

❖ There Is **Power** In God's Word... Speak It & Believe It

❖ You Are Divinely Orchestrated By The Creator.... Compare Yourself To No One

❖ According To Your Faith Be It Unto You... (*Matthew 9:29*)

❖ The Lord Has Established His Throne In Heaven And His Kingdom Rules Over ALL.... (*Psalm 103:19*)

❖ Grace & Mercy, The Angels That Follow You All The Days Of Your Life

ABOUT THE AUTHOR

SHARON MCWILLIAMS

Having "accidentally" stumbled upon a miraculous second journey during her baby boomer life, Sharon McWilliams traveled into her very own Grand Wise Woman adventures, with the grand desire to use the power of an elder wise woman to make a difference in the lives of others, to selfishly focus on creating a peaceful healthy planet for her children and her grandchildren.

She took the journey of heart and soul, exploring deeply, expanding her courage muscles to continuously take just one more step. Each step of that journey pulled her deeper within, finding her own wise woman compassionate soul with natural healing and intuitive and creative abilities ready to reawaken. Sharon learned how to combine these God-given abilities with her Grand Wise Woman years of experience, honing them into the gentle wisdom place as a wise woman elder to use and share in her later years as a master Wise Woman!

Sharon is a speaker/performer, author, singer/songwriter, educator, certified master retreat coach, life & woman's empowerment coach and Reiki Master-Teacher. She is the PRG facilitator for *A Mother's Guide to Self-Renewal* in Kentucky and surrounding areas. A co-creator with wise women, Sharon shares her discoveries with you in her multifaceted experiential retreats and programs known as the Wise WomanSoul Grace in Action!

Sharon takes you on the journey of yourself with your life stories into safe retreat surroundings using compassionate playfulness. She shows you how to rediscover your natural intuition and your natural healing abilities, something all wise women have! Sharon has you rebuild and refill your wise woman toolkit, the one you forgot you had. Believe it or not, you were not put here on this planet without those wise woman tools!

Books:
Celebration of Life Inspiration for Women
Releasing Strongholds Letting Go of What's Holding You Back
The Power of a Woman Embracing the Woman Within
The Power of Change Reinventing Yourself at Any Age
Daddy, I Remember Hope and Healing for Families of Alzheimer's
Freeing Godiva A Woman's Journey of Self-Empowerment!
CSI Courageous Stories of Inspiration
The Power of God
The Power of God Daily Devotional 2013

Expertise:
Life, Retreat and Wellness Coaching for Women
Women and Empowerment
Personal Exploration for Women
Retreats for Wise Women
Essence Journaling
Women and their Stories
Sound Healing with Solfeggio Tuning Forks
Stress Reduction for Women
Mother's and Self-Care

Seminars and Topics offered (also in retreat style):
Releasing Strongholds Letting Go of What's Holding You Back
The Power of Change Reinventing Yourself, Wise Woman!
The Power of a Woman
The Gift of Your Stories: Your Stories are Your Music on the Journey of your Life

Wise Woman Essence Journaling
The Labyrinth Within
Retreating: the how's and why's and when's
Journaling: The Power of Presence in Writing
Visualization: The True Self Discovery Process
Intuition and the Wise Woman

Contact:
The Gift
PO Box 941
Pewee Valley, KY 40056
Telephone: 502.541.3106
Email: sharon@wisewomansoul.com
Fax: 502.742.1977
Website: www.wisewomansoul.com
Blog: http://wisewomanessence.com

TWENTY-TWO

THE SOFTER SIDE OF GOD

By Sharon McWilliams

Take a breath
Close your eyes
Come with me....

How is it that we wise women like to complicate our lives? How is it that we think there is so much more we have to do to reach God? How is it we wise women think we are not enough to do that? What have we forgotten?

To a place
Deep inside
Where you're free....

Where is that place? Where do we learn there is a path to freedom?

Where do we find peace and joy and honor for ourselves?

What do we need to remember?

> *There's a Wonder there you'll see---*
> *A special gift*
> *The secret key...*

When do we discover there is a gentler way to living our lives? When do we find that we don't have to 'work it 'til we drop'? When do we find we don't have to be the man to get the job done? When do we finally realize that the feminine side of God is the most powerful place to spend time? When do we understand that living our lives, every moment of our lives, starts from a softer place? When do we know that we as wise women were actually *meant* to live life from a gentler, kinder place----a place that *honors* us and *how* we are meant to live our lives.

> *Take a breath*
> *Close your eyes*
> *Come with me.*

So many of us have had to step up to the plate and take major steps for ourselves, for our babies, for safety and protection, caretaking, financial support, etc. And many times in doing so we have had to make decisions that resorted in hard, hurtful steps, unknown to us at the time. Many of us have tried it solo. Many of us have had to put on the man's shoes and pants and get out there in the 'hard-at-it' work field. Many of us have fallen flat on our faces only to get back up and start again, determined not to fail.

Resilience is an energy that lies in that soft place, waiting to be used gently. Take a breath right now with me...a deep breath down through your heart to your belly. Place one hand on your heart and the other on your soft belly, connecting these two brings you to your 'soft' place. Breathe here deeply, gently, repeating until you become calm. You may have to practice over and over for a little while until you can slide into that 'calm'. You may question, "When do I have time for this?" It is a valid question to be considered as you live that question, carving out tiny pieces of time and space:

- before bedtime,

- when you set down to a meal or TV,

- before you rise in the morning,

- before your 10 minute power nap,

- instead of your 10 minute power nap,

- when you are waiting for your children from their lessons,

- when you are waiting in traffic.

As you can see, there are many moments you can create to practice your 'calm' breath in that soft place.

Take a breath
Close your eyes
Come with me...

You are now finding yourself beginning to live from the softer side of God. It's called the 'Feminine'. Anderson and Hopkins share this with their book, *The Feminine Face of God*. The Bible calls it 'Sofia' or 'Wisdom'. The Talmud calls it 'Shekinah'. Some call it the Divine Feminine. It is your soft place, your Sacred Space. It is that calm quiet place of Knowing, of Wisdom. It is where you live your life, where you create each moment consciously, if you so choose. It is where Grace remains. It is where your gifts and talents lie with all the beautiful essence of a wise woman. Of what does that essence consist?

Feel that sweet
Calm within,
Simply be...

Take a look at these qualities, the energies that flow in and radiate out of that calm place where the essence of the Feminine...your Divine Feminine Self --- rests:

Peace   Love   Joy
Healing   Forgiveness   Understanding   Wisdom
Harmony   Balance
Prosperity   Abundance
Gratitude
Grace

All wrapped in compassionate playfulness...

These vibrational energies of your wise woman essence penetrate deep into your soul where a beautiful inner peace, charged with courage, strength and the healing power of the Divine Feminine rests. This essence steeps magnificently in the earthy sensuality of Mother Earth and the ethereal sweetness of Heaven, forming the remembrances of the beauty of the Wise WomanSoul *(my word)*, qualities so long forgotten. This essence brings out the 'healer, lightworker, wayshower, peacemaker, channel of grace' qualities of the Wise Woman. She takes the walk of the labyrinth deep into her soul and rests in that center where compassionate playfulness occupies her heart and soul as she breathes in the splendor of her wise woman essence. The Wise WomanSoul is the epitome of Heaven and Earth, Heaven on Earth--- grace in action.

Here's your light
For all to see
Where Grace abides
Eternally…

Wow! You may be thinking---surely she is not speaking about me. Lots of phrasing that appears ideological---maybe even a little nonsensical with a touch of the mystical? What do we do with that, especially since we, more than likely, do not live our day-to-day lives with thoughts about essence, the soul, or what it takes to be a wise woman? We have programmed ourselves right out of the beauty of who we are, ions ago. Proof of that is in the world around us. Take a look. What do you see? All around the planet, there is abuse and rape of the earth, women, children; constant fighting and war; starvation and too little water; major family dysfunction; terminal illnesses with cancer, and the lingering diseases like multiple sclerosis and fibromyalgia. Public education still misses the boat. Healthcare costs are outrageous. Many of us work two jobs. Television and computers raise our children. And how many single mothers are there these days? And how much support are they receiving? I am sure you have many of your own thoughts that you could add here. So…

> *Take a breath*
> *Close your eyes*
> *Come with me…*

How can we and how do we change the absurdities and atrocities that have hung on for so very long? We can only begin with ourselves. We go to the calm place…the softer side of God --- that feminine face of God. We take back and reestablish what is rightfully ours and who we are as Wise WomanSouls…as 'grace in action'.

To begin with, you can't fill an already full glass. So we must begin a cleansing, an emptying, a letting go of some things that don't fit into the real definition of who we are. We can physically take action with drinking lots of water daily, eating healthier foods, getting the rest we need *on purpose*. We can journal our thoughts as to what we need to release, maybe tweak our schedules some, change little by little habits that hurt us. We can walk---not a marathon, but a gentle walk in nature---focusing on the beauty of Mother Earth instead of the thousand and one things we have to do when we get back, letting go of that audio book or jamming music with our headsets….just keeping it ever so simple.

> *Just let go*
> *Breathe again*
> *Soothe your soul*

I have always loved the quote by Martin Luther King Jr. where he speaks of his busy day ahead so he needs to spend more time on his knees. I read somewhere how that is a purposefully physical position of prayer for our bodies. I remember doing that before bedtime as a little girl. I still do it sometimes, keeping me safe in a beautiful humble soft place, that softer side so I can listen deep. But I want to share with you that for wise women like you and me....we don't have to do that unless we just want to. For our God-given make-up is so amazingly wonderful, that we *do* embody prayer naturally; upon reestablishing our wise woman beauty, we *are* walking prayers of grace in action. We still have our delightful personalities, traits, gifts, talents to use as tools for living in this world. The difference is we operate not from the outside of ourselves but from the inside, deep within. I call it 'the labyrinth within'. I've heard it called the 'well', where we quench our thirst.

- It's where we listen to the Whispers.

- It's where we hear Guidance.

- Is where we Know.

- It's where Wisdom rests.

- It's where the softer side of God resides.

- It's the Divine Feminine within.

- It's who we really are.

And, once we get that, once we understand, we can never go back--*never*. The old way is hurtful to our bodies and our souls and our children and our relationships. The softer side of God is a magnificence to celebrate quietly with gratitude, then move forward as we live our daily lives as grace, in action.

Touch your heart
Feel Love's Song
So you'll know...

A few years ago I attended my high school reunion; I was a teacher at that time. A good dear male friend of mine in the military smiled and winked and said he bet I was a 'soft' teacher, slightly derogatory. I laughed and got it...then shared with him my 'soft' approach. I shared with him a different viewing where 'soft' is not weakness, in fact more powerful than the usual forceful push of living from the outside. The author and scientist, David Hawkins, shares that information in his book *Power versus Force*.

Recently I was given the honor to present at an international woman's conference where I met the most gracious wise woman. Only a few months before had she lost her husband of many years. Yet, to be around her presence, to talk with her, to spend time with her, was a most calming peaceful place to be. She was grieving her loss, at the same time a caregiver for her ailing mother with Alzheimer's *and* a writer *and* author, too, in service to God *and* living her life. Such a powerful presence she is----the softer side of God reflecting from her beautiful spirit self. She brought all that she does from the deeper place---that calm place...that 'peace, be still' place, where she operates her life on a daily basis.

You see, the softer side of God is the place where Power originates. We get so confused with thinking and feel that that power lies somewhere out there, with someone else, at some other time. Not so, sweet Sister, not so.

> *God sings to you*
> *In every way*
> *Such Love*
> *Be mindful*
> *Everyday*

One of the loveliest gifts I have been given recently is discovering I didn't have to use the old rules anymore. I didn't have to work so hard. I didn't have to make that list and check it twice…never worked for me anyway. How many of you have made lists and still forgot something?

Now I am not saying I don't work and that you don't have to. We work diligently in service with honor and integrity, laced with patience and kindness---as best we can. We are human with lots of moments that don't come close; we do our best.

When I trained in Reiki, a beautiful soft, feminine energy work, I found the Reiki precepts so appropriate. Take a look at these:

> *Just for today, I will not be angry.*
> *Just for today, I will not worry.*
> *Just for today, I will be grateful.*
> *Just for today, I will do my work diligently.*
> *Just for today, I will be kind to everyone.*

Such simple tenets to focus on upon arising in the morning and at bedtime! Simplicity helps us stay focused. These are easy to memorize.

They can be printed out or as a screen on your computer desktop. I like these. They are not scary. And I can do my best to live this way.

So stop what you're doing in this moment. Take a breath of these precepts. Notice the gentle energy behind them....the softer side of God. Breathe in. Breathe out. Deeply.

These precepts also remind me of Miguel Ruiz's *Four Agreements*:

- Be impeccable with your word.

- Take nothing personally.

- Make no assumptions.

- Do your best everyday...(your best will be different everyday, depending on where you are at the moment)

I had memorized these a few years back. They calmed me. I shared them many times with friends and family members. The softer side of God is what you experience when you take these agreements to heart.

Again, take a moment to breathe in these agreements. Breathe in. Breathe out. Ever so gently. Deeply. Notice how kindness and nonjudgment seeps in. Notice the lightness you feel now. The softer side of God has a much sweeter flavor and it works with us better, similar to those newer mattresses that conform to the body as we move in comfort and support. Much, much better.

A Course in Miracles has many 'powerful' prayer affirmations that move me to the softer side of God. One of my favorites that carries a beautiful vibration is: '*I could choose peace instead of this.*' When I am struggling and pushing and in the world too much, breathing and whispering this small prayerful phrase to myself brings me to that calm, that softer side. I don't know about you; but I do much better work from this place than from the old 'hard at it!' I have observed many, many of my dear wise woman friends continue on the hard way, especially after age 50, only to end up with major stress, illness and loss --- heart-broken. I travelled there myself a few years ago.

Breathe into this beautiful 'soft' prayer now:
I could choose peace instead of this.

Just sit with this moment. Repeat and breathe deeply with your eyes closed. Relax into moment out of time.

One thing I need to clarify is this. Life is messy. Life hurts and laughs and cries in sorrow and in joy. Life is what it is, incoming and outgoing, no matter what. We, as wise women, have a choice in how we see our lives and how we live our stories out. We have a choice to live on the surface, forcing and pushing and beating ourselves up. We have a choice to live from deep within, as a prayer form, co-creating each moment with God, in the sacred space of the feminine energy, the softer side.

- You will find Trust there.

- You will find Safety.

- You will find Comfort.

- You will find Courage.

- You will find a Friend.

- You will also find Joy,

- Delight

- and Laughter

- and Loving Life Deeply!

You see---we, you and I, are powerhouses of the softer side. And once you find your soft spot, you won't want to return to the way of the sharp edges.

Take a breath
Close your eyes
Come with me.

So let's get started. Now that you have read all the above, here are some strategies, exercises with activities to get you moving into the softer side....that feminine sacred space just for you. Yes, (you know me by now,) you need your journal and a comfortable place to be, preferably outside in nature. Nature is very healing and uplifting, naturally! And, you need to stay hydrated. Doing breath work requires oxygen, which is in H2O! Sometimes I literally forget what is right in front of my face as I and all women are so giving away of our time, space and energy. Do your whole body a favor----drink up.

Activity One:

As you have been reading this chapter you may have noticed a verse flowing in and out about the breath: *"Take a Breath"* (© 2007 lyrics and melody Sharon McWilliams BMI). I received this simple song as my own mama was passing. She had always told me to slow down, Sharon, and take a breath. I finally did, honoring her sweet precious soul.

This activity is so easy yet the most powerful 'soft' gift you will ever receive. All you have to do is breathe. There are some parameters with this breathing.

1. Find a quiet spot, comforting and supportive, preferably in nature.

2. Sit straight and tall with feet on the ground, so spine is straight. Use a pillow(s) for support, a blanket for warmth if needed.

3. Relax into this pose, your neck but stay tall, your jaw, your shoulders, yours arms & hands, your belly, thighs, knees, feet & toes. Relax your eyes---soft gaze.

4. Take a gentle breath in through your nose all the way down through your heart to your belly.

5. Allow your belly to expand like a balloon slowly. Hold for just 4 seconds.

6. Allow your belly to deflate slowly as you exhale with a sigh.

7. Repeat this breath work 4 times.

8. Know this…the breath, a gentle calm naturally rebalances you.

What do you notice?

Activity Two:
This activity builds on the first one.

1. As you breathe in, focus on the breath. Let thoughts ramble past. Keep coming back to the breath.

2. Listen to your breath---the inhale, the exhale, the sighs---your aliveness

3. Now feel your breath--- with your whole body.

4. Imagine every pore, every cell breathing with you now.

5. Repeat this sequence 4 times.

6. Know this: Your whole body *really* is doing the breathing; time for practice.

What do you notice?

Activity Three:

This activity builds on the last two. You will need some extra time for this one...possibly even another day. Just make certain to do the first two activities in the same timeframe with this one.

1. Now that you are considerably calm and more focused, think of a dream you have or something you really want to happen.

2. Write down all the specifics----experience it on your journal paper with color, sounds, feelings, tastes, using descriptive words and phrases, maybe even cut out pics from magazines or photos...to collage in your journal. As you do this, pause and breathe as if you already have it, already live it, already are it.

What do you notice?

Activity Four:
This activity builds on the last three activities.

1. Review your dream that you have put in your journal. Pull in the experience of the senses with each part. Breathe into it just like you have previously learned, deeply and slowly 4 times.

2. Bring that experience into your body with your breath as you close your eyes and visualize it as a daily occurrence for you. See and imagine every wonderful nuance about it. Sense your day from the time you arise until you retire daily.

What do you notice?

What is there that is more important than the breath? Even the airline attendants share to put your oxygen mask on first, before that of your child. Even in childbirth are you taught to breathe for easing pain and for moving the energy to help that sweet baby arrive. What is there that is softer than the breath? What is there that doesn't charge for breathing? What is there in you that can take charge of your life with something so simple and God-given as this?

Move into the softer side of God, the softer side of your Divine Feminine, the softer side of your sweet self. Live your life from this place. Breathe out the old...breathe in the new. For **you** literally _are_ the Softer Side of God. You've just forgotten. So let's remember now:

Take a breath
The holy breath
Be still and know.

Sweet and strong, courageous and gentle…
Wise WomanSoul, **you** can do this.

Notes:

_____

_____

_____

_____

_____

_____

_____

_____

_____

_____

_____

_____

_____

_____

_____

_____

_____

_____

_____

_____

_____

_____

_____

_____

ABOUT THE AUTHOR

EVANGELIST BRENDA DENNIS

Evangelist Brenda Dennis was born in St Petersburg, FL. She is a servant of The Most High God, a mother, grandmother, poet, author and ordained minister. She is the founder/visionary of Brenda Denise Ministries and Empowered2Inspire and is a sought after conference speaker and workshop facilitator. She holds a degree in Communications/Journalism and has a certificate of completion from UCLA's Mass Media program. Brenda has also completed extensive studies in counseling and psychotherapy. In 2004 she was called into the ministry and was ordained as a Minister of the Gospel in 2009. In early 2010, Brenda inspired thousands of listeners on Praise 1590 radio station with Brenda's Biscuits & Butter; a daily word of scripture and encouragement. Brenda co-authored her 1st book; which was the anthology Victorious Living for Women. Her highly anticipated 2nd book **"Get Real With God & Get Real with Yourself!"** will be released in 2012. Her favorite quote was given to her by the Holy Spirit - "Meet a person where they are, and let the Holy Spirit deal with who they will become" Read about Brenda's incredible story of redemption & restoration at www.empowered2inspire.com.

Contact:
Twitter: User Name - 2Cor517
Facebook: Minister Brenda Dennis
Email: brendadeniseministries@gmail.com

TWENTY-THREE

TRANSPARENCY – THE KEY TO BREAKTHROUGH

By Rev. Brenda Dennis

We refuse to wear masks and play games. We don't maneuver and manipulate behind the scenes. And we don't twist God's Word to suit ourselves. Rather, we keep everything we do and say out in the open, the whole truth on display, so that those who want to can see and judge for themselves in the presence of God.
—2 Corinthians 4:2 (MSG)

Living behind a mask in these days and times has unfortunately for most, become a normal way of life. We attempt to measure up to society's standards. We try to fit into certain cliques; but continue experiencing rejection. Some of us have become so worn out and discouraged in our attempts therefore, we choose to stay complacent, instead of confronting the true issue at hand. It has become easier to settle than to sever! If you are basking in denial; look a little deeper. I pray this portion of the book will give you new insight and revelation that will cause you to begin to sever faulty perceptions. I pray that you may be set free from not only the battle in your mind, but also labels that have been attached to you due to the trials & tribulations of life. Or you may have self – medicated yourself for so long that you are numb to reality. Self medication does not only come in the form of medicine. It can come in the form of sex, illegal use of drugs, chocolate cake, or even having a humorous attitude can even be your medicine. For example, do you know someone who jokes about everything? I mean they are always joking and kidding around! Can you say – you know this person? Probably not! This is to camouflage the real so that the issues will not be revealed.

B's Biscuit – God desires to know you inwardly

The more honest you become with yourself, the more honest you will be with God. It is in transparency, that true intimacy is found.

Becoming transparent requires you to embark on a journey of self -discovery. You will travel though life experiences and circumstances that is designed to bring forth your authentic self. Authentic means genuine and original, as opposed to being a fake or reproduction. Just as a seed when planted into the ground remains dormant without the proper water, oxygen, and climate; your life will also remain dormant without the proper water (the word of God), oxygen, (the breath of God), and climate (positive environment) to become the best you that you can be! Starting today, allow yourself to come from behind the mask that covers your flaws and insecurities. Unfortunately, many of us spend many years in the mirror concealed…..or should I say disguised.

The journey isn't always easy

Psalm 40:1 says "I waited patiently for the Lord; and He inclined to me, and heard my cry.

God predestined me to live a victorious life before the foundation of the world. I was imputed righteousness because of what He did, not what I did. God knew the end from the beginning. He is Alpha & Omega. He just never told me about the transition in the middle. Fasten your seat belts as we take a turbulent journey down a middle lane of deception, defeat & destiny.

I was the perfect daughter; at least my parents thought so.

To my father, I could do no wrong. My mom was the best mother in the world! She was encouraging, and we spent a lot of mother and daughter time together. Being an only child afforded extra time to study, therefore I excelled in school. I recall when I was in third grade, I was selected to advance to fifth grade, but my mom declined that idea. I was spoiled, but I wasn't selfish. It brought joy to my heart to share everything I had. (except mom's homemade banana pudding) Every summer; after vacation bible school was over, I was given the privilege of inviting a friend to share my family vacation. I loved and enjoyed my childhood.

Moment of Thought: What feelings emerge as you think of your childhood?

As I became a teenager, I began to observe my parents arguing and the perfect world that I knew seemed to crumble. After graduation, I dated, became engaged and eventually married. It was a form of escapism. During this time, hidden feelings of lesbianism began to emerge. I had a very open relationship with my mom, yet I never discussed it with her until many years later. During the early years of my marriage, I was dying on the inside. The conflict was excruciating. Dealing and using drugs was my way to escape. I started smoking marijuana, snorting cocaine and then finally smoking crack. There were times when I would smoke $500 crack a day! Amazingly I was never addicted. I wasn't doing it to get high. I was doing it to feel numb. What most people don't understand is when a person turns to drugs, most of the time they are doing it to survive, to stay above the water; even though the outside world only see a 'druggie'.

Trying to escape again; I would find myself in drug holes and crack houses. Not because I had to, but I was to embarrassed to allow my parents see me living a reckless life. There was still a flicker of light within me that knew this was not the end. The years of being raised with a strong foundation was still there. The girl who had everything is now bumming on the streets with the homeless to understand life from a non materialistic point of view. Ironically, I still chose to feed the hungry and buy toys for children whose parents were strung out on drugs. I also met people who actually chose to be homeless. They were beautiful people and they appreciated life. Some, actually chose to be homeless, a decision to let go of the weights of the world. The world that I knew, the world I was raised in appeared to be fabricated. Was I the only one looking through rose colored glasses? What happened to my playground? Existing stepped in and Living stepped out.

Moment of Thought: Was there ever a time in your life where you felt as if you were just existing? Can you reflect back or look deeper and see more to be thankful for?

The only thing keeping me alive was the memories in my heart, yet they seemed so distant. There was one thing that was close; the 23rd Psalm. My mom read it to me nightly. With that said, I knew who my Shepherd was and in a chaotic world that consisted of weeds that seemed to choke the life out of me, He was the only one who could provide still waters and green pastures. In the midst of a world surrounded by crime, drugs, homelessness, and sexual sin; I began declaring that I was the righteousness of God and Satan had no authority over me. I was calling those things that were not as though they were. It definitely got worse before it got better starting with being held at gun point by a crack head. As he attempted to pull the trigger the second time, his eyes got as big as a pancake and he ran. I was told he was found dead 3 days later. Knowing what I know now, I was surrounded by protective angels. Psalms 91:11 (NIV) says "For He will command His angels concerning you to guard you in all your ways" The 2nd incident was a crack cocaine overdose. My body went numb and as I lay comatose and immobile, a bright light circled and embraced me. The next day, I awaken as if nothing happened. Grace stepped in and Mercy said no. Despite my low life living, mom never gave up on me. She and my best friend Bernice would come looking for me. My mom didn't care if it was a drug hole or a crack house. Nothing stopped her from finding me to let me know I was loved and that I could come home. She was saddened by the choices I made, but she never condemned or ridiculed me. She would always say 'God has a plan'. Only the unconditional love of God could be better. My prayer life intensified and I knew there was a better blueprint for my life. Jeremiah 29:11 (MSG) says "I know what I'm doing. I have it all planned out - plans to take care of you, not abandon you, plans to give you the future you hope for"

Stop! Take a moment and thank God for His faithfulness. Regardless of the situation, He has a Plan and it is always in effect!

While my spirit had a 16x20 blueprint, my mind and imagination was still stuck on 5x7. But I had a faith that spoke to everything, even though I physically saw nothing. I couldn't wait for my situation to become favorable; I just began to pray for a way out. God knew that I was tired and He gave me rest. 57 days in county jail. I found out I was pregnant and my husband ended up in prison. Miraculously, my son was born healthy without a trace of drugs in his system, even though I used drugs the first trimester of my pregnancy. In no way do I condone the use of drugs, alcohol or smoking while pregnant. I did not know I was pregnant. Without the grace of God, I don't know where I would be today or what deformed state my child, whom I call 'my angel' would be in. His grace is truly sufficient for every situation. I never went to counseling or any other treatment. I walked away from drugs and never looked back. Afterward, God began to open doors and I went back to college and received my degree in journalism. I won a writing contest and received a scholarship to attend UCLA for a summer internship in Mass Media, BUT I still was attracted to women. I returned home from California due to my parents' illness. I couldn't keep a job because my parents were constantly hospitalized. Finally, my father passed away. By this time I was dressing like a man. There was no abuse, no molestation, none of the circumstances that are associated with being gay. I even contemplated having a sex change because I felt like a boy trapped in a girl's body. I eventually had a nervous breakdown from the overwhelming responsibility of taking care of my mom, being a parent, dealing with my father's death, dealing with a stressful relationship & gender confusion. Panic attacks were occurring daily. I became suicidal and was admitted to a psychiatric hospital. I was diagnosed bipolar. They wanted to give me lithium, but I refused. I prescribed my therapy by writing poetry daily. The vision that was only 5x7 was now 8x10. I wrote poetry that spoke life; even in situations that appeared morbid and hopeless. If I could perceive it, I could receive it.

Reflection: What are some hobbies that has proven therapeutic to you?

After leaving the hospital, all femininity was gone. I thought, dressed, acted, walked & moved like a man. I felt the only choice in life was to be paid or played. Within the year, I moved 5 times. Nothing seemed stable. Nothing made sense. My father, the only man I trusted has died; I am born as a woman while feeling like a man. My thoughts were masculine; I even began to grow facial hair! God finally spoke and said 'go home.' I went home and my relationship with my mom was as beautiful as ever. I shared with her a secret that I had been keeping for over 30 years. When I was 10 years old, I was told that I was adopted. Everything that was concealed was revealed. I was healed and delivered from the anger and abandonment that I camouflaged for over 30 years.

Moment of Reflection: Has there been an event in your life that has caused you to have toxic feelings and behaviors? If so, take a

moment and release it to God. He understands the feelings of our
infirmities, heal every area that hurts, and collect every tear.

Even though, my teenage years consisted of arguing among my parents, I remained their priority. They encouraged me to love and believe in myself. You are probably wondering how could I love myself yet I was damaging myself. It's as simple as a toothache. The tooth appears fine; it is the inner living pulp that is contaminated with toxins. Separating healing from deliverance has a slim chance of survival. You may be delivered out of a situation, but if you are not internally healed, you are still mentally bound. By confessing to mom what I knew, she provided clarity to the deception. What the enemy used all of those years to perpetrate abandonment, God used as a blessing of purpose and acceptance. 3 months later, mom passed. I trusted no one. I began behaving promiscuously and was dating 3-4 girls at one time.

I found a new way to escape; the casino. I was "lucky" not "blessed" to win several jackpots. Winning the jackpots was the bait that hooked me. Some people feel that it is permissible to gamble once all the bills are paid. I have been raised up for such a time as this to tell you to **RUN!** The casino has an affect on you mentally and emotionally. This is not the place to go when you are dealing with grief, overcoming an addiction, coming out of a bad relationship, or just trying to escape the chaotic events of life. The lights, action, screams of excitement all contribute to a mystified sense of belonging. This translates into you not understanding why you cannot leave, even though you are broke! You know that you have bills to pay, but you are $50 short for your electric bill – so you justify that if you play your last $20 on the slot machine – you might just win.

Reflection Time

Gambling was another one of my issues. *In this moment of transparency; ask yourself – What is my issue? What is it that I cannot resist even though it is violating my value? It is causing division within my spirit and subtracting any trace of peace.*

Even though 'it' makes you miserable, you enjoy the company. In other words, it has become a liability!

What this means is a stronghold has developed in your mind. A stronghold is a mind that is resistant to change. A mind that has been taken captive by thoughts that is out of the alignment of Gods Word. Sin is something you need forgiveness for; a stronghold is something you need freedom from. How do I become free? Many repeat "you shall know the truth and it shall set you free." The beginning of the scripture which is found in John 8:31 says: If you hold to my teachings, then you are really my disciples. THEN you shall know the truth and the truth shall set you free. I must become an image of the Word of God. Every problem that I may have, there is a solution found in the word of God.

Because I trusted in the casino, I developed a disillusionment of believing all of my problems, worries, and concerns were gone....... until I was broke! Winning then became necessary! Let the sick cycle begin. I pray this is setting someone free in the name of Jesus. Everything that has a name has to bow to the name of Jesus. I demand the stronghold of gambling & the strongman of addiction to be severed right now in the name of Jesus!

Repeating this sick cycle is absolute bondage. *Proverbs 25:28 (AMP) says, "He who has no rule over his own spirit is like a city that is broken down without walls.* I was broken with no walls of defense to protect me. I operated from a carnal mind by attempting to fill a void from the grief of my mother's death. The voices of "tonight's the night, "I am going to hit it big", are the only voices I was able to hear. I even had the audacity to pray! Before I understood that the worlds system and God's system operated contradictory to each other, I thought my luck was actually a blessing.

**B's Biscuit – *What you consider a blessing,
may very well be your bondage.***

I would cry out; ***"God it's not fair- how is it that I win sometimes and other times lose everything? You did say the wealth of the wicked is stored up for the righteous!" Five minutes later - Ching Ching! Jackpot! $2250.00! Thank you Jesus!*** Is this not deception to the highest degree? Yes it is! But it is also the bait that I bit. The enemy is a master manipulator; his strength is in his strategy. If the enemy cannot get you in your strength, he will get you in your weakness. He seeks whomever he can demolish and I come with warning to you – if there are any cracks in your foundation such as feeling unloved, unfulfilled, or searching for meaning in all the wrong places, seal it up with the Word of God. Snakes do not have backbone; they can slither through the smallest crack to get to their destination!

What the enemy attempts to pervert, God has a plan to convert. One day while sitting quietly, The Holy Spirit spoke to me in a still small voice saying, "you are My child, I chose you, therefore you shall not use the casino to obtain your wealth. If that happened, then you would be able to say 'look what I won at the casino', not 'look what God has blessed me with". The Kingdom of God says give; the world says get. They are in total opposites of each other. God does not operate in winning by chance. God is no respecter of persons and He shows no personal favoritism for anyone.

Looking for man or the world to do what only God can, only gives you a dose of counterfeit love. One day during the winter of 2004, a sweet calm voice gave me a scripture and whispered in my ear that I was the "vessel ". The scripture was 2 Tim 2:20-22 which says "But in a great house there are not only vessels of gold and of silver, but also of wood and of earth: and some to honor, and some to dishonor. If a man therefore purge himself from these, he shall be a vessel unto honor, sanctified, and meet for the master's use, and prepared unto every good work. Flee also youthful lusts: but follow righteousness, faith, charity, peace, with them that call on the Lord out of a pure heart". I found a church to attend and began to study the Word. I slowly began to trust people and met someone who was active in ministry. She befriended me and before I knew it, we were sexually involved. During this time, I was vacillating between codependency on a person and dependency upon the Holy Spirit. I was looking for mom in everybody. I don't say this to turn anyone away from church, but just understand when you make up your mind and decide to follow Christ - spiritual warfare begins. He's not intimidated by you attending church, he's intimidated when you discern your moment and walk into destiny! I immediately recognized that Satan was dropping bait to take me out of position. It was easy to not trust the church. It was easy to become offended and leave the church. But it wasn't easy to stay still and stand! It wasn't easy listening to the foolishness that God didn't make Adam & Steve jokes. I just had to do it. I had to press forward, not in my strength, but in Him that strengthens me. The enemy was firing darts to push me back into the pain and misery that I decided I would never be apart of again. I was in a God moment to discern what **WAS** right, not what **FELT** right.

B's Biscuit ~ Never allow your emotions to take the steering wheel;
they will always cause an accident!

What the enemy tried to use as a setback was really a setup. From that point on, I didn't focus on the world, the church, or people. I focused on the Word. No more running! I went through 20 years of drugs and homosexual activity, today I am free.

Reflection: As I have transparently shared my exodus with you,
ask yourself - Who are you in Jesus Christ? What labels have you
allowed life to attach to you? What fruit are you producing in
your life because of a toxic root?

When Jacob wrestled with God, he didn't get blessed until his name was changed from Jacob to Israel. Even the woman with the issue of blood went from being "who" touched my clothes to "daughter' thy faith has made thee whole. What name are you answering to?

I am who God says I am. Deut. 28:13 says "I am the head and not the tail", 2 Corinthians 5:20 says I am an Ambassador for Christ, 1 Thessalonians 1:4 says I am Beloved of God, Colossians 2:10 says I am Complete in Christ, 2 Corinthians 2:14 says I am always Triumphant, Matthew 5:13 says I am the Salt of the earth and Romans 8:37 says I am more than a Conqueror. Identifying with Gods perspective illuminates how he views you rather than your perception. Perception can be dangerous, because it is your understanding based on thought, which is influenced by your circumstances and environment. When you identify with God, you become synonymous with His Word. You realize that you don't have to be a prisoner of your circumstances and because you go through it; you don't have to become it. Your illumination has now become revelation.

To live your life is to lose your life. Therefore, wake up to die daily. It is only when there is a death that there can be a resurrection. When you walk in the Spirit, you identify with God's perspective. Walking in the spirit is not based on feelings because some mornings I feel like running folk over with a bulldozer. But....The Power of God!

Finally, when my mom passed, I found a letter stating that on December 25, 1964, I was a Christmas gift given from my biological mother to my mommy at age 6 months. Immediately, I looked up to heaven and I promised mom and dad that the life and the foundational structure of unconditional love I received, I would find a way to help those that are bound due to the issues of life. Someone has to be crucified, in order for someone to be resurrected. It was never about me. Trials and tribulations are prerequisites for the treasure that is within the vessel. Therefore, for every mother who has a child who is gay, love them unconditionally. All the bashing and harshness by man only causes division and sends them into a world where the enemy is waiting to embrace them and then erase them. Change can only be done by the transforming power of the Holy Spirit. If you know someone that is going through trials that are weighing them down, reach down and lift them up. Every mother that has a child on drugs, prostituting or living a life of promiscuity, tell them they are loved. Pray for them, encourage them. To every person that is trying to fill a void, understand if it is not the love of God, it is counterfeit. Embrace the love of God if you are feeling condemnation, hurt and shame because of life's issues; understand that nothing catches God by surprise. He's always there patiently waiting to comfort you. Issues in life are only a platform to bring forth God's glory, God's grace and God's compassion. It is in your transparency, that true intimacy is born!

Notes:

_____

_____

_____

_____

_____

_____

_____

_____

_____

_____

_____

_____

_____

_____

_____

_____

_____

_____

_____

_____

_____

_____

ABOUT THE AUTHOR

KAMALA C. MCGEE

Kamala C. McGee is a Registered Nurse with the Department of Veterans Affair. She received her education from the University of Phoenix completing a dual degree Masters in Nursing/Business Administration/Health Care Administration. She also attended Saint Leo University obtaining a Bachelors of Arts in Psychology and Patrick Henry Community College, Martinsville, VA where she obtained her Associates Degree in Nursing. She is currently pursuing a Masters in Nursing Education at Liberty University.

As a 31 year Veteran of the U.S. Military, where she has held leadership position, Kamala understands what it means to be disciplined to be of service and her being a member of Professional Woman Network has opened the door to more engaging and enlightening opportunities.

Ms. McGee has obtained the following certifications:

* Certified Professional Coach (2011)
* A Journey to Wellness Certification & Training (2005)
* Diversity Certification & Training (2005)

Further Kamal has been given the gift of co-authoring the following books published by PWN:

(2007) Survival Skills for the African American Woman: *"Sister to Thine Own Self Be True! Know Your Values"*

(2009) A Journey Within: Self-Discovery for Women: *"Ten Attributes of an Emotionally Healthy Woman"*

(2010) Living Your Vision and Purpose: *"When Jesus Touched My Life"*

(2011) The Power of a Woman, Embracing the Woman Within: *"Embracing Strength & Courage"*

Kamala also holds the following professional affiliations:

Professional Woman Network and was appointed to the Board of Directors

The Virginia Nursing Association

National Association of Female Executives (NAFE)

Academy of Medical Surgical Nurses (AMSN)

My life has been immensely blessed by every individual, circumstance and situation encountered. I hope use the lessons I have learned to communicate how awesome Life is through respect, education and God's guidance and blessings.

Each one should use whatever gift he has received to serve others, faithfully administering God's grace in its various forms. **1 Peter 4:10**

Contact

Kamala C. McGee

434.770.0007

kamichar63@gmail.com

www.protrain.net

TWENTY-FOUR

LIFE IS SHORT............

By Kamala McGee

In the beginning God created the heaven and the earth... So, God created man in his own image, in the image of God he created him; male and female created he them.
—Genesis 1:1; 1:27

God had a plan for his design of heaven and earth; he provided specific instructions for life to exist. So it is a wonder that on the day of your birth there has always been a plan, a design for your life. You ever wonder what that plan is and how and when you would accomplish it? Time is of the essence and your life is comprised of numbers; so what does a life look like broken down into the components of time?

1,546, 387, 200 seconds
25, 773, 120 minutes

283

429, 552 hours

17, 798 days

2556 weeks

These numbers identify the seconds, minutes, hours, days and weeks of a life and it all seems so expansive, but in actuality time has continued to progress no matter what state of being we in. How awesome is it to know that time of your life there a plan already in place? Fulfilled or unfilled, what remains are that we all have moments when we reflect on our life's purpose is. Have you made any strides to become who God intended you to be?

Time is continuous and in the blink of an eye life can change, Can lead you to question all that is! Psalms 39:4-5 states "Oh Lord make me know the end and what is the measure of my days; let me know how fleeting I am! Behold you have made my days a fine handbreadths and my lifetime is as nothing before you. Surely all mankind stands as mere breath! Selah." Imagine just a breath is all it took to create man, to create a life.

How to synthesize the processes of life – processes that can be seen as abstract concepts through which we look for meaning and relationships in situations. The concepts I will label as challenges, joy and promise. These areas, although not inclusive of what makes a life, are in my opinion the areas which people struggle with in efforts to find meaning.

******

"Count it all joy, my brothers, when you meet trials of various kinds, for you know that the testing of your faith produces steadfastness. And let steadfastness have its full effect, that you may be perfect and complete, lacking in nothing." —James 1:2-3

Challenges can appear in two (2) forms: trials or temptations and it all seems a matter of the flip of a coin which. But each has a distinct purpose in your life. Trials are the tests that are intended to bring out the best in your character; whereas temptations are those situations that bring out the worst, the doubt in you. It is a struggle of virtually good and evil. Wisdom of choice is what it takes to make it through any situation.

Be not mistaken though, challenges may make you feel as though you want to give up, especially when all around you is dark and you are blind to what God has already set in place for you. Further, challenges can cause you to sabotage yourself and break your spirit. For sure it can be assumed that the turmoil within your spirit is manifested outside throughout your interactions in life and in the choices that are made. So it is important to know that you cannot escape the consequences when you know they are coming, but there is a way.

During your valley experiences, you must learn to pray and ask God to guide you, to make you careful in your choices, and for what you are praying for. Ask Him to be your guiding light of understanding – understanding the behind the challenge. God knows what you need and if he brings it to you, He most certainly will bring you through it and when all is said and done it will lead you towards your peace and joy.

My Challenges

******

"I have told you this so that my joy may be in you and that your joy may be complete." —John 15:11

It is one thing to feel bruised, but when God finds you weak and broken it changes your whole outlook. The world is filled with so much sorrow, worry, and people who will steal your joy; but knowing that through God's grace and mercy you are able to find inner contentment and purpose inspite of what has happened in your life. Only God who is the author of all things will come to you in loving kindness and give you a place to really live – to live in Jesus.

Sing praises unto God even during the valley times because the joy is in the testimony. The acknowledgement of God in all things opens doors and your heart to greater experiences with God. He will pull you towards deeper depths and higher heights of faith and expectation in your relationship with Him.

The joy of the Lord is fulfilling your every need according to his will, but He knows exactly what is needed and when to provide. You have to trust tin God because "he who kneels before God can stand before anyone." Continue to serve him with an open heart willingly and He will lead you to your promise.

My Joy (Tea Cup Moments)

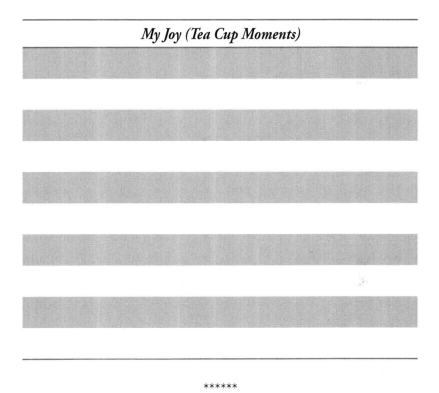

******

"For I know the plans I have for you, says the Lord. They are plans for good and not for evil, to give you a future and hope." —Jeremiah 29:11

I speak life; I speak life; I speak the cost of following God's plan is high because in doing so your life will not be the same. God endorses a product that when you wear the full of armor, you are able to do things as he does in the name of Jesus.

Through God's promise of life everlasting all things that are in his will are possible. What other promises does God provide us?

1. Luke 17:11-15 – "When praises go up blessings come down."

2. Romans 8:28 – "Things work for those who love the Lord."

3. Psalms 138:7-8 – "The Lord will perfect that which concerns me."

4. Haggai 2:6 – "Delight yourself in the Lord; he will give you the desires of your heart."

5. Matthew 11:28-29 - "Come to me, all you who are weary and burdened, and I will give you rest. Take my yoke upon you and learn from me, for I am gentle and humble in heart, and you will find rest for your souls."

6. John 14:27 - "I am leaving you with a gift—peace of mind and heart. And the peace I give is a gift the world cannot give. So don't be troubled or afraid. "

7. Proverbs 1:33 – *"But all who listen to me will live in peace, untroubled by fear of harm*

The Bible is filled with Gods promises and more, but to be receivers of His gifts you have to make preparation to serve Him. Let these promises work into your heart as you continue to study Gods words. Ask yourself am I standing or the promises of God? Is He my all and all? Life is short, forget those things which are behind and reach forth unto those things which are before. Believe that you deserve everything God has to offer and choose to live on purpose in God.

My Promises

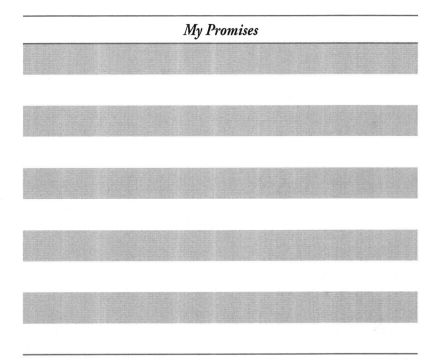

Dear God,

I am desperately struggling – struggling with what I need to do and how so that I can have a better relationship with you. I feel like am running, running away from myself from you towards nothingness. I have dreamt of falling through a tunnel in which I am reaching out for someone to help me, but everyone there only turn away. I have trusted in people, allowed them to share my life and attempted to be someone who is willing, oh so willing to be a support for others, yet I am alone. It hurts so much and I do not understand why.

I have overwhelming emotions stirring inside my very core, emotions that feel like such turmoil (a ball of fire) waiting to erupt, to explode at the next hurt. I am ashamed that I feel this (what you suffered for me was greater), that I am even writing you this letter telling you of my problems, but I need to stop the tears and acknowledge all that makes me who I am and try to move forward.

God, I also am struggling with this writing, as I am in a place where I have the opportunity to encourage others yet I feel so discouraged and defeated. How can I even think of assisting another in their transition when I am stuck in my own?

I have and continue to give so much of myself to others to the point that I have very little if anything left for me. You created the heart within me and I know that there is a purpose and promise in that, but at this point Lord, I am questioning so much and for that I apologize.

Lord I pray you continue to guide me and that I learn to better hear your voice and understand. Surrendering to your 'Will" has not, is not easy – I ask that you have patience with me.

Finally, Lord for all who may read these words let them be of encouragement and give them comfort in   knowing that as Isaiah **40:29-31 states** "*He gives power to the weak and strength to the powerless. Even youths will become weak and tired, and young men will fall in exhaustion. But those who trust in the Lord will find new strength. They will soar high on wings like eagles. They will run and not grow weary. They will walk and not faint.*

Thank you Lord for considering me worthy.

Blessed Be

Reference

Holy Bible, New Living Translation (NLT)

Notes

ABOUT THE AUTHOR

REV. PHYLLIS ALSTON, M. DIV.

Rev. Phyllis Alston has been an ordained priest in the Episcopal/ Anglican Diocese of Pittsburgh for the past ten years.

Rev. Phyllis Alston holds a Master's of Divinity from Trinity School for Ministry, Ambridge, PA, a Bachelor of Science Degree in Business Administration from Robert Morris College (now University), Coraopolis, PA, and four units of Clinical Pastoral Education (CPE) from the Veterans Administration, Pittsburgh, PA. She is currently working towards a Ph.D. in Educational Psychology from Walden University, Minneapolis, MN. She is a member of The International Honor Society of Psychology (Psi Chi). Rev. Phyllis believes her greatest credential is her personal relationship with Jesus Christ, the Son of God.

Rev. Phyllis Alston's knowledge of business and professionalism is supported by over 30 years of real world leadership acquired from business administration, organizational management, social service, spiritual care, and personal experience. She has worked in companies including LTV Steel, Jones and Laughlin Steel, United Parcel Service (UPS), and various hospice and social organizations.

Rev. Phyllis Alston is a member of the Professional Woman Network (PWN) and has acquired certifications: Certified Professional Coach, Certified Women's Empowerment Coach, and Certified Diversity Trainer. She is President and CEO of The Alston Institute of Self-Care. This institute provides workshops, seminars, and one-on-one coaching and consulting under two umbrellas: The Women's Terrace and The Widow's Pillar. The Women's Terrace offers strengthening techniques to help individuals embrace self-care, including recovering from abusive relationships, formulating a life plan, and creating a terrace oasis mentality. The Widow's Pillar is designed to support widows and comprises three components, the widow's grief, the widow's transition, and the widow's victorious new identity.

Rev. Phyllis Alston is a proud mother of three grown children, Phillip, Brandi, and Joelle and surrogate mother of two grown children, Marianne and Joe, and a blessed grandmother of six, Isaiah, Jasmine, Mikah, RayMichael, Ayden, and Sabrina. Her husband, William F. Alston, Jr., a councilman and retired police chief, passed away in 2008. She dedicates this chapter to her dear friends, confidants, and supporters Oliver and Gloria Hall of Pittsburgh, PA.

Contact:
Rev. Phyllis M. Alston, M. Div.,
Professional Coach, Consultant, & Key-Note Speaker
The Alston Institute of Self-Care
(724) 630-8750
Email: alstoninstitute@gmail.com

TWENTY-FIVE

WHAT SHALL I RENDER?

By Rev. Phyllis Alston

Introduction

There are many occasions during the year when we find it appropriate to give gifts to our family and friends, sometimes even to acquaintances or work associates. Gifts can provide a message to the recipient, perhaps a message of love, blessings, or consideration. There are times that we may feel driven or obligated to return the love, blessing, or consideration to that person at a later date in time.

When Jesus was obedient to Father God in taking it upon himself to die upon the cross for our sins and the sins of the entire world, he provided many gifts for us. According to John 15:13, Jesus considered us his friends and bestowed upon us the greatest gift, the gift of love: "Greater love has no one than this, that he lay down his life for his friends.".

In this chapter, we will review the inspired Word of God to take a look at the precious gifts God has provided for our taking, free gifts and decide what we shall render unto such a gracious and loving provider out of the goodness of our hearts. Of course, we cannot ever repay God the Father for his sacrifice through his Son, our Savior Jesus Christ. There is no requirement to return his favor, however out of our overwhelming appreciation, what shall we render unto the Lord for his goodness and mercy?

The gift of forgiveness

Jesus said, "Father, forgive them, for they do not know what they are doing." Luke 23:34

No matter how much effort we put forth in trying not to sin, we all sin and fall short from the glory of God. Read Romans 3:23. Jesus offered his life, shed his blood and paid our debt in full. Read Psalm 103: 8-12. When we pray with repentant hearts and ask God to forgive us, he is gracious in forgiving our debt of sin, can take away our guilt and shame, and also as far as the east is from the west he removes our transgressions from our memory.

One of the most precious gifts of forgiveness is that we can go to the Lord in prayer at any time and in any place. We do not have to wait to enter a church building/sanctuary to ask God to listen to us for the forgiveness of our sins. Through a personal relationship with Jesus Christ, we are required to produce fruit in keeping with repentance. Read Luke 3:8.

Find other Scripture passages that support forgiveness and note here.

_____

_____

_____

_____

_____

_____

_____

The gift of healing

> *"He himself bore our sins in his body on the tree,*
> *so that we might die to sins and live for righteousness:*
> *by his wounds you have been healed."* —1Peter 2:24

Can you imagine the magnitude of all of the weight of all the sins Christ carried so that we might be free to live for righteousness? As the result of the fall in the Garden of Eden, sin carried with it the infirmities and brokenness of humankind. However, thanks be to God, Christ Jesus carried our diseases to save, heal, and deliver us from them. It is important that we realize that Jesus has provided healing for our mind, body, and spirit. Read Isaiah 53:4-5. Seeking your own healing is paramount in grasping obedience to the Holy Spirit's direction. Ultimately as believers in Christ Jesus, we look forward to the Day of Resurrection when our bodies will be fully healed and changed. Read 1Corinthians 15:50-53.

Find other Scripture passages that support healing and note here.

_____

_____

_____

_____

_____

_____

_____

_____

The gift of justification

> *"The words "it was credited to him" were written*
> *not for him alone, but also for us, to whom God will credit*
> *righteousness – for us who believe in him who raised*
> *Jesus our Lord from the dead. He was delivered*
> *over to death for our sins and was raised to life*
> *for our justification."* —Romans 4:23-25

There is simply nothing that we can do on our own merit to save ourselves from our transgressions. It is essential for us to believe in the work Christ Jesus has done on the cross in order for us to get to heaven. Jesus is "the way and the truth, and the life. No one comes to the Father except through him." Read John 14:6. God sent his Son to die on the cross for our sins and through this action treated us as if we had never sinned. Read Romans 4:25 and Romans 5:18.

Find other Scripture passages that support justification and note here.

_____

_____

_____

_____

_____

_____

_____

The gift of adoption

> *"For you did not receive a spirit that makes you*
> *a slave again to fear, but you received the*
> *Spirit of sonship."* —Roman 8:15

We have a choice to become children of God through adoption. When we repent of our sins and make a choice to receive Jesus into our hearts, Jesus accepts us into his family and through the process of adoption we are transferred from the clutches of Satan into the privilege of sonship. At this time, we receive the Spirit of his Son. Read Romans 8:14-16. Read Galatians 4:4-7.

Find other Scripture passages that support adoption and note here.

_____

_____

_____

_____

_____

_____

_____

The gift of redemption

*"In him we have redemption through his blood,
the forgiveness of sins, in accordance with the riches
of God's grace that he lavished on us with
all wisdom and understanding."* —Ephesians 1:7-8

Redemption means being brought back through a purchase from our current position. In other words, God through his Son "has rescued us from the dominion of darkness and brought us into the kingdom of the Son he loves in whom we have redemption, the forgiveness of sins." Read Colossians 1:13-14. Believers of Jesus Christ have been redeemed from paying a penalty for sins. God chose us, he personally chose each one of us by giving his son Jesus who paid the penalty for us.

Find other Scripture passages that support redemption and note here.

_____

The gift of atonement

"And they sang a new song: You are worthy to take the scroll,
and to open its seals, because you were slain,
and with your blood you purchased men for God,
from every tribe and language and people and nation." —Revelation 5:9

When Jesus died on the cross for our sins, he paid our penalty and made right the relationship that we had broken between God and humans. In the Old Testament, people atoned symbolically for their sins by offering sacrifices to God. In the New Testament, Jesus corrected the relationship between God and people once and for all by dying for our sins and the sins of the whole world. Read Leviticus 17:11, Leviticus 23:27, Romans 3:25.

Find other Scripture passages that support atonement and note here.

_____

_____

_____

_____

_____

The gift of substitution

*"And he took bread, gave thanks and broke it, and gave it to them,
saying, "This is my body given for you; do this in remembrance of me."
In the same way, after the supper he took the cup, saying, "This cup is the
new covenant in my blood, which is poured out for you."*
—Luke 22:19-20

In the Old Testament, sinful people of faith confessed their sins and transferred them onto unblemished innocent animals. God's judgment then fell upon the substitutes as their blood was shed and their bodies were burned in fire. God then accepted this substitution as payment for sin in place of the lives of sinful people. Read Leviticus 1:1-5, 16:21, 22. This was a temporary solution. Read Hebrews 8:5-13. In the New Testament, Christ loved us so much that He voluntarily became our substitute. Read John 10:14-18, 18:1-6.

Find other Scripture passages that support substitution and note here.

_____

_____

_____

_____

_____

_____

_____

The gift of righteousness

God made him who had no sin to be sin for us,
so that in him we might become the righteousness of God.
—2 Corinthians 5:21

Jesus was obedient to God in giving his sinless nature to pay our penalty of sin. Jesus suffered so horribly that he sweat great drops of blood and he needed an angel to strengthen him. Read Luke 22:43,44. Jesus knew he was the only One who could deliver us from the penalty of sin because he was the only sinless one who could offer his righteousness to us. As we pray and repent of our sins and trust in Christ, it will be the righteousness of Christ that will provide us entrance into heaven through God's abundance of grace. Read Ephesians 2:8-9

Find other Scripture passages that support righteousness and note them here.

_____

_____

_____

_____

_____

_____

_____

_____

The gift of reconciliation

> "...we also rejoice in God through our Lord Jesus Christ,
> through whom we have now received reconciliation."
> —Read Romans 5:8-11

God has a standard for us to live up to, however we all sin and fall short from the glory of God and miss the mark. Read Jeremiah 17:9 and Romans 3:9-18, 23. God used his Son to make us acceptable, reconciling us to him. When we repent of our sins and receive Jesus into our hearts as ruler over our lives, we are his children and enjoy peace and friendship with God.

Find other Scripture passages that support reconciliation and note them here.

_____

The gift of salvation

> *"The Lord is my light and my salvation –*
> *whom shall I fear?* —Psalm 27:1

If Jesus had come down from the cross and saved Himself, He would not have been able to save us. Salvation means deliverance from the guilt and power of sin. By his death and resurrection, Jesus brings salvation to people who believe in him. Read Luke 2:30, Acts 4:12, 2Corinthians 7:10.

Find other Scripture passages that support salvation and note them here.

_____

_____

_____

_____

_____

The gift of direct access to God

*"At that moment the curtain of the temple was torn in two
from top to bottom."* —Matthew 27:51

We learn from the Old Testament, that priests were permitted
on the Day of Atonement to enter beyond the curtain and the Most
Holy Place to offer sacrifices on behalf of their people for the sins
that were committed. Read Exodus 26:31-35 and Hebrews 9:6-12.
However when Jesus died on the cross for our sins, this curtain was
torn completely into two giving us direct access to God through our
mediator, Jesus Christ. Read 1 Timothy 2:5, Hebrews 9:11-15.

Find other Scripture passages that support direct access to God
and note here.

_____

_____

_____

_____

_____

_____

_____

_____

The gift of eternal life

*For God so loved the world that he gave his one
and only Son, that whoever believes in him
shall not perish but have eternal life.* —John 3:16

God is eternal. He is the beginning and the end. He was before the beginning and will be after the end. In other words, God is without beginning or end. God is so gracious that he has provided the opportunity for his believers to have eternal life, forever life. When believers in Christ Jesus die worldly death, they do not cease to exist. Our physical bodies house our soul and spirit which will live on eternally. However, unbelievers who are dead in their relationship with God will perish at the time of death.

Find other Scripture passages that support eternal life and note them here.

_____

_____

_____

_____

_____

_____

_____

_____

The gift of the powerful Kingdom

"I am the Living One: I was dead, and behold I am alive for ever and ever! And I hold the keys of death and Hades" —Revelation 1:18

Jesus holds the key to the Kingdom in his hands and has the power to empower us with authority to live victorious lives as well as eternal life. We are no longer controlled by our sinful nature but by the Spirit. Read Romans 8:11, 1John 3:8. The reason the Son of Man appeared was to destroy the devil's work, the power the devil had over death. Read Hebrews 2: 14, 15.

Find other Scripture passages that support God empowering us with authority and note here.

_____

_____

_____

_____

_____

_____

_____

The gift of the ultimate sacrifice

"When he had received the drink, Jesus said, "It is finished. With that, he bowed his head and gave up his spirit." —John 19:30

When I graduated from seminary, all classmates were welcomed to wear a tee-shirt with the Greek word, *telelestai,* from the New Testament used for "It is finished." This was an appropriate message to wear because seminary was all work and very little play and we had finally completed our seminarian mission.

When Jesus said the words, *"it is finished,"* what did he actually mean? Jesus was obedient to Father God and had completed the mission of dying for the sins of the whole world. "He has appeared once for all at the end of the ages to do away with sin by the sacrifice of himself. Just as man is destined to die once, and after that face judgment, so Christ was sacrificed once to take away the sins of many people; and he will appear a second time, not to bear sin, but to bring salvation to those who are waiting for him." Hebrews 9:26-28. After Christ had offered this all time one sacrifice for sins, he sat down at the right hand of God. Read Hebrews 9:26-28; 10:12-14.

Find other Scripture passages that support the ultimate sacrifice that God provided for us and note.

_____

_____

_____

_____

_____

_____

_____

Conclusion

Now that you have read about some of the wonderful gifts God has bestowed upon us through his Son, Jesus Christ, what are some of the thoughts that come to your mind? Please note.

_____

_____

_____

_____

_____

_____

Can you think of what you could render, offer to the Lord for the sacrifice he has made? I do have some suggestions.

(1) Acknowledgment – the realization that you are a sinner and fall short from the mark that God has set as a standard. Read Romans 3:23, Romans 6:23

Notes _____

_____

_____

_____

_____

_____

_____

(2) Confession – acknowledging before the Lord and others that you need the Savior and would like to have eternal life. Read Revelation 22:17

Notes _____

_____

_____

_____

_____

_____

_____

(3) **Ask**- ask for the forgiveness of sins. Read Matthew 7:7, Ephesians
   1:7, John 3:17

Notes _____

_____

_____

_____

_____

_____

_____

(4) **Accept** – accept Christ as your Savior. Read John 6:47, Romans 5:8

Notes _____

_____

_____

_____

_____

_____

_____

_____

(5) Continual Confession – after accepting Jesus into your heart, it is imperative to go to him in continual confession for the forgiveness of sins. Pray to Jesus, your mediator. Read 1 Timothy 2:5, Hebrew 9:15

Notes _____

_____

_____

_____

_____

_____

_____

_____

(6) Offer a thirsty heart to God – Seek the kingdom and God's righteousness with a thirsty heart which is pleasing to Him. Read Matthew 6:33

Notes _____

_____

_____

_____

_____

_____

_____

_____

(7) Offer continual praise and thanksgiving with a heart of gratitude – Read Psalm 100:4, Philippians 4:6, 1Chronicles 16:8-11

Notes _____

_____

_____

_____

_____

_____

_____

_____

What shall you render unto the Lord, for he is good, and his mercy endures forever? Can you think of other things you might offer to the Lord?

_____

_____

_____

_____

_____

_____

_____

_____

Reference

Skeba, David (1990). Discovering Treasures from the Cross. Discover Ministries.

ABOUT THE AUTHOR

KIMBERLY CARTER

Kimberly Carter is a woman known for taking up great causes. She served her country faithfully for 6 years as a member of the Air Force National Guard and cultivated her sense of duty. She takes a similar pursuit of a higher calling as she volunteers to improve the lives of inner city youth along underprivileged young ladies. She also impacts her community through outreach with local church members. When not spending time reading a book, she continues to a build a foundation for future generations with her loving husband. She holds a MBA in management and is currently pursuing a degree in Christian Ministry.

TWENTY-SIX

GOD'S PLAN

By Kimberley Carter

Have you ever wanted to know God's plan for your life? It's always been my biggest question. My story starts at birth; before I could even talk…I was born and left the hospital that same day. I've always felt like Moses you know? Born and left in a basket to float up a river alone, unaware of the danger that surrounded me. I was probably guided by the prayers of my Mother to safety as well.

Sometimes I've even imagined myself to be like Esther…born for such a time as this. I just could never pinpoint exactly what time that meant for me! Of course Moses helped to free his own people from slavery and Egyptian bondage. Esther ensured that her people were not wiped off the face of the planet through the plot of an evil man who hated her entire race. But as for me, I have never even come close to attempting such heroic acts. So this leaves me back at square one; God, what is your plan for my life?

I was placed in foster care shortly after my birth for about two years. I was then adopted into a loving home and raised in a supportive and loving environment. I grew up and did most things that all kids do.

315

I went through school without giving too much thought to my destiny and God's plans for me. I started making my own plans! Now how many of us do that? Make our own plans, to serve our own purpose? It has nothing to do with God or His purpose. We may pray and ask for His guidance…to our destination. We may acknowledge His existence. We may even thank Him for all of His blessings. But most of us never stop and ask Him to show us where we fit into His world. The one He created. We never ask for His plans and purposes for our life; at least not initially. For most of us, it takes one hard "bump in the road" after another. Then we stop and pray. We suddenly remember that we didn't ask the Creator of everything for direction. We just got in the car and started going the way we pleased.

Well, my world came to a stop at the age of 18. Before that, I had little hints along the way that perhaps I may be going the wrong way…but like most people, I tried my best to ignore it and continue along the path I had mapped out on my own. It wasn't easy to continue along my own path though. As you know, God always sends warnings. He sends people into your life to point you in the right direction. He'll send circumstances, hints, or anything that will grab your attention. We somehow manage to ignore most of these warning signs. Still, he persists out of His unconditional love for you.

So, getting back to my journey to God's plan; My Mother died of lung cancer when I was 14. That same year I started High School. This was all around the time when God started really tugging on my heart to follow Him. "I know the Plans I have for your life, Kimberly", He would constantly whisper to my heart. "Plans of Peace, Plans to give you an expected end"…. I would dismiss it as my imagination. After all, I would say to myself, you're too young for God to want you to follow him. You're just 15, 16, and 17…whichever age I was at the time. I am sure you've been there too, in the place where God desires you to follow Him. You talk yourself out of it by saying that you're too young or old. You may say to yourself that it's a phase. You ask yourself "what will my family and friends think about this newfound relationship with God?" I just kept pushing it aside until I eventually thought it was gone forever. Honestly, I should have been more eager for God to tell me His plans for my life, because I did not have any for myself. I had the usual I guess. Go to college, graduate, get a nice career. I went to a small, Christian college and joined the military part time.

It was in basic training for the military where God started tugging on me again. While I was in Basic Training for the Air Force, God dealt with me. Not in a harsh way, but He did separate me from everything and everything familiar. It was a hard time for me. I did not finish Basic in the six week time period that I was supposed to...I was held back. While being held back, I had people asking me to pray for them and to encourage them. Talk about God's Plan! I was thinking, what kind of plan is this! He always knows what He's doing though. I made it to my last week, and I met a young lady who told me that God held me back so that I could minister to other young women. She told me that God had a Women's ministry inside of me. I was devastated. I did not know that His plan could include you ministering to people even though you were in despair. Apparently I had not read Joseph's story!

I finished Basic and my undergraduate studies and moved out on my own. By this time I had gotten engaged to a wonderful young man, however, marriage was never in my plan. Don't get me wrong, I've settled into my marriage to Paul Carter, and he is a wonderful man, but it took me a while to wrap my head around the idea of marriage. I just hadn't incorporated that into MY plans.

So, I continued searching for God and this "Plan to prosper and not harm me", and my journey led me to Kentucky. There I met Linda Ellis Eastman, and became certified in Women's issues. I went back a second time for the Save Our Youth training. It was remarkable. I was fairly blown away. She actually revealed something to me that is in the process of unfolding as I write this. She told me that God was going to use me in the church. I thought "she must be mistaken....ME!! I am not CHURCHY at all!"

Sometimes it takes a journey for God's Plan to completely unfold. Sometimes it takes YEARS for God's plan to unfold. Sometimes it takes people speaking things that "Be not as though they were" into your life for God's plan to unfold. But have no doubt...it ALWAYS unfolds.

I soaked in all the information I could from the certification classes, and I went home. I did not immediately use any of the information. The few times I have used the information, it's been in a women's ministry that I am a part of, R.A.I.N. (Releasing Authority and Identity Now). When the opportunity to be a part of R.A.I.N. presented itself, I thought "Surely they don't want me to help! I'm not even 30!! What could I offer to these women?" Yes, I was intimidated and scared. I still wasn't seeing that God's Plan was unfolding right before me. The truth is that we would all like to be healed from own "issues" before we attempt to help anyone else with their issues, but you know by now that God's Plan does not work like that. He wants us to help someone else, even when we have not conquered our own problems. He watches to see how we handle other people needing prayer before He sends someone to pray for us. He watches to see if we will pass by the homeless person and offer them some money or food, before He allows us to be "fed". How will you handle forgiveness when you don't think the other person deserves it? Will you be faithful over the few things He's placed in your hands?

We can guess by now that God has his own system in place to measure our maturity. He has a system in place to judge the intents of our heart. He watches what we do; but not only that, WHY we do it.

As my personal journey continued, I found myself asking God what His plans would be for my life. As I mentioned earlier, I had completed my undergraduate studies, and I thought that I was finished with school. Of course God had other plans, as usual. I found myself pursuing my graduate degree. It was a difficult journey, not due to the workload, but, due to the fact that, once again, this was not a part of the plan that I had in mind.

God always uses people to help in your process of healing. It's funny because we always think that we are doing much better than we are. God will place people along your journey's path to point out areas that need to be improved. I met several of these people while working on my graduate degree. I refer to them as life changers. You may call them something else, but we can agree on one thing, we are grateful for these people and the impact that they have on us. You should stop right now and say a prayer for the people in your life that fit this description. Where would you have ended up without their intervention? I will tell you that there is absolutely no telling where I would be.

I am still seeking God to unfold His complete Plan for my life, but there is one more thing that I must mention to you. It's the most critical component of asking God for His Plan for your life. You have to accept and embrace His Plan and let go of your own plan. This,* my friend, is the difficult job. Oh yes, it sounds like something that would come naturally; ask for God's Plan, relinquish my own plan, but it's not so easy. You have to constantly surrender yourself to God. You must constantly pray and ask for help with this. It's the key to actually seeing God's Plan unfold. If you don't obey in something God tells you, He may not reveal the next step in His Plan to you. It's critical.

Seeking God's Plan is a lifelong journey. After He reveals one Plan, there will be another one. Then once we accomplish that Plan, another one may unfold. The best thing to do is be flexible, open, and willing to follow through on the Plan that God reveals.

I have one question for you: What is God's Plan for your life?

Discussion Questions:

1) Have you ever sought God for His Plan for your life? If so, do you feel like He has shown it to you yet?

2) Do you ever discuss God's Plan for your life with close friends and family members? Are they supportive?

3) Have you ever had doubt about the direction that you feel God was leading you to go? If so, how did you proceed?

4) Have you sincerely surrendered your plans for your life and accepted what God has shown you? If not, how can you begin today to change this behavior and line up with God's Plan?

Notes:

ABOUT THE AUTHOR

CYNTHIA BLEVINS

Cynthia Blevins is President & CEO, of the CB Experience (CBE), a professional consulting firm. She is known throughout her career as the consummate authority in Customer Service skills. Ms Blevins customizes and conducts workshops and seminars that have been presented throughout the United States and abroad. The workshops and seminars conducted consist of topics such as Customer Service Professionalism, Diversity, and Leadership Skills for Women.

Ms Blevins is a member of the Professional Women Network (PWN), where she received her consulting credentials and co-authored her two book. Her knowledge of business is supported by years working with top corporations. She has 30+ years experience developing business processes, call center training, and management, and 7+ years consulting experience creating training programs, and assessments. Ms Blevins, has educates groups and mentored individuals one-on-one including marketing Product Managers, in the logistics of successfully launching new products within the highly competitive Medical Device industry.

Ms Blevins is passionate about helping others as a Professional & Spiritual Life Coach, accentuating the needs of Women and Singles.

Her educational accomplishments include currently pursuing her credentials in Project Management, University of California, Irvine; is an Alumae of Biola University, California. Keeping her faith evident, she earned an Associates Degree in Biblical Studies, Visions International School of Ministry, and holds certificates in Human Resources Management, University of Phoenix, and Project Management with American Society of Training & Development (ASTD).

Ms Blevins resides in southern California. She is mother to a beautiful adult daughter who mentors her to stay young. She enjoys family, friends, jazz music, golf, networking and traveling. Ms Blevins is available for individual and group speaking engagements, seminars and consulting assignments, on local, national, and global basis.

Contact:
Cynthia Blevins, President & CEO
The CB Experience Consulting
P.O. Box 503192
San Diego, CA 92150-3192
Tel 858.880.8671
Fax 866.370.6740
cjblevins@gmail.com
www.cbe.whenseevicematters.com
www.protrain.net

TWENTY-SEVEN

OH... YES HE DID...

By Cynthia Blevins

Give us life, to make wise confident *choices*, to deliver trustworthy *communications* with everlasting *compassion* for one another. It is by GOD's designed that we possess the authority to connect or reconnect with Him on an intimate and individual level. It's important to remember, often, all the things the LORD has done for us.

I encourage you to get your writing instrument of choice pen & paper, journal, laptop or IPAD, then take a moment and write a declaration of how would you finish this statement?

OH... Yes HE Did...._____

_____! I believe that Jesus is the Anointed Son of GOD, within my heart, soul and body... I think He is always coming towards us or passing by us. It's up to you, to decide when, to stop Him and receive His healing power to be whole and complete. GOD's mercy is infinite and His grace is sufficient for anything we may encounter in the physical or the spiritual life. **Ephesians 6:12** reminds us that we do not struggle with flesh and blood (physical) but instead we are inundated by unseen powers of darkness and wickedness of the supernatural arena. It's like being in a good mood and suddenly your mood changes to a negative for no apparent reason. Or everything you try to do, fails or isn't as successful as you planned it.

Jeremiah 1:5 reminds us that before we were a "thought" to our parents or a seed inside our mother, we are all born on purpose and for a purpose, no one is here by accident and everyone has a specific assignment to solve specific problems in this world. Consider this: GOD does not make mistakes, blunders, errors or slip ups. He never says oops, my bad or loses sight of us. Until someone has a problem, the person predestined to solve it, is unnecessary. So every time you solve a problem no matter how small or how big, understand GOD knew and designed each of us to solve that particular issue, everywhere there is a problem we have or are the solution.

*Take a moment here and write a declaration of all the things you believe you are/were born to solve.*_____

_____.

Example: I was born to give life to my daughter, who is sure to love and encourage the world one person at a time, with the love of Christ living on the inside.

CHOICES:

As Christians' we understand that GOD is able to do exceedingly and abundantly more that we can imagine or ask of Him; we just need to remember He is NOT a genie; He is GOD! The Creator of giving and receiving, the God of exchange and of choices. And in all we do in life for the most part requires we give, receive and make choices.

Example, GOD the Father, made a choice and gave us (humanity) His only Son, Christ Jesus (**John 3:16**) and although He (Jesus) was a gift, a response of acceptance or rejection, is required. This is a reminder to those who have already made the choice to accept Him as LORD and Savior. But for those who have not yet responded to the LORD...let me explain. In *I Corinthians 15:45[AMP]* when the first Adam made a choice to eat of the tree that caused humanity to be physically born into a state of spiritual death, separated from GOD for all eternity. This initiated an action by the last Adam (Jesus), Who made it possible for us to reconnected with GOD, the Father. Imagine everything wrong you have ever done, is erased, forgotten <u>permanently</u> and you can be restored with the Heavenly Father <u>by accepting</u> Jesus. He FORGIVES us for every negative, illegal, illegitimate, and destructive action ever committed and only GOD has the ability to forget all of them as well. For those who are visual like me, see illustration, when Adam sinned, he broke a covenant (promise, contract) between humanity and GOD. With the miracle birth of Jesus, His death on the cross, and His resurrected life, Christ made a way for humanity to reconnect with our Creator.

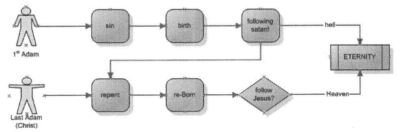

Make a choice: Heaven with GOD or hell without Him. By the way, saying you don't believe in hell, doesn't mean it not exist I pray no one ever finds out.

If you want to receive Jesus as your LORD and Savior right now, pray with your mouth and believe with your heart.... *Father, Thank You for salvation. I recognize Jesus is the true Son of GOD, Who takes away and forgives me of all my sins. Thank you for Your forgiveness, mercy and grace. Thank you for saving my soul, and with my Faith; (trust & belief in You) I am saved, Amen.*

Isn't it amazing how we experience life changing moments that we remember as milestones, where moments in time, solve problems or where promises are fulfilled.

WISDOM:

Proverbs 4:7 we are instructed to get skillful and godly wisdom which is a principle thing and in getting wisdom, we get interpretation, discernment and values of life. Individually and corporately, people talk of and desire success without knowing its true value. But when we choose to pursue wisdom, GOD shows us how to succeed. He gives us the ability to recognize the honor in people, to see differences in people, to recognize pain, attitude and purpose. There is wisdom in honoring it's the willingness to reward someone for their distinctions. Recently I heard, failures in life can usually be tracked to someone we dishonored. Think about it, corrections facilities (prison, jail) are full because someone chose to dishonor someone. Teach people to be honorable, especially our children. There was a time when honor was an established custom. We need to get back to teaching honor to our successors in life. When you look at the **10 Commandments** they are all about honor, **Exodus 20:3-17**. The first four (4) are about honoring GOD and the other six (6) are about honoring people. GOD gives each of us the choice again to succeed or fail just in making decisions with wisdom, of value and of honor.

Sowing seed: (the) **Genesis 8:22** states that while the earth remains, seedtime and harvest, cold and heat, summer and winter and day and night, shall not cease. When we understand seeds are sown and we reap the fruits of our labor, we are strategically positioned to plant seeds for all kinds of things. I believe knowledge is the seed for change, repentance (remorseful apology) is the seed for forgiveness and there's also the seed of our time and money into growing the Kingdom of God. It is vital that ANY time you sow seed; it should always be with an expectation (specific purpose).

Write a statement of expectation

My expectation is to be a giver and in turn I become a receiver. I give of my time, my knowledge and my finances as the LORD leads me. As a receiver, I am continuously blessed to be a blessing to others and realize daily, that Oh yes, He did make be a receiver!!

TRUSTWORTHY COMMUNICATIONS:

In my awe of GOD, I recognize the gift of communications He gives to some of us. It's not by chance that you are reading this chapter or this book. GOD knew before you or I that this deed would take place. In working with clients and customers, remind us constantly they expect and deserve reliable, truthful and consistent communications. The best strategy is to also provide incentive and consequence. In project management, meeting the expectations supporter/sponsors also means understanding requirements and the vision. I begin with asking and understanding the end goal, expectations and clearly document the vision not just a plan. Understanding the vision is important to fulfill the project, timely within budget and accomplish the intended purpose. In my opinion, it's important that the reward and consequences be relevant to drive the right behavior. Life decisions are the same way. Whether it's the natural life or the spiritual life, we need to set expectations, open ourselves up for GOD to use our talents, skills, passions and expertise not to mention our spiritual gifts. This is where GOD can show up, show out and position us to be whole and complete.

COMPASSION for OTHERS:

When I was invited to participate in this awesome Power of GOD project, my primary goal was for GOD to reveal Himself to you in whatever area you require. To be sure you know GOD loves us all unconditionally and He NEVER stops loving any of us no matter what we do or in some cases don't do. The consequence however can be more about our lack of obedience to the Word of God. It's said often, important to realize we're living in *dangerous times* and it's time for us to change both spiritually and naturally. People are starving to be healed from the physical and emotional traumas of life as well as being delivered and set free from the decisions of the past. Beware of false teachers and false doctrines; get in the Word of GOD. Knowledge is power. Most of us don't understand it's not the clothes, jewelry, cars, false nails or more shoes we need, don't get it twisted I like things and God is okay with things we like, but those are all temporary and empty methods the world throws at us to distract us from understanding it's about having a truly personal, intimate relationship with GOD! Once that decision is made, the joy and our new life begins. Put GOD and His interests first and He will give us the power to overcome the past (where so many of us need to also forgive ourselves). This will help in receiving His divine healing, wholeness and completeness; to be more like Jesus and pursue the Power of GOD. Important we seek the gift of knowledge which becomes revelation. At some point in our lives, we share the Gospel, learn scripture, are release from evil spirits that are on our lives before we accepted Christ into our hearts; understanding the prophetic spirits of the LORD. Did you know that **Psalms 23** is about Christ and how He walked through the valley of the shadow of death as well as **Psalms 91.** We can make the same claims as He instructed us to ONLY in Christ can we claim the promises of GOD in the scriptures. It's all about Jesus and not about me or you. It requires the anointing (power) of Christ in order to have the Power of GOD on our lives. HIS-tory is about the plan of redemption and the life of Christ. The other areas of power are in Praise and Worship. There is serious power when individuals gifted to sing and who are "called" of GOD. You can hear the power in their voice, we are moved to surrender all of our being to GOD when the anointing exists. But without the anointing, people are just gifted to entertain as they harmonize what is just a nice song.

FAVOR of GOD:

Let's not forget, we receive the awesome favor of GOD, where He restores EVERYTHING we lost. When we give up things in life for His sake, He repays us back for all we have lost. I heard a man of God say recently that in **Job 22:21[AMP]** "Acquaint now yourself with Him [agree with GOD and show yourself to be conformed to His will] and be at peace; by that [you shall prosper and great] good shall come to you and in, **Job 33:11.** It's fascinating to know that if we obey and serve Him, we will receive abundance of His promises.

Keep in mind we need to also understand what GOD wants for us and how to know how to tell the difference when satan is trying to destroy / distract us from our purpose.

Write out a list of things that are distracting you from accomplishing goals you have set or that the LORD has placed before you and how you plan to get back on track.

As for me, it is my prayer that every plan of satan on my life is destroyed only the plans of GOD for my life, business ministry is established and fulfilled! I pray for the biblical knowledge to prepare for the times we live. It's amazing to see prophecies of the Bible come to past. It's imperative to see the TRUTH of GOD not the deceit of the enemy.

It's crucial we play our part to pray and seek the will of GOD and understand we play part in the times we're living. When I think about the impact He has had on my life, it's difficult to contain it yet we live in a world that is offended by the Originator of life. I want to share His goodness with all who wish to hear it. I am not one to force the LORD on others, however, if you hint to needing Him or ask me about my joy, passion, love for others and willingness to help...I promise to share His Love for me and invite you to join His Family. Again, don't get it twisted I am not religious and I don't belong to a specific denomination. I have a personal relationship with GOD. If you are saved you know what I mean. I you are not save, reading this book is destiny. Making a conscious choice for your eternal life will forever change you and your circumstances. I am privileged to share with you my heart's desire. Getting into a Bible-based church is the next vital step **II Timothy 3:16-17**. You know, not long ago, I was content and unknowingly on my way to hell (separated from a relationship with Jesus), then the LORD touched my life and drew me into His way of life. I realized hell is lost hope, lost dreams and life not fulfilled. Humanity is burdened with wrong decisions where choices are not recanted, repented or corrected. Think about the hottest most miserable day and unluckiest times of your life. Multiply that by 100 and think about what it would be like to experience that <u>forever</u>. The world gives the appearance of being wonderful, attractive and inviting, but none of the alcohol, drugs, or vain promises can compare to the promises of GOD and having a personal relationship with His Son, Jesus Christ the Anointed One.

Here is some other areas of focus:

PRAY – connect, declare and decree your needs to the LORD. Set aside time, daily to have private heart-to-heart conversations with God. He will direct your path if you let Him.

FAITH – increase your level of forgiveness is the best and most sure-fire way to increase your faith. NOTHING pleases GOD more that our faith, **Hebrews 11:6**.

WORSHIP - the LORD in song, praising Him and in our giving. It is truly the joy of the LORD. Pursue Honor!

WISDOM – is our hammer, prudence will be our nails...courage never fails.

SPIRITUAL LIFE - with the LORD is a process that takes a lifetime, from Repentance, Forgiveness, Acceptance, Deliverance, Restoration, Accountability, and understanding Spiritual Warfare.

My friend and spiritual mentor, recently shared a profound word from the LORD, we can no longer afford to play church any more. Un-repented sin in the pulpit, open sin against the commandments of GOD can no longer be tolerated by the staff and workers of the church (Altar workers, hospitality, greeters, deacons, etc. It's time to ask GOD and the congregation for forgiveness. Make peace with GOD, and stop doing things we don't want to answer to GOD for. As agents of the church, please realize that you are a representative, an advocate and an Ambassador of GOD. You have a responsibility to live sanctified lives that honor GOD and to meet the expectations GOD has set for you and your life. He never gives us more that we can handle and He knows what we are capable of managing. We are all gifted to do what He has established. I know that I am not perfect. I know that I have come a long way from how I was, and because of all the LORD has done for me; I have made a conscious choice to live GOD's way. I implore you to reconnect with the GOD and receive all that He has for each of us and do not be afraid to share His love with others.

Take a moment; write out the vision for your life; includes sound choices, respectful communications and how to maintain compassion for all you encounter:

Godly Choices	Respectful Communications	Compassion for Others

Notes:

ABOUT THE AUTHOR

ELIZABETH M. WATERBURY, P.E., P.P., C.M.E.

Elizabeth Waterbury is the President and founder of E. M. Waterbury & Associates Consulting Engineers, a successful Consulting Engineering firm specializing in Land Use and Land Use Development. The focus of her career is to provide quality professional engineering services with a commitment to innovation and personal attention. Ms.Waterbury's firm consists of a talented group of professionals and support staff who have made their mark in this specialized field of engineering which is highly competitive and dominated by larger engineering firms.

When not working in her firm, Ms. Waterbury mentors others in professionalism, leadership and balance. This is accomplished through her many and diverse roles that vary from university professor to providing speeches as a member of The Professional Woman International Speakers Bureau. Her unique ability to channel her technical mind into creative and down-to-earth communication allows her to mentor to a broad range of individuals. One of her most honored rolls was to be the keynote speaker for the Southwest Regional Conference for the Society of Woman Engineer's. She has also been honored as a member of the International Advisory Board for The Professional Woman Network since 1990.

Her most cherished role is that of mother. She has worked hard since her daughter's birth to raise her daughter while running her firm. She is well versed in the difficulties that face women who wish to pursue their career, as well as be active in their family's lives. Her message of balance, defining personal success, and personal empowerment is carried through in all of her endeavors.

Contact
Elizabeth Waterbury, P.E., P.P., C.M.E.
E. M. Waterbury & Associates, P.A.
17 Monmouth Street
Red Bank, NJ 07701
(732) 747-6530
Fax (732) 747-6778
EMWAssoc@aol.com
www.protrain.net

TWENTY-EIGHT

I ASKED
WHY....

By Elizabeth Waterbury

"Why, Lord-why is this happening...Why us...Why here.... Why now?" My mind and heart has asked these questions in many forms, consciously and sub-consciously too many times in my life. It usually enters my mind when I am feeling a very heavy heart and through many tears. These are the times that the pain of the event tempts me to doubt God's presence or will. I become a doubting Thomas. Along with the pain comes a darkness that seems to limit my ability to see, hear or feel my loving God. To ask this question is to be human.

I spent this past weekend taking my daughter to summer camp. Her best friend talked her into coming to camp with her in Pennsylvania, 320 miles away from our home. This is close enough to tempt us to drive, but far enough that it is a full weekend of driving. We live in NJ. The area we live in is across from NY harbor. The communities in our areas have always been bedroom communities for "The City", as we call it. 'The City' of course being New York City, NYC. We have always enjoyed the benefits offered by 'The City". Besides work opportunities, 'The City' gives us access to some of the world's best foods, theater, Christmas lights, and my daughters favorite, shopping. On September 11, 2001, however our proximity came at a cost. Our area was the second hardest hit for losses during the terrorist attacks on the Trade Center Towers. We asked, our neighbors asked, our towns asked, our country asked "Why Lord?" on that day.

We arrived at camp a day early to give us time to feel out the area. My husband and I took a walk from the hotel to stretch our legs and we saw this huge flag on a flagpole tucked behind a commercial building. The flag's size peaked our curiosity, so we walked over guessing along the way what it was for. In casual chit chat my husband offers that a friend told him that the flight 93 crash site was somewhere near us in western Pennsylvania. We climbed up into the memorial that surrounded the flag and saw that it had been constructed by the County of Somerset to honors the heroes of that flight. We realized we were near the site and quickly worked to find the location. We were drawn to the site and felt an immediate link to the community. Their community too had felt the direct impact of the events of that day. They too had had their landscape permanently changed. They too had their hearts filled with the pain of the day. We quickly packed and jumped into the car to find the site. We drove out of the town, over the hills, and into the country until we found the memorial field. We took a heavy breath and got out of the car.

Flight 93 had left Newark airport heading for California on Sept 11, 2001. Half way across Pennsylvania the Terrorists had taken over the plane and redirected the flight toward Washington. It is assumed that the intended target was the Capital building where our legislators were in session. The passengers had heard of the attacks in NYC and the Pentagon and figured this plane too was intended to be used as a weapon. The passengers said good bye to their families on their cell phones and took action against the attackers. The plane crashed in a field, upside down, at a speed of over 500 miles per hour. The flight had lasted about 20 minutes. No one survived at that site, but the intended victims, the leaders of our country, were saved by the heroic efforts of the brave passengers on that plane.

Our area is full of stories of that day. We all know people who survived and we all know people who did not. We all questioned if more attacks would occur in our area on that day. We all scrambled to gather family, friends and neighbors to see who was ok and who was not. We waited to hear about those who were missing. We anxiously waited for news. The local TV stations had been knocked out when the antennas were destroyed that were on the towers. We did not have cable at that time. We gathered clothes for the people covered in the dust of the area to wear after cleaning up. Hospitals readied themselves to receive thousands of injured that did not come. We gathered to pray and you heard people ask "Why God?".

Our journey to answer this question for us began earlier that year and in some ways decades before. My mother had died of cancer when I was a teen. My father was devastated and his life fell apart. He was the breadwinner of the household and did not know what to do with the 4 kids he was now to take care of after she died. He was lost in his own grief. He had also been self employed with no health insurance so he lost everything due to the medical bills. He did his best, but he was so full of grief that his life slowly sank into darkness. In some ways it was like we lost both parents at once.

My father had one sister, Aunt Betty. She was married to Uncle Walt and had a disabled son, Larry who had MS and was slightly mentally challenged. Larry was much older than I. They lived in a small 5 room house. Uncle Walt worked sometimes 2 to 3 jobs to maintain the household. They had grown up during the depression and knew the difficulty life can offer. Sometimes the only food they had to eat was what they grew. Uncle Walt had a huge green thumb. They knew selflessness. They opened their doors to become our new parents. Their door was always open. Some of my siblings lived on and off with them. They would give you whatever food they had and always give you their love regardless what crazy thing was going on. As you can imagine we were pretty lost and at times would get into some crazy things. After my Uncle retired (my uncle was 10 years older than my dad), they would watch soap operas. This was fortunate as the craziness of the stories luckily were usually one step above what we would be going through so it prepared them for the events of raising modern children in the 1980's.

Although we would joke when we were young about what we perceived as their boring and predictable life, it was a god sent for us. As we got older and had our kids it was something we tried to replicate. They were our rock. Uncle Walt was simple, brave, strong, loving and practical. In February of 2001 at the age of 88, he went to the doctor and they found an abdominal aneurysm in his main artery to his legs. They told him it could burst any time, or he could out live it. He could not live with the vision of what his wife would find if it burst, so he wanted it removed. We went to Robert Wood Johnson Hospital in New Brunswick NJ and in March of that year he had surgery. The surgery was a success. He was relocated to a rehab hospital that was so horrible that in 3 days he almost died from poor conditions. We got him back to Robert Wood Johnson in time and he recovered, but was too weak to breath on his own. He went on the ventilator. The ventilator is a breathing tube that goes down the throat and forces air into the lungs. He was conscious, aware, able to think, and able to talk to us (by mouthing words). He just could not breathe on his own well enough. So it began.

The hospital was about 45 min away from the house. Neither his son nor his wife was able to drive at that time. My Aunt went to the hospital every day. She was 85. They had been married for over 65 years and had only taken one weekend away from each other. My sister and I took over the primary responsibilities of the household, medical care, legal ramifications and transportation responsibilities. We had two other siblings and we would have a rotating schedule for getting Aunt Betty to the hospital and back. My dad would help at the house with his nephew. Uncle Walt would get stronger and begin to breathe on his own. We would discuss him coming home and then he would get an infection, become weak again and go back on the vent. This happened over and over. It was an extreme roller coaster. I was self employed so I would bring my laptop to the hospital and try to stay on top of everything while traveling back and forth. We all had families of our own so it was a balancing job for all. Many times I would ask God why? We did not want him to die, but we did not want him living like this either. We would joke that if nothing else at least, it can't get any worse.

In the middle of the summer my sister and I got a call late in the night. My Aunt had had a heart attack at home. After getting her settled, my sister and I were in the local hospital elevator going home. It was probably 3 am. We looked at each other and began a pact that we would never ask "what else could happen?" again. We now had the two people we loved most in separate hospitals 45 minutes away from each other and a disabled person at home to care for. I would ask God for a sign as to why this is happening. I would ask God for strength.

The beginning of September Uncle Walt went through another round of hopefully getting off the vent and then getting an infection. It was apparent that each time he went through this he took a hit and became weaker. He would ask us to please take him of the vent, but his wife maintained hope and was not able to hear the requests. Finally her heart was able to hear him. She accepted it was time to take him off the vent. We scheduled to go up to talk to the doctor about taking him off the vent the next day and for the family to come and say good bye before we did that. The next day, on September 11, 2001, I was getting ready to take her up to the hospital to talk to the doctor about taking him off of the vent when the first plane hit the towers. No one knew what it was. They thought "How could a plane go so off course? What a horrible accident!"

It soon became evident that this was no accident. NYC is visible on a clear day when you are on the loop exiting the NJ Parkway onto the NJ Turnpike. The smoke was rising from the side of the one tower. Shortly after we rounded the curve onto the NJ Turnpike, the second plane hit. The radio was alive with excitement about the disaster. When we got to the hospital I made the mistake of just letting my Aunt out of the car at the drop off without getting out to help her. She stepped out of the car and fell. We then ended up in the emergency room. Robert Wood Johnson hospital is a regional trauma hospital. We were now in the middle of the emergency room of one of the hospitals preparing to take on the thousands from the attack. Rumors flew about the attack. There were rumors that the Sears building in Chicago had been hit. There were no TVs. People were working at their jobs, yet trying to find out about their families and the events. There was talk of them shutting down the city of New Brunswick to allow only emergency response into the hospitals. My sister was with me, and we were trapped.

We could not use cell phones in the ER so we were limited to the few phones that were in the hospital. I went to my Uncles room. The news on the cable TV was alive with the events. We watched the video of the towers fall over and over. He was disgusted and asked to have it turned off. He was the protector of the family. He was a doer. He was a prisoner in his bed. He shut his eyes and would not speak.

In the course of the morning we had gotten through to the rest of the family. All were safe, although scattered in the State. We decided to wait on taking action with my Uncle until the next day to allow the family to say good-bye. In the course of or discussions with siblings we found out that my brother, whom had a securities company at the time, was to be in the towers that day. Like so many stories we heard, something interceded that day to keep him from there. Early that morning, before the planes had even taken off, he had canceled his meeting with his partners and peers at Cantor Fitzgerald in the towers to be able to say good-bye to my Uncle. The strength given to my Uncle for all those months had saved my brother. We were the lucky ones. Besides our brother being safe, our prayers from all those months had been answered. We knew why.

After hearing that and understanding what that meant, I returned to my Uncles room. I told him that he had been our hero again. That he had saved our brother by being so strong. He had cared for us.

The next day we all met and said good-bye. Later that afternoon he was removed from the vent. He had asked to just be kept comfortable and to sleep. In the middle of the second night, early in the morning of September 14, 2001, he passed. We shared this story at the funeral. That at a time when the world seemed to have no God, that God was there, saving those that were saved, and for those that passed, God sent angels to escort and welcome into a peaceful and loving heaven.

It is in times of deep pain that we wonder "why" from God. Thousands who lost loved ones on that day have their own journeys to reconcile the event with God. Ten years later many are still struggling with that question. It's a personal journey. For us, we got to see God's hand.

Over the years many have shared their stories. It was noted during the news accounts of the tower attack, that the death toll should have been thousands greater. On a normal day thousands more should have been there. For some reason those thousands more were not there. Many whom I spoke to, like my brother, indicated something had interceded and kept them from being there that day, or got them to leave. For people that were there, the day was full of heroes; people that sacrificed themselves to help others. I believe they were all helped by God's angels. The angels were in NYC, they were at the Pentagon, and they were there with the passengers on Fight 93.

When I get in difficult situations I remember that day. The event reminded us all of what's important. We were all equalized that day. The events of the day impacted rich and poor, old and young, man and woman, and many races. And out of it the communities all pulled together. It is the grace of God that helped us to rise up from the ashes and continue on. We are asked to not fear the future. To live each day like there is no other. To help others. To believe.

I still have times that life's events feel so large, feel so difficult. As I write this the country is dealing with the Colorado movie theater massacre. Seemingly senseless killings by ones that believe it is justified. Human acts observed by God. I believe he cries on these days. I listen to the stories of heroes saving others. God's angels at work. I listen to the stories of the community pulling together to rise above and recover. God's grace at work. And I believe God welcomed those that died into heaven and will be there to soothe their survivor's hearts if they let him.

Although I speak of extreme events, we all have our hard times and difficult events that we go through. My story above is not intended to minimize or invalidate the impact we feel from what may seem like comparatively minor but difficult events; whether it is a death of a loved one, a divorce, addictions, bullying, economic difficulty or other. We all are frozen at times with challenges, hurtles, heartache or fear. My minister always tells us that life is hard. No one is immune. God is there to help us with the difficulty. We have to be willing to open our hearts and ears to hear him, and have the courage to trust and move forward as we are guided.

That may sound easy, but its not. When I have a heavy heart due to overwhelming challenges, or feelings of despair, hopelessness or inadequacy, it is heard for me to listen. I want it to be over when I want it to be over. My timing is usually not God's timing. I need patience to carry on until it is Good's time. If we had changed anything with my Uncle's illness, he may have passed earlier and my brother would have been in the towers on September 11, 2001. I tell myself this when I am impatient with a difficult situation. I look to remind myself that I do not know the big picture. That picture can be greater than me. When I tried to act within my frame of reference I am restricted by only what I know. God knows all. If I allow him to guide, then I have seem that I am lead to things greater than I could imagine.

It takes work to let God lead. My job is to work at the following so that I can keep myself open to hear his word and to let him lead:

- <u>Know myself</u>- I need to know myself so that I know my baggage, weaknesses and triggers. It is my job to not let my baggage run my life.

- <u>Give myself time to listen to his guidance</u>-if I am always running in chaos then I do not have time to stop and listen. I need to give myself permission to stop and listen. I can not depend on others around me to give this to me; I have to give it to myself;

- <u>Strengthen myself so I can have the courage to follow as asked and stand up to my beliefs</u>- sometimes we are criticized for our beliefs. Don't let criticisms of others make you deny your beliefs or keep you from doing what needs to be done;

- <u>Educate myself to his example so I can separate his voice from destructive voices-</u> I have always regretted decisions made in the heat of a dark emotion. Voices of revenge or retaliation separate me from my God. I am to educate myself with the knowledge of how I am to act to stay connected. For me I stay connected by going to church and learning about the bible. I am Presbyterian so I believe in my direct relationship with God. The information I take in helps me to understand my relationship with God and what it is I need to do to keep myself connected to God.

- <u>Surround myself with a support group</u>-When I am in a dark place, I need help to stay connected. When I let the thoughts from those emotions just stay on my head without voicing them they get more power. Sometimes I need others to guide me and to not let those emotions take over. I note though it is important whom I choose to share these emotions with. If I am trying to avoid addiction, I should speak to those that are trying to do the same and have been successful. If I choose to speak to active addicts about wanting to quit, I will not get support for my task. It is my job to pick the right support system;

- <u>Be willing to volunteer to help others.</u> - When I help others, even when I need help my self, it opens me up to hear God word. I have many nephews and nieces whom have lived with us over the years and we always tell them that volunteering is important to make changes in their own lives.

- <u>Be thankful for all I have</u> -I have found that during my darkest moments I can open myself up by giving thanks at night for all that I have every day, even when I feel there is nothing good. It makes me focus on the good God has given. It can be for the family I have, the shelter, the clothing, the food or even something as simple as a gentle jester from a stranger on that day.

- <u>Don't beat myself up for being human</u>- No one is perfect. We all have our weak moments. We all have our individual journeys. We all have our chapters that guide how we think, feel and have as a frame of reference for processing things. Look at yourself and your actions with a loving eye. We may not like some of our behavior, but we can still love ourselves as we get closer to God. As noted above, life is hard. We don't need to make it harder by beating on ourselves as well. We don't want others to do it to us so why do it to ourselves.

I work for myself and I always tell people that I have a tough boss. Sometimes I will give my workers more of a break than I will myself. God loves me just the way I am. Why not give that to myself as well! Also if we are beating up on ourselves we will most likely not be open and available for those we love. We need all the love we can get when we are having a hard time.

- Lastly- Trust in God – When I ask "Why", I am not trusting. God is too big for me to wrap my head around so I do not believe I will always understand 'why' even if he told me. It's like a parent with a kid. My experience is far greater, deeper and longer than my daughters. When I offer instruction in behavior it is coming from experiences that she maybe can't comprehend yet. I have decades more years of living then she has had as a teenager. My advice and guidance is based on all that background. God's background and experiences are from the before the beginning of time. Our human mind can never understand or comprehend all of that.

  The teenagers in our lives question all we do, feel they know better, think they should be in control, and are impatient. Sometimes I am like a teenager with my relationship with God. I think I know better, my timing is the most important, and I think I am in control. All I can say is MISTAKE. Let go let God. When I let my heart trust him, I have gone places I never would have envisioned.

We are human, so we will always consciously or un-consciously ask "Why". The answer is we may not always know why. Some pains and experiences that cause us to ask this are the result of human actions; some are from life's events that do not seem to be fair at the time, like the loss of a child. On a human level the pain caused from these events will never seem to make sense to us. It is during these times that God offers us Grace. He is there to help us to rise above and to make the lemonade from lemons. Like a loving parent we are embraced and guided through the difficulty, if we let him. When I start to ask "why", I work to stop myself, trust that I am in loving hands and work to keep myself open to his guidance. It is hard work, but so worth it.

ABOUT THE AUTHOR

LaWanda Hill

LaWanda Hill, founder of Preserve Life Ministries in Baton Rouge, Louisiana, is a respected spiritual leader, co-author, speaker, life coach, mother, wife, philanthropist, humanitarian, and minister of the Word of God. She has impacted people from every walk of life.

LaWanda brings excitement to ministering, helping individuals bring clarity, joy and balance into their life and business while enhancing personal and professional relationships and creating fulfillment in every area of their life.

LaWanda believes that we as "Believers" are living epistles and should be winning others over to God through our lifestyle. She strives to be an example of Christ and follows the Truth. She seeks the honor that comes only from God and is always striving for more of God. She is strong in the faith, always giving glory to God; and fully persuaded that what He had promised, He is well able to perform in her life. She does not bow to circumstances, circumstances bow to her. Her nature is love, for love fulfills the whole law. All men are to be like God, filled with God and ruled by God.

LaWanda is dedicated to creating and providing programs, resources, and services to help those in need. LaWanda founded Preserve Life Ministries on a passion and love for people and a drive to see change in the world.

LaWanda has a degree in Divinity. She is married to Darius Hill, who has a degree in Divinity. They have six wonderful children.

Contact:
LaWanda Hill Ministries
P.O. Box 318177
Baton Rouge, LA 70831
www.lawandahill.com
info@lawandahill.com
Tel. 225-341-5438

TWENTY-NINE

"BUT GOD!"

By LaWanda Hill

"You intended to harm me, but God intended it for good to accomplish what is now being done, the saving of many lives." (Genesis 50:20)

Have you ever been in a situation where death was near, but God kept it from taking you out? There have been times in our lives where the enemy came in like a flood, but God lifted up a standard against him.

As I sat back and thought about how good God is I recalled a time when I had a blow out on the interstate. It was around 5 o'clock in the evening when most people are getting off work and I was driving down the highway. My husband gave me the nickname "lead" foot because he said I drive a bit fast. So, I was driving my usual speed, when all of a sudden I heard this loud noise and my car began to spin continuously in the middle of the interstate. As I was spinning around and around and around, I wondered if it would ever stop and when it did, what would happen next? All kinds of thoughts went through my head. Well, the car finally ceased spinning and then went expeditiously off the interstate and down the hill. When the car came to a complete stop all I could say is, "Thank you Lord!" I was still alive and I had not been injured at all. Of course, I had a dent on the back side of my car, but that was minor.

Perhaps you may be wondering if challenging life events are really an accident or a coincidence and you're wondering " Where is God? What's really going on:? or "Lord, why me"? "But, God....!"Don't you know that whatever trial you're experiencing in your life right now is for a divine purpose? Whatever it is, no matter how it feels or what it looks like, it just doesn't matter. I know it's painful, but there just may be good behind it after all. And if you just hold on you'll see that God's hand was in it all the while.

Look back over your life 5 years ago, or 10 years ago at the situations you encountered and how although some of them didn't feel too good and how uncomfortable they were, you survived. How many times did you say to yourself "God, Why?"

That thing that you went through years ago, it doesn't even bother you now, as a matter of fact you had forgotten it even happened. It doesn't even have an effect on you anymore. Well, don't you know that just as you made it through that situation, this too shall pass. So, whatever it is you're going through right now, next year or the year after that it will not have an effect on you IF you take on the right attitude. You may have to deal with another issue, but it won't be this one.

You must get the right attitude and know that if God brought you out of past situations, He will bring you out of this one. The Word of God lets us know that we have the victory. We triumph in all things, not some things, not half of them, but in ALL things. God declares, "It is well with the righteous." So, if God say's it's well, then it is well.

It is well with you. God goes beyond our circumstances and beyond our situations and manifests His glory in our life even when we don't deserve it.

So, whatever it is you're going through, it is to strengthen you. It's to build you. It's to make you and mold you. I don't know about anybody else, but if it weren't for hell; and all I've been through, I wouldn't be who I am today. I may not be all that God wants me to be, but I can tell you one thing, *I'm not what I used to be.* God has brought me a mighty long way and I'm just going to keep on in my journey with Him because I know that this time next year I'm going to be a better woman than I am today. And the year after that, I'll be a better woman than I was the year before.

All Things Work Together For Your Good

We must learn to yield to God and allow Him to do what He wants to do in our lives. When we do, we'll experience a level in God like never before. We will become better people and fit for the Master's use. So, just let God do what He wants to do in your life. God didn't promise that it was going to be all sugar and cream or a piece of cake or whatever it is that you like. He did promise that, "I will be with you. I will never leave you neither will I forsake you. I will be with you until the end."

Being broken doesn't feel good. It appears disastrous, but if you just hold on to God's unchanging hand you shall come out as pure gold. You must take on the attitude of " Lord, I know one thing, that you're here with me, and that you will never leave me or forsake me. And although it doesn't feel good, I know you're working out for my good. Therefore, I won't be moved. I won't be sway to the left, I won't sway to the right, but I will remain steadfast and immovable and always abounding in the things of you Lord. "

You must know He's working it out for your good. Weeping may endure for a night, but joy comes in the morning and, the morning is going to come; no matter how long the night is, morning has to come. And when morning comes it will come with the good. With morning comes your breakthrough, with morning comes your peace, with morning comes your joy, with morning comes your healing. Are you waiting on morning? Just hold on because morning has to come. It won't stay night forever. Morning has to come!

Be Strong and Courageous - Trust God

"Be strong and courageous. Do not be afraid or discouraged because of the king of Assyria and the vast army with him, for there is a greater power with us than with him. With him is only the arm of flesh, but with us is the LORD *our God to help us and to fight our battles." And the people gained confidence from what Hezekiah the king of Judah said."*
(2 Chronicles 32:7,8)

It is major that the people of God learn to rest in God. When you learn to rest in God you begin to see things differently. You begin to see circumstances through the eyes of God. And you take on the attitude that no matter what it looks like, you're resting in God. Don't you know that at night while you sleep, you're getting your rest. So change your attitude. Look at the situation differently.

It's okay to cry, get it out. Don't let anyone tell you, 'don't cry'. You better get it out. If you keep all of that stuff inside of you and don't release it, you will be a bomb waiting to explode. Have you ever seen a bomb explode? You know that's not pretty! Some people lose their minds. Get it out. Don't hold on to that stuff. Get it out and move on.

That situation is bigger than you, but it's just right for God. "Baby, God got this". When we learn to cast our cares on the Lord, it is no longer our problem, but God's. Therefore, it is not my battle to fight, but God's. I'm just going to rest in and wait until my change comes.

It Shall Come to Pass

"Then he continued, "Do not be afraid, Daniel. Since the first day that you set your mind to gain understanding and to humble yourself before your God, your words were heard, and I have come in response to them. But the prince of the Persian kingdom resisted me twenty-one days. Then Michael, one of the chief princes, came to help me, because I was detained there with the king of Persia. Now I have come to explain to you what will happen to your people in the future, for the vision concerns a time yet to come." (Daniel 10:12-14)

In Daniel Chapter 10, Daniel was frightened by a vision, but was reassured by a messenger. Daniel had prayed and fasted, but the enemy tried to oppose the plan of God. However, Daniel did not stop praying. He prayed fervently and earnestly expecting a answer. Daniel's answer was detained for three weeks. God's messenger eventually arrived assisted by the archangel, Michael. The name Michael means, "Who is like God."

There are times when prayers may be hindered by evil forces. Although they may be hindered they cannot be stopped. Like Daniel, expect God to hear and answer your prayers. Trust God to come through for you just as He did for Daniel.

Just as there are spirits that are assigned to try and keep you from getting to your next level, to keep you from conquering, or possessing the goods, there are also angels assigned to you, 'your posse' to help you get to your next level and to possess all that God has planned for your life. So tell the devil, "Go ahead and play with me if you want to, but, my posse, has my back. My posse got you! You have a cloud of witnesses cheering you on. They are your cheerleaders, saying, "go ahead and conquer that thing, we have your back. Handle your business girl. Handle your business boy, we've got your back. You can do this! And they just take us on in.

Daniel was going through some stuff. Daniel needed to hear from God. He needed a word from the Lord. Perhaps you are saying, "Lord I need to hear from you right now! What's going on, I haven't heard from you in quite some time? I need you to talk to me right now. I need answers for this situation that I'm in now. I need you to give me some answers for these issues that I'm going through. I need a word from you Lord. I need to hear from God." You may be having a Daniel experience and the devil doesn't want you to get your answer. But God... The enemy might hold it up but he can't stop it!

That's alright, you can play with it for a little while devil, but you can't have it. You have to lose it, you have to release it, you've got to let it go. Because my God says that it's mine, my name is on that. He promised it to me. God is not a man that He should lie. Neither is He the son of man that He should repent. If He said he's going to do it than He's going to do it. God says you can play with it if you want to, but you've got to let it go!

The devil knows that if you get that word, it is over! He is going to have to hang it up. And there is nothing he can do about it. It is over. He knows that once you get the word you need, it's over. So, he plays with it in the spirit realm. They were warring in the spirit and Michael was saying, "Oh, but Susan need this right now". Jason needs it. Paul needs it. Whomever, call your own name out. They need it. They have to have it. My Daddy promised it to them and they are waiting on it. They were warring in the spirit for 21 days!

How Will You Respond?

See, the devil knows that your future is bright. He already knows. He knows. That's why he causes the turmoil to go on in your life. It's just a distraction. That's all it is. It's just a distraction. But guess what? How you respond to it determines how fast you will come up out of it. If you respond with a positive attitude then you will come out faster.

It's time to stop letting the enemy come into your life and do what he wants. I dare you to get up and gird yourself with the Word of God and prayer and take back everything that the enemy has stolen from you. The devil has got some of your stuff and it's time for him to let it go. All you have to do is just go in and get it. Some of your stuff isn't even a struggle for you to reach. All you have to do is go get it. But, there is some stuff that God says will come through only with fasting and prayer. Some stuff we are just going to have to pray and fast for. But, He has some stuff that all we have to do is just go get it. Stop being lazy and go get it. Quit being rebellious and just go get it. From the very first day you spoke it out of your mouth, when you made your request known, God heard you. Oh yes, He did! He heard you. And from the first day you spoke it , the day you made your request known,

God started working on it. Do you believe that? It's true. The Word says, "The first day". *"For from the first day, thou didst set thine heart to understand and to chasen thyself before thy God, though words were heard."* Your words were heard! Your words were heard! God heard you! The God that I serve tells me that whatsoever I desire will be mine. Believe it. Receive it. And thou shall have it. He didn't say when, He just says you shall have it.

When I make my request known, God hears me and he starts working on the situation and working on me. He's working on me to prepare me to receive it, so that I will appreciate what He does for me. Now how long it takes you to get prepared, that's on you. Ask God for help if you need help. Tell God, "Lord, I need your help" and then keep holding on.

When we choose to do things our way God just sits back and say, "Oh, I just wish they would just get out of my way and let me do it." We must learn to give it to God and to wait on God. The word of God declares, that we have need of patience, that after we have done the will of the Father, we shall obtain the promise.

When we get the attitude that God wants us to have He can release it to us. How quick you respond with the right attitude is how quick you will get whatever it is you desire from God. God has to equip us to be able to handle, manage, and take care of what He places in our care or puts in our hands. Many Christians right now, when making a request of God really can't handle it. You do know that, right? If God gives certain things to us, it would be like He has never given it to us. Have you ever heard of people winning the lottery, millions of dollars, and the next year or so they're broke? I mean, who can spend that kind of money in a year? And what are they buying? They got that money but they didn't know what to do with it. This has been the case for some athletes, actors, actresses, and singers; some of them just dabbled in all kinds of stuff and they got all messed up in their minds because mentally they are not prepared to handle what they obtained. That's because mentally they were not prepared to receive that amount of money. Therefore, God prepares and equips us to receive His blessings.

God says, "You are mine and I don't want you to waste this or I don't want it to take you over and to take you out, I need you to be ready for it". God loves us enough to prepare us for whatever it is that He is about to bless us with in this life. God doesn't just want you to be blessed by it, but He want your children, and your children's children to blessed by it as well. He wants our generations to be blessed so He prepares us to be able to handle it. You must be prepared spiritually, physically, and mentally so that when you receive the promise you're going to be well-balanced and enduring. You won't have a little of this and a lot of that. God wants us to be balanced spiritually, physically, mentally and financially. He doesn't want you to have so much in the natural world that you aren't any good in the Spirit world and you can't even help anybody. God doesn't want that. He wants us to be balanced. He doesn't want us rich and all broken down and we can't even enjoy our money. He says, "Balance". So, let God do it! Let Him do it!

Ask for Help

Thy words were heard. Oh yeah, He heard you! And I am come for thy words. I come to get them. I come to get your words. He moved this out of the way and got that out of your way. He opened that door and closed that door. Even as I speak right now your words are working for you. You're going to have your mind so right that you're next in line for a miracle. Some of your words will go farther than somebody else's but that's okay; that means my blessing is going to be bigger than somebody else's. Do what you do, Lord.

Sometimes you might need to call on Michael. I'm telling you, Michael will fight for you! Michael can throw down in the spirit. Let me give you some wisdom, the next time that you are going through something and you feel overwhelmed, just say this, "Lord, I'm just tired!" Then, do this for me, say, "MICHAEL...I NEED YOU RIGHT NOW, BOY!!! I need you to fight for me, Michael. I know you said you had my back, Michael, I need you to fight for me"!!

When you begin to trust God, you and your household will be delivered.

Notes:

_____

_____

_____

_____

_____

_____

_____

_____

_____

_____

_____

_____

_____

_____

_____

_____

_____

_____

_____

_____

ABOUT THE AUTHOR

PAMELA DENISE GRAHAM

Pamela Denise Graham is the mother of two son's Rhoshe and Rhamelle Jackson, grandmother of four grandchildren. She is an Ordained Minister at Word of Life Ministries where she resides in one of the seventh wonders of the World Niagara Falls New York. She has served as a Youth Sunday School Teacher, Christian Growth Teacher, one of Niagara County Jail Ministries Bible Study Teachers for Women. She is also the founder of Woman in Travail Ministries Newsletter/Magazine; she holds a two year Associates Degree in Communications and Media Arts, currently enrolled at Buffalo State College to get her Bachelor's Degree in Journalism. Ms. Graham is also a Member of the National Society for Leadership and Success Alpha Sigma Pi. In August of 2011 she received her Certification as Life Coach for Women's Issues from (PWN).

Her passion in life is to be a blessing to Women from all walks of life that have been abandoned, abused and forgotten. Pamela's mission is to bring healing to women and restore them back to living their lives in wholeness Body, Mind, and Spirit. Ms. Graham loves God and puts Him first in everything that she does; then her Family, she lives to be an example for all people.

Books:
- Releasing Strongholds: Letting go of what's holding you back.
- The Celebration of Life: Inspiration For Women

Contact:
pamelagraham31@yahoo.com

THIRTY

BROKENNESS / A SHATTERED LIFE / A PERSONAL TESTIMONY

Pamela Graham

While the spring rain fell against my window, as I sat praying and pondering my past experiences. I began to thank God for where He had brought me from. Every now and again the Lord takes me back to my yesterdays, to remind me that He is yet worthy in my life. That it's not by chance that I am saved by grace today. As I sat in the presence of the Lord He started ministering to the very core of my being. I could hear the Lord speaking expressively to me, "It's time to be made whole." While the Spirit of God was speaking I could not grasp what He was trying to say to me. Knowing that I had given my life to Him well over seven years at the time, I thought I was fine, I thought that I had been delivered from something's in my past. Yes I was going through like my fellow Christians in the Lord, as it turned out the longer I sat in the presence of the Almighty God; He just began to strip, uncover, and reveal old hurts and wounds. The tears began to flow the Lord said to me, "you have been wounded all these years and went around hiding and covering up what you endured in your childhood." In reality I needed mending on the inside my life was just broken and all messed up, I was overwhelmed with the fact that I could be saved and still not be whole and complete in God. Suddenly my past came flashing back as though the hurt happened yesterday; the blessing this time around was that what the devil meant for evil God turned it around for His good. God was exposing my brokenness so that I would be able to tell someone else about deliverance.

Being a child of domestic violence, coming from a dysfunctional family watching Mom and Dad fighting and arguing all the time, many times alcohol would be the root cause of everything. Back in the day My Parents were the type of people that worked very hard during the week, but by Friday they would wont to let their hair down and party and drink, one thing lead to another and before the night was over a fight would break out. My sister and I were so accustomed to the violence until we thought it was just common place for a women and men to be abusive to each other. But in essence it was not normal behavior; there was something wrong with that picture. When arguments and fights broke out my sister and I would grab each other and run out of the apartment looking for anyone that would help us or our parents. I can remember people opening their doors and seeing us and just closing their doors, as if to say that's them fighting again. Often times my mother would have a black eye, a cut and a bruise of some sort, but my mother fought back at all times and my dad would have some marks on him as well. I can remember my father holding knives to my mother's that and guns to her head he would say, "if you breathe I'll slit your through, or I'll blow your brains out." the domestic violence was getting serious I still can hear my sister and I screaming to the top of our lungs with fear. When I look back those were desperate cries from two little girls that were frightened for their Parents lives.

They were so caught up in their lives that they didn't know that their youngest daughter was being molested at the age of six to eight years of age. My abuse would always happen at different family functions; I got to the place where I knew when to expect it at times I would prepare myself mentally. I would act like it didn't matter; it was just look playing house (except this was real life). I learned how to keep a secret, I remember growing up and mother would tell us girls it wasn't good to keep secrets; nevertheless I did keep this secret because my family was already going through so much. I chose to keep the abuse to myself, until this very day I never told my mother or father what happened to me. My mother and father were still caught up in themselves, I can remember the last time my father raised his hand to hit my mother, and my sister jumped in the middle of them and said, "If you hit my mother one more time I'll kill you." (What a thing for a child to say) After she spoke her peace, mom and dad were quiet they began to go to different areas of our apartment, softly you could hear my mother crying. She thought about everything that was going on in our family, and how dangerous it would be to keep living like this they really did love each other but this life was not good anymore. Surely there was more to life than this, after a couple of weeks had passed mom and dad still weren't talking or on speaking terms, so this particular morning we got up for school and got dressed my parents did the same. My father left for work first then my mother began to pack we had no idea that she was planning on moving, she explained to us girls that we would be leaving and would not be coming back. I tell you it was the best decision that she could have made, but it bothered me that I would be leaving so many of our cousins and friends. Nevertheless it was working out for my good because not only did she come out of her abuse I also came out of my own (Praise God).

Looking back over my childhood I can honestly say that I was never a child. Mt childhood had been stolen from me never to get it back again Even as a young child I was living with a broken spirit. I was never able to play with my peers; I always wanted to be around older people way beyond my years to lose that part of my life was devastating and the impact was great. As a little girl I said that, "I will never hurt another child like I was hurt." I can boldly proclaim that I have never hurt or abused anyone. By the worlds standards once you have been molested chances are that you will become an abuser, but I beg the difference, praise God you don't have to become what you've been through.

As a direct result of going through such much in my short life, I began to smoke cigarettes when I was eight years old. Living a fast paced life at the age of eleven I was already smoking weed running the streets whenever I felt like it I was off the hook. No one could tell me anything, feeling hurt at time not being able to share what happened to me; defiant saying harmful things to people because of my wounds. Found myself at the age of thirteen drinking liquor, ("see the weed wasn't enough high for me to cover up the pain.") Sneaking out to parties and dances, staying out all night long (enjoying the devil), going to bars and didn't need ID. On the road to destruction education was not important to me trying to be grown was important to me and staying as high as I could get was what I was living for. My mother could never figure out why I was so out of control, but only if she knew what happened to me. I was so disobedient it had to be Pam's way or no way. When I ran the street it was a source of comfort, because I didn't have time to think about my issues, grown men would give me money, buy me cigarettes. I wasn't in to the sex thing but I knew sooner or later that those men were not just going to keep giving me their money they were going to want something in return. Nevertheless I kept taking the money, you might be wondering where my mother was in all of this, she was there right there I was just an out of control kid looking for a way of escape from the pain. As time went on my behavior was getting a little better I was now about seventeen years old some said that I would never make it to that age, but I made it. It was the Power of God that had begun to start changing some things in my life. I was getting good grade in school on commendable achievement just a step down from the honor roll. Things were really looking up until someone close to my heart my cousin my best friend was hit by a driver that was on drugs and alcohol, subsequently she passed away at the age of fifteen years old. That experience was enough for me to straighten up and fly right. That was the first time I heard the voice of God He was trying to give me a wakeup call. People for years had been telling me to slow down, but it took God to say it's time to slow down it was something about hearing that voice that made all the difference in my life. I began to feel the hand of God on my life, so I started changing people places and things. Finally I was graduating from high school a task that I never thought I would accomplish, but

I have my mother to thank for that she pushed me to finish school. After graduating I found out that I was pregnant at the age of eighteen, my dreams of going to the Fashion institute of New York was delayed. Although I was disappointed it dawned on me that I was going to be someone's mother and I had to deal with it to me that was the easy part. The hard part came when the father had to be told and I was able to get through it, and at the age of twenty-one I was the mother of two. It was an hard thing to have to be a mother of two at such a young age, but God saw fit for me to have my children at an early age because at the age of twenty four I had an Hysterectomy and my body totally went in to menopause, I had no ovaries or uterus after having this surgery it did not go well and I was back in the hospital because I had a blood clot that had broken off and was traveling through my body. I was on the verge of death, my doctor advised my mother if you did not bring her to the emergency room when you did she would have died. This is the Power of God working on my behalf even though I did not know Him, he had spared my life just for my children not to have to growth up without a mother and the Lord new how much I loved and adored my son's.

After the Lord healed my body and things began to get back to normal my children were happy that they had their Mommy back it had been years and months that I had struggled with my health, all though things were not perfect it had improved. But there was still something that was missing from my life, I could find it in a man I could not find it in a job, I could not find it in my family I tell you I had searched for something in the natural to satisfy the spiritual, not knowing that I really was having a God problem He was wooing me, and begging me to come to Him and I yet ignored Him time and time again. So I began to smoke a little crack I began placing it in my cigarettes, I even started smoking it with friends in a pipe, I never had to spend any money on it, it was free. Until one night there were no friends around and for the first time I coped some crack for myself, after putting my babies to sleep and making sure they were ok. I found myself in my bedroom with a dim light lacing the crack in my cigarettes; I can hear God say, "You know this is not you, why are you taking yourself there". I finally realized that I wasn't going to be comfortable until change took place in my life; it is hard to kick against the prick when God wants your life.

The Lord was slowly intervening in my life, He had sent a lady my way while paying rent one day, and she was so excited about her salvation that she asked me to come out with her to service. I didn't actually go with her I ended up going to their Wednesday night Bible study I can remember the study was on the rapture. it was so good until, when I returned home I said I am going to go to their Sunday service, so that Sunday my son's and I attended the service as soon as we hit the building you could feel the love of God the people were so pleasant and they greeted us with such kindness that I had never experienced before. So it got to be alter call and the Preacher said if anyone needs prayer they can come up at this time, and so my youngest son got up off the Pugh and went up for prayer he couldn't of been no more than 6 years old, even he knew that there was a need for prayer. After all he was a part of my brokenness, so my son stood there by himself and my motherly instinct kicked in and My other son and I found ourselves on the altar too; the Preacher asked me what did I want the Lord to do for me and I said I wanted to give my life to the Lord, I can remember the song that was playing in the background it went something like this. I been revived for the first time in my life I am alive and I'm never going back to my old life ever again. The tears of repentance began to flow down my face and I could feel the burdens that I had carried so long just lift and I felt so free I tell you the Power of God fell in that place and my life was changed forever. I tell you the Power of God was unto salvation. I pray that something in my testimony will bless you and encourage you that God is an awesome God, and that He can do the impossible in your life.

Notes:

_____

_____

_____

_____

_____

_____

_____

_____

_____

_____

_____

_____

_____

_____

_____

_____

_____

_____

_____

_____

_____

_____

_____

_____

ABOUT THE AUTHOR

DR. VERONICA EDDY

Dr. Veronica Eddy, President of Dove Consulting and Counseling Group, LLC, is as RN, who earned a BA in Psychology from St Leo University in St Leo, Florida. She earned a Masters in Religious Arts, was ordained into ministry, and continued on to earn her PhD and NCCA licensure as a clinical pastoral counselor from Jacksonville Theological Seminary.

Her nursing career has spanned more than forty-six years with half of that spent working in the Oncology field where she not only administered chemotherapy and counseled patients and their families through very difficult times, but also helped families through the death of their loved ones.

Dr. Eddy has also worked as an administrative assistant in a successful nursing company providing IV services to the nursing home communities around the state of Florida, as well as in MD., VA., Washington D.C., and other regions of the Northeast. Her ability to understand and relate to women in this highly stressful environment keeps her continually in the forefront of providing the necessary tools to work smarter, not harder. About two years ago, she has relocated to Pennsylvania, is working as an Intake Coordinator in a growing home health agency and continues to attend to the needs of the nurses under her care.

Professionally, she is a member of the National Association of Professional Nurses (NAPN), a Certified Trainer with Professional Woman Network specializing in the area of Women's Issues, is a member of The American Association of Christian Counselors (AACC), and The National Christian Counselors Association (NCCA).

Dr. Eddy has had the privilege of being the women's ministry leader in her church in Florida where she applied her expertise in the many areas of the needs of women. She has also designed and implemented a grief recovery program to minister to the countless people needing support after experiencing loss, as well as help to train others to help those in the depths of their grief. After her relocation, she continues to be involved in her church singing on the praise team and ministering to wounded and grieving women. As a licensed clinical pastoral counselor, her understanding of one's emotional needs propel her forward to help minister to and help meet the needs of the physically and spiritually battered women.

Contact:

123 Carriage Dr.
North Huntingdon, Pa. 15642
727-247-7944 or 724-989-9311
Email: dccgroup07@aol.com

THIRTY-ONE

HOW GREAT IS MY GOD

By Dr. Veronica Eddy

We read of God's great power and awesome works in both the Old and New Testaments. Some examples are the parting of the Red Sea, Joshua's answered prayer for the sun to stand still, the provision of manna and quail for the Israelites while they wandered in the wilderness, Peter walking on water and the resurrection of God's son Jesus Christ to name a few.

But we fail to recognize or give Him credit for all He does for us each and every minute of each and every day. Just because they do not appear to be extravagant and elaborate, our everyday "coincidences" are the hand of God guiding, protecting and delivering our daily unexpected miracles.

God is looked on by many as cruel and vengeful but that is far from the truth. He is our Creator, our Father. For a moment think about your role as mother (creator) – a parent, and what extent you would go to in order to protect your child. You would move mountains, (if you could) and remove threats and danger to ensure your child's safety. Well, so does God. All who call Him Father, believe in Him as the one true God and are covered in the blood of His son Jesus Christ are afforded His divine protection, and He will do what He deems necessary to protect, guide and direct away from evil influences or danger. And He will use His creation to accomplish His purposes just to show us His power in and through us.

Let's look at some of the Bible greats, who at their time, were as ordinary as we are today, and see how we can relate to them in the difficulties and dilemmas they faced, and how we can draw from their experiences and courage to help in our own walk. Were they more courageous than we are? No! Were they endowed with supernatural power? No! Were they better equipped intellectually and spiritually than we are? No! Well then, what did they possess to thrust them into God's hall of fame? What made their lives and decisions so memorable that they became examples for centuries of great and mighty people? What did they possess that we all have as well?

I don't think they were physically stronger than we are today, nor do I think they possessed supernatural intelligence. In fact, I think today we are so intellectually advanced that it gets in our way of faith and trust. And ladies, we have become so fiercely independent that we find it hard to lean on anyone for support, even our own Creator God who yearns for us to fall into His embrace and allow Him to be our protector and provider. So, what was it that made these people so memorable through these many centuries? I personally believe it was their faith and trust in God, their unwavering belief that He would provide what they needed to accomplish what was set before them.

So, let's take a look at several of these "greats" who in their day were as ordinary as we are today. But to do that, let's look at some of the issues they dealt with as well. Issues not so different from the ones we face today – fear, anxiety, guilt, shame, depression, danger and grief, to name a few.

Fear/Anxiety/Danger:

The first person I thought of was Queen Esther. She wasn't born a queen; in fact, she was as far from royalty as one could get. Esther lost her parents as a young girl, was taken in by her cousin and guardian, and was raised in a quiet, unassuming home. She was just an unknown orphaned girl but God had great plans to use her. The King of Persia was looking for a queen and many young women were taken to his palace and presented before him. Esther captured his eye, won his favor and was his chosen one. Unknown to anyone was the fact that she was a Jew. As today, there was much prejudice against her race and one high ranking officer in the king's court was the most prejudiced of all. He convinced the king to institute destruction on the Jews by telling him there was rebellion brewing against him. Esther's uncle heard of this decree and went to her telling her she needed to intercede on behalf of their people.

Now for Esther to go into the king without his request could mean her demise and that same fate would be hers when he discovered she was a Jew because the edict would apply to her even though she was the queen. How afraid she must have been! What could she, a lowly peasant girl who became queen, hope to accomplish? How did she overcome her fear? She knew she did not possess the wisdom and courage to do this on her own; she knew she needed strength from a source greater than anything she possessed. She turned to her God. She fasted and prayed and had her uncle and all her people fast and pray as well. When the time came, she stepped forward in God's power and was used as His instrument to accomplish what only God could do. She was willing to perish to be God's instrument to accomplish His purposes.

So, what does this have to do with us today? Well, we are all afraid of something at one time or another; or some of us may live in a continual state of fear. Is courage a lack of fear? Absolutely not! Ambrose Redmoon said, *"Courage is not the absence of fear but rather the judgment that something else is more important than fear".* We must recognize that there is strength within each of us to overcome our fears. If we recognize that important something then we will be able to go forward and rise above that which would try to overpower us. In my own personal experiences, and there have been many, I learned just how fearful I was. I was never on my own – I always had someone to depend on, someone to make the decisions, someone to provide, and then I found myself alone. That wasn't bad enough; I also realized I had no self-confidence, no self-esteem and no identity. So, how could I have courage? How would I ever be able to do all I need to do, to stand on my own two feet and make a life for myself?

I knew God and I knew He was closer than my next breath, but was I ready and willing to put my money where my mouth was, so to speak. Was I ready to reach out to Him and believe He would never let me down? How would I do that? I knew I would have to push down my fear and reach into that place of faith, and then trust and believe He would be my guide, my protector, my provider – my All.

In Romans 12: 3 we read, *"....God has dealt to every man the measure of faith"*

And in Matthew 17:20 Jesus is speaking and saying, *"....if you have faith as a grain of mustard seed you shall say unto this mountain remove hence to yonder place and it shall remove, and nothing shall be impossible unto you."*

I pulled these scriptures out and they became my mantra as I went through one trial after another. God never failed me, He always provided and when I trusted His word the fear began to melt away and slowly over time I came to believe in myself and my ability through Him to live and go forward and to accomplish all He created me to be. Was this transformation an overnight accomplishment? No! Did I fall back into my fearful ways? Yes, many times over and over again. But my great God is patient and loving and never tires of lifting us up, brushing us off and sending us forward again with His power and strength to accomplish that which has been set before us. No one is inconsequential to God. Each and every one of us, walking in God's providence, will be guided by His hand and protected by His mighty band of angels.

Guilt/Shame:

When I think of shame I think of Rahab, the harlot. Not much is said about her except for one courageous but dangerous decision that cast her into the hero's hall of fame. She was born into a pagan culture in Jericho, a woman of the world. However, she heard of the great miracles of the God of Israel and how He delivered and protected them. Because of this knowledge and her decision to trust this powerful true God, she chose to hide two Israelite spies and protect them from being killed. But, being a very wise woman she exacted a promise from them. She asked that when they invaded they would spare her and her family. And they did! Because of her belief she would experience the beginning of a new life. And because of this new found faith and life she is a great example of II Corinthians 5: 17 "*Therefore if any man is in Christ, he is a new creature, the old things passed away; behold all things become new.*" Rahab was an immoral pagan woman but her faith in the one true God caused her to be spared, and to be memorialized through these many centuries.

There isn't much written about Rahab but for three references in the New Testament. In Matthew chapter 1 we read that she was an ancestor of King David and of God's son Jesus. WOW! From harlot to a person in the lineage of Jesus Christ.

It is important to remember that a life of shame doesn't have to remain a lifestyle; that a shameful past does not block us from being close to God or being used by Him. Our bad choices do not have to cripple our entire future. There is redemption, forgiveness and healing for us if we would only humble ourselves before our Father God. He is waiting with open arms to welcome us back and apply soothing salve on all our wounds. As we surrender our past failures to God, we may find that they become the very things that make us of use in His kingdom's purposes. Our experiences become the catalyst to open avenues of communication with otherwise hardened individuals because we then have credibility with them that others don't. We have walked through the fire of adversity and have come out the other side a bit smoky but not burned up. When they witness our joy at how God has delivered us through a particular trial their small measure of faith will be sparked and begin to be fanned into a flame of victory.

Danger:

We all face danger everyday whether we are aware of it or not. Just driving on all the congested highways and interstates pose daily threats. We don't know the condition of the drivers around us, nor do we always concentrate on our driving as we should. An accident can happen at any time due to faulty equipment or driver distraction.

We can also find ourselves in dangerous situations because of the foolishness of others. Another lesser known woman in the Bible that found herself in just such a situation was a woman named Abigail. She was both beautiful and wise, and it was this God-given wisdom that enabled her to deal with the foolishness of her husband. Abigail's story is found in the Old Testament in the book of 1Samuel chapter 25. Abigail's marriage was arranged by her parents, as was the custom, to a man, who on the outside appeared to be a great catch and an industrious man, but what looked good on the outside covered something horrible on the inside. He was a rich, drunken fool of a man but Abigail carried herself with a rare poise and behavior. Because of her love and commitment to God, she was given the power and the ability to deal with the circumstances her husband created. I'm sure she didn't think she had any more ability to deal with the many issues he created than we would today, but when she stepped out in faith and tested her God's word and promises, the way was there as was His guidance.

Have you found yourself in a similar situation? Or are you currently in this situation? Well, let's see what Abigail did to protect herself and her family from the danger this foolish man caused.

Abigail lived in a time when Davis was soon to be king of Israel. Everyone knew who David was. He and his army of six hundred were in need of food and water, and were in the vicinity of Abigail and her husband's property. They approached one of the farmhands asking for food and this request was conveyed to Nabal – Abigail's husband.

Nabal's response was a rude, blunt and degrading response because Nabal was not only foolish but he was proud and selfish as well.

David was angered beyond description. His anger turned to foolishness as well when he set out to kill Nabal and everyone on his land. David, the anointed one of God, who wrote many of the Psalms and is described as a man after God's own heart was in a rage and was bent on murder. Nabal's foolishness, insults and refusals did not give David the right to kill, but David's temper raged out of control and murder was his path at this point. Have you found yourself in a similar state of mind? How interesting that the great men and women of God were as human as we are today and did not live in ivory towers removed from the same issues that we face today. That is why God's Word is alive and so relevant today as it was so many centuries ago. God is the same yesterday, today and forever, and His hand is guiding and delivering today as it did all those many years ago if we would just trust Him.

This is the situation that Abigail finds herself in the middle of – a foolish husband and a king acting like a fool! "But God!!" There are many "but God" moments in the Bible – this is just one of them.

God again has a plan even though Abigail does not see it; and it is the same with us today. We are in the middle of a messy situation, not necessarily caused by us but by the foolish people in our lives and we are thrust into danger – what do we do? What will happen? When we trust God, He intervenes; He gives wisdom to move in the situation in a particular way with an idea or a person that comes alongside to help prevent that foolish one from doing something that could be very damaging.

Let's look at what God did through Abigail to prevent David from doing a foolish, costly thing and to protect her foolish husband from death. Abigail loved her God and was willing to do all He directed her to do. She humbled herself before her God and before King David, and was used to accomplish God's divine plan. She did what her foolish husband refused to do putting herself in danger from him because she did not tell him before doing it. Abigail prepared and personally delivered food and drink to David and his army, and then as she bowed humbly before her king she took full responsibility for her husband's foolish words and actions in hopes of disarming David's anger. And you know what – she did just that. We read in Proverbs 15:1 *"A soft answer turns away wrath; but grievous words stir up anger"*

When we are offended we think we are entitled to react harshly against the offender but when we do we become as foolish as they. However, when we are in tune to God and His hand is in and on our lives, and we surrender to become His willing vessel, God always has a way and a plan. We never know how our humble, peacemaking ways are being used by God to lead and direct and protect another or even ourselves.

Abigail's husband died and David remembered her and her kindness to him and his men. He remembered her beauty and her humility and he sought her out and took her as his queen. God saw the wife of a drunk and a fool as a queen; what do you think He sees in you that you do not see in yourself? He doesn't look on the outside as we do but He looks on the heart. What situation, event, fear or danger has your heart so encased that you have forgotten its capacity to love, serve and provide? Allow my great God to take it and release it to serve Him and all He places in your path. Allow Him to release you to soar to heights only He can see. A caterpillar is entombed in a cocoon so it can be transformed into a beautiful butterfly, but the butterfly does not emerge easily. The struggle out of its cocoon is deliberate so that its wings will strengthen enabling it to fly.

As with us, our struggles are not meant to destroy us; they are meant to strengthen us so we can soar as on wings of eagles to accomplish all that our great God has prepared for us to do to bring Him honor and glory. God's power is matchless and His love is limitless. Give Him a try, if you haven't already – let Him show you how precious and special you are and what He can do to you, for you and through you. Because my God is great!

Barber, Rasnake & Shepherd, <u>Women of the Bible I</u>, Cahttanooga, TN, AMG Publishers, 1999

Barber, Rasnake & Shepherd, <u>Women of the Bible II</u>, Chattanooga, TN, AMG Publishers, 2002

Swindoll, Charles, <u>A Woman of Strength and Dignity – Esther</u>, Nashville-London-Vancouver-Melbourne, Word Publishing, 1997

<u>The Holy Bible</u>, Indianapolis, Indiana, B.B. Kirkbride Bible Co,. Inc., 1957

Notes:

THE PROFESSIONAL WOMAN NETWORK
Training and Certification on Women's Issues

 Linda Ellis Eastman, President & CEO of The Professional Woman Network, has trained and certified over two thousand individuals to start their own consulting/seminar business. Women from such countries as Brazil, Argentina, the Bahamas, Costa Rica, Bermuda, Nigeria, South Africa, Malaysia, and Mexico have attended trainings.

Topics for certification include:
• Diversity & Multiculturalism
• Women's Issues
• Women: A Journey to Wellness
• Save Our Youth
• Teen Image & Social Etiquette
• Leadership & Empowerment Skills for Youth
• Customer Service & Professionalism
• Marketing a Consulting Practice
• Professional Coaching
• Professional Presentation Skills

If you are interested in learning more about becoming certified or about starting your own consulting/seminar business contact:

The Professional Woman Network
P.O. Box 333
Prospect, KY 40059
(502) 566-9900
lindaeastman@prodigy.net
www.prowoman.net

Women's Empowerment Series

Creating a Blue Print for Inner Change: Tools for Personal Growth
Tapping into Your Inner CEO Self-Leadership
Leaders in Pearls: Becoming a Change Architect
Releasing Strongholds: Letting Go of What is Holding You Back
The Power of a Woman: Embracing the Woman Within
How to Break the Glass Ceiling Without a Hammer
The Power of Change: Reinvent Yourself at Any Age
Life is an Attitude. The Power of Positive Thinking
Transformation: Reinventing the Woman Within
Learning to Love Yourself: Self-Esteem for Women
A Journey Within: Self-Discovery for Women
The Woman's Handbook for Self-Confidence
Remove the Mask! Living an Authentic Life
The Woman's Handbook for Self-Empowerment
Becoming Your Own Best Friend
The Self-Architect: Redesigning Your Life

The African American Library

Single and Loving It! Secrets for the SINGLE African American Sister
Boys to Men The Guide for African American Boys
Sister to Sister A Guide for African American Girls
Bruised But Not Broken
Learning to Love Yourself: A Handbook for the African American Woman
Wellness for the African American Woman: Mind, Body & Spirit
Life Skills for the African American Woman
Raising African American Boys
Raising African American Girls
Living Your Vision and Purpose

The Professional Woman Network - Book Series
Becoming the Professional Woman
Customer Service & Professionalism for Women
Self-Esteem & Empowerment for Women
The Young Woman's Guide for Personal Success
The Christian Woman's Guide for Personal Success
Survival Skills for the African-American Woman
Overcoming the SuperWoman Syndrome
You're on Stage! Image, Etiquette, Branding & Style
Women's Journey to Wellness: Mind, Body & Spirit
A Woman's Survival Guide for Obstacles, Transition & Change
Women as Leaders: Strategies for Empowerment & Communication
Beyond the Body! Developing Inner Beauty
The Young Man's Guide for Personal Success
Emotional Wellness for Women Volume I
Emotional Wellness for Women Volume II
Emotional Wellness for Women Volume III
The Baby Boomer's Handbook for Women

Youth Empowerment Series
Raising Healthy Children in an Unhealthy World
The Teen Handbook for Self-Confidence

Christian Series
The Power of God

These books are available from the individual contributors, the publisher (www.pwnbooks.com), www.amazon.com, and your local bookstore by request.